Dan W Bannister

LINCOLN

and the

COMMON LAW

A Collection of Lincoln's Illinois Supreme Court Cases from 1838-1861 and their Influence on the Evolution of Illinois Common Law.

Dan W. Bannister, J.D.

This book printed on recycled paper

Additional copies may be ordered from:
HUMAN SERVICES PRESS
P.O. Box 2423
Springfield, IL 62705
(217) 528-1756

Introduction

Abraham Lincoln practiced law in Springfield, Illinois from 1837 to 1861, when he left Springfield to become President. Even after that time his partnership with William H. Herndon continued, as he intended to resume his practice after serving his country. His earlier partners were John T. Stuart (1837-1841) and Stephen T. Logan (1841-1844). His practice before the Illinois Supreme Court had a great influence on the common law of Illinois as it evolved, and his masterful performance before that appellate court belied the popular image we have today of Lincoln only as a rustic, quick-witted trial lawyer.

He practiced before all levels of courts, from the justice of peace courts, to the trial courts in the state circuits and Federal districts, and the supreme courts of both the state and Federal governments. There is comparatively little about his law practice in biographies of Lincoln, and much of what is written pertains to his famous jury trial criminal cases. The popular image of his practice featured his home-spun yarns and tactics, enhanced by his humor and talent for argument, which combined to win victories for his clients. However his most significant successes occurred in the Illinois Supreme Court, and this collection of cases is presented to support that conclusion.

Historians comment favorably on Lincoln's performance before the Illinois Supreme Court. Stephen Oates says: "Though Lincoln labored diligently in the federal and state circuit courts, he did his most influential legal work in the prestigious Supreme Court of Illinois. In all he participated in 243 cases (Ed. note: since that was written many more cases have been found. There are 333 in this collection about which written decisions exist, and many more about which all we know is that he participated.) before that tribunal and won most of them. It was here he earned his reputation as a lawyer's lawyer, adept at meticulous preparation and cogent argument."[1] John J. Duff wrote: "Contrary to

---

[1]Oates, Stephen B.: With Malice Toward None. Page 104.

popular belief, it was in the Supreme Court, and not in the circuit, that Lincoln had his greatest impact as a lawyer. During the period when the outlines of the state's jurisprudence were being established on an enduring basis, he helped to mold, in a significant way, doctrines of law laid down by the state's most authorative court. If the principles involved seem commonplace today, one needs to be reminded that Lincoln had no encyclopedia of law, no digests to go by--only the maxims of the English common law as set forth in Blackstone and applied in the older sister states. It would not be rash to claim for him that, in exploring areas that the Illinois courts had not yet clearly delineated, he hacked out important precedents in the law of that state and, more than any other Illinois lawyer of his generation, made a distinct contribution to law that governs today. Herndon's statement that Lincoln was a 'great lawyer . . . in the Supreme Court of Illinois' is, for once, no exaggeration. He was an uncommonly fine appeals lawyer."[2]

The other interesting facet of this collection of Lincoln cases should be the insight it gives us into the development of the common law in Illinois from 1837 to 1865. A general definition of "Common Law" is a body of law that develops and derives through judicial decisions, as distinguished from legislative enactments. These cases cover a broad spectrum of subjects, many of them deciding issues for the first time in Illinois. The cumulative body of supreme court decisions, together with statutes passed by the legislature, established a framework for protection of the rights of our citizens. The common law of England was established for that same purpose, and continues to this day.

Illinois became a state in 1818, and in 1819 the first act of the First General Assembly of the state, meeting in Kaskaskia at its second session was "An act declaring what laws are in force in this state: that the common law of England, all statutes or acts of the British Parliament, made in aid of the common law, prior to the fourth year of the reign of King James the First, except the second section of the sixth chapter of xliii, Elizabeth; the eighth chapter xliii, Elizabeth, and the ninth chapter of xxxvii, Henry the Eighth, and which are of general nature, and not local to that kingdom, shall be the rule of decision, and shall be considered as of full force, until repealed by legislative authority."

That enactment served as the basis for all supreme court decisions. Decisions from states with appellate courts established earlier than Illinois, and whose jurisprudence was also based on the English common law, were also cited to assist the court to interpret what specific examples of English common law were of such a general nature, and not merely

---

[2]Duff, John J.: A. Lincoln Prairie Lawyer. Page 243.

local to England, to be properly the common law of Illinois. In our narrative descriptions we have included what we deem pertinent direct quotations from the Justices showing the influence of English common law on our system of jurisprudence.

The cases are presented in chronological order. As the state grew in population, and made social and economic progress, the subject matter of the cases reflected that growth. Most of a person's wealth was measured by land holdings, and disputes over land frequently ended up in the supreme court. Women's dower rights affected land ownership, and Lincoln was involved in several appeals on this subject. Corporations first came into being in Illinois during this period, and the railroads were the most prominent of these. Lincoln was involved in many cases involving railroads, and represented the Illinois Central Railroad in some major cases. As commerce developed, actions involving negotiable instruments were very common. A topical index is included so the reader can identify cases of special interest.

Lincoln had some involvement in each of the cases presented in this collection, and when we could identify a definite contribution by him in a particular case, we have done so. We have also included direct quotes from some of the opinions which we have enjoyed as either good writing or wry humor.

We hope the presentation of these cases is of interest to any reader, lawyer or non-lawyer, and/or history buffs or casual perusers of anything of interest. My background includes a law degree in 1946; after a short practice, a long career in insurance company management, with outside reading devoted to perusal of anything of interest; followed by volunteer work with the Lincoln Legal Papers, when I briefed every known Lincoln case before the Illinois Supreme Court. It was during this activity that the cumulative impact of the development of the Illinois common law enhanced my appreciation of its importance, and that the Lincoln cases constituted a good cross section of this evolution.

To the best of our knowledge, briefs of these cases have never been published before. One can reference any case from the alphabetical index, any generic group of cases from the topical index, or can read the cases in chronological order to share appreciation of the relationship of the cases to each other as the common law of Illinois was formed, and the relationship of these cases to other known details of the history of Illinois in all its facets as it developed.

We recognize these are merely summaries of cases. There is so much more that could be included to add more depth and enjoyment to these cases, so we plan to publish quarterly commentaries on this subject starting in 1992. These will include new Lincoln cases as they are found; observations about the relationships of specific cases in the collection;

additional special interest, such as testimony reported in a case report, or items on a given case from other references, including Lincoln - Day by Day, published by the Abraham Lincoln Association; a review of each copy of the Illinois Reports (through 1861 at least) to include other cases with specific references to the development of the common law, and/or quotations from cases written by the Justices who wrote the best; explanations of legal terms and concepts as necessary to add clarity to some cases; and other pertinent things, especially comments by readers who hopefully will be stimulated enough to share thoughts and opinions with all of us. Details on how one can participate in this can be obtained by writing the editor of this collection c/o Human Services Press, P.O. Box 2423, 2631 North Grand Ave. E., Springfield, IL 62702.

We thank Lincoln Legal Papers, and its Director and Senior Editor, Dr. Cullom Davis, for encouragement and assistance in this project. The readers of the quarterly comments will also learn more about this important project, and how it is funded.

Dan W. Bannister, J.D.

Lyon v. Barney
orig. ed. 2 Ill.287
(Ill. Rep.: Lyon v. Barney 2 Ill.287)
December Term 1837

Barney brought an action of assumption against Lyon, who filed his plea of non-assumpsit (denying he owed the money sought by Barney). On the same day Lyon filed his plea, Barney was granted a judgment by default against him. Barney contends the fact these occurred on the same day justifies the presumption the default judgment was rendered before the plea was entered.

The supreme court, in an opinion written by Justice Smith, reversed the judgment and remanded the cause. The record showed the plea was entered before the default judgment was rendered, and no presumption can be raised to contradict the record. The form of the judgment was also erroneous, which should be straightened out if the case is tried again.

These early cases contain more procedural and pleading errors than later cases. Probably this was due to the comparative inexperience of the lawyers and the trial judges.

Grimsley & Levering v. Klein
orig. ed. 2 Ill.343
(Ill. Rep.: Grimsley et al. v. Klein 2 Ill.343)
June Term 1837

This was a trial of the right of property brought by Klein against Grimsley and Levering before Judge S.T. Logan in the Sangamon circuit court. Klein, the landlord of Bailey, distrained his goods for rent due. These same goods were afterwards taken in execution in a suit against Bailey brought by Grimsley and Levering. Klein, in order to prove the indebtedness of Bailey to him for rent, was permitted to read in evidence, without any proof of its execution, a lease from him to Bailey. Grimsley et al. objected; the judge overruled the objection, and gave judgment to Klein. J.T. Stuart represented Grimsley et al. on the appeal at least.

The Supreme Court, in an opinion written by Justice Wilson, reversed the judgment, and remanded the cause for a new trial, because the judge erred in overruling the objection to the reading of the lease as evidence. Grimsley and Levering were not parties to the lease. A lease cannot be read in evidence, except as between the parties to the same, without proof of its execution.

Covell et al. v. Marks
orig. ed. 2 Ill.391

(Ill. Rep.: Covell et al. v. Marks 2 Ill.391)
December Term 1837

Marks brought an action of assumpsit to recover on a note against Covell et al., who filed a plea of non-assumpsit. The court gave a judgment by default against them, and they appeal to the supreme court.

The supreme court, in an opinion written by Justice Lockwood, reversed the judgment and remanded the cause with directions to the circuit court to set aside the default. Covell et al's. pleading was adequate to try the case.

For further action on this case, see 2 Ill.525.

Covell et al. v. Marks
orig. ed. 2 Ill.525

(Ill. Rep.: Covell et al. v. Marks 2 Ill.525)
December Term 1838

Marks brought an action in assumpsit against Covell et al. The action was originally reported at 2 Ill. 391, when Covell et al. had the default judgment reversed in the circuit court. The cause was remanded for trial. Marks then received permission from the court to amend his declaration (the pleading by the plaintiff, [Marks] which recites his cause of action) by adding to the description of his note: "with twelve per cent, from the date until paid." Covell et al. made a motion for a continuance of the cause, which was refused. Judgment was again rendered against them by default.

The supreme court, in an opinion written by Justice Wilson, reversed the judgment, and remanded the cause. The rule is, that where the amendment to the pleading is a substantive one, it entitles the defendant (Covell et al.) to a continuance. The addition of the interest in the declaration was substantive because it increased the defendant's liability.

There is no record of subsequent attempts by Marks to recover on the note in any Supreme Court cases. It seems the default judgments in both attempts at this case were based on assiduous attention to technicalities. The English common law had very formal rules about pleadings, which were applied in Illinois. However, in later years more flexibility was granted, recognizing the importance of saving time and effort for both parties. The importance of formal rules of pleading is to define and refine the issues, so a clear cut question is presented for a decision. Flexibility in interpreting the rules, when no advantage is gained by either party through such flexibility, was deemed proper as the common law evolved.

Beams & Archer v. Denham & Buckmaster
orig. ed. 3 Ill.58

(Ill. Rep.: Beams & Archer v.
Denham & Buckmaster 3 Ill.58)
December Term 1839

Beams and Archer filed a bill in chancery seeking an injunction against Denham and Buckmaster. Buckmaster, for the use of Denham, had commenced an action in law for replevin against Beams and Archer. Shortly before the case was to be heard, Beams became ill, and sent an agent to Buckmaster's attorney to ask to have the lawsuit delayed. The attorney agreed, but proceeded to take a default judgment against Beams and Archer for $600. The bill further states "that complainants do not mean to charge the attorney for the plaintiff in said suit with fraud in taking judgment by default, but suppose that the judgment by default was taken by mistake or forgetfulness, in consequence of pressing and multifarious business." A temporary injunction was granted, but was dissolved after the trial.

The Supreme court, in an opinion written by Justice Lockwood, reversed the judgment, and remanded the cause since the issue of the attorney's mistake or forgetfulness was not considered at the trial. The default was against good faith and deprived Beams and Archer of a fair trial on the merits of the case. The dismissal of the bill was consequently irregular.

An appeal from a subsequent trial of this issue is reported as Buckmaster v. Beams, 8 Ill.97.

Field v. People ex rel. McClernand
orig ed. 3 Ill.79

(Ill. Rep.: Field v. People ex rel. McClernand 3 Ill.79)
December Term 1839

This is an appeal from an action of quo warranto (in common law, a claim against an incumbent office holder to inquire by what authority he supports his claim to office) brought in the Fayette circuit court before Judge Breese, by McClernand against Field to ask by what authority he holds the office of secretary of state. Field was legally appointed secretary of state in 1829, and remained in office in 1838 when Carlin was elected governor. In 1839, Carlin, by virtue of his authority as governor, appointed McClernand in place of Field. Field refused to leave office, so this action was brought. Judge Breese held for McClernand.

The judgment was reversed in the Supreme Court. Chief Justice Wilson wrote the majority opinion (44 pages); Justice Smith wrote a dissenting opinion (27 pages); and Justice Lockwood wrote a concurring opinion with the Chief Justice (44 pages). The opinions each were based on interpretations of the logic of the Illinois constitution, and at least nine attorneys represented the litigants. It is obvious there were many points made at the trial and on appeal, that had to be agreed with or contravened by logical argument. There was little case law on this subject in Illinois at the time.

Justice Wilson's opinion stated that neither the executive nor the judiciary could execute any authority or power, except such as is clearly granted by the constitution. Under the Illinois constitution, the appointing power does not have automatic power to remove from office. The secretary of state is a constitutional officer, whose role and powers are specified in the constitution, and his tenure is undefined and unlimited. The legislature has the power to limit his term, but until it does so, he can hold office. He cited two cases in Illinois which he said were indistinguishable from this case, and held the incumbent in a government office could not be removed from office at the will or pleasure of his superior officer. The circuit court judge (Breese) said he knew about these cases, but since he didn't agree with them, he wasn't going to comply with them. Wilson impliedly rebuked Breese by stating what he thought was very clear--when the Supreme Court has declared what the law is on a given point, when the same point comes again in litigation, all other courts in the state are bound to conform to the decision. "A different rule would destroy all the stability and uniformity in the rules of law, which is so essential to the administration of justice, and the safety of the citizens. If every judge can decide according to his private sentiments, without regard to precedent and authority, there may be as many rules of decisions as there are circuits, and the decision of one day would furnish no rule for the decision of the next."

Justice Smith dissenting stated that under the U.S. constitution the president could dismiss the secretary of state. The Illinois constitution was patterned after the U.S., and "as the state constitution was adopted in the year 1818, thirty-one years after that of the United States, it is a fair legal inference, that by that adoption, it was intended to adopt the construction given to that from which it was taken, and to which it is in so many essential parts entirely analogous." Thus Field could be dismissed by the new governor.

Justice Lockwood, in agreeing with the majority, pointed out the essential differences in the secretaries of state for the U.S. and Illinois. The U.S. secretary of state assists the president in performing his management of peace and war, negotiation of treaties with foreign nations, and in the regulation of commerce. There must be a confidential relationship between the two, and the president must be able to control the secretary. Implied power to remove the secretary of state is highly necessary to carry on the duties of the U.S. government. The secretary of state in Illinois has duties specified in the constitution, rendered to both the governor and the legislature. He has no confidential role with the governor, and is not under his control. The settled doctrine is, that construction for the purpose of conferring power, should be resorted to with great caution, and only for the most persuasive reasons. Such are not present in this case.

James & Leonard v. Hughill
orig. ed. 3 Ill.361

(Ill. Rep.: James & Leonard v. Hughill 3 Ill.362)

December Term 1840

This is a case in which Logan represented James and Leonard, and a writ of certiorari was granted to the court below to transfer the record of a case in which judgment had been entered against James and Leonard by default. It was indicated the court below had permitted the sheriff, who had served process upon James and Leonard, to add his signature to the record, where it had been omitted, subsequent to the taking of the appeal in the case and after the record had been transmitted to the supreme court.

The facts are minimal in this case, and nothing indicates any results after the records were received by the supreme court pursuant to this issuance of the writ of certiorari.

Bank of Washtenaw v. Montgomery
orig. ed. 3 Ill.422

(Ill. Rep.: Bank of Washtenaw v. Montgomery 3 Ill.422)
December Term 1840

Montgomery executed a promissory note to the Browns, who assigned the note to the Bank of Washtenaw, a foreign corporation (meaning it was authorized and organized in a state other than Illinois). The note is in default, and the Bank brings this action of assumpsit in Cook county. Montgomery demurs (a pleading which says in effect that even if what the other party alleges is true, there still is no meritorious cause of action), because a foreign corporation cannot bring an action in Illinois. His attorneys submit three and a half pages of precedents and reasoning in support of his position. The court agrees, and sustains the demurrer. Judgment for Montgomery.

The supreme court, in an opinion written by Justice Smith, disagrees, reverses the judgment and remands the cause. The cases cited by Montgomery's attorneys were not applicable. Smith said there could be no doubt: "The numerous adjudged cases in which this right (for a foreign corporation to sue in another state) has been recognized and settled, as well as on grounds of public policy and comity between the several states of the Union, ought to be conclusive and satisfactory. It is supposed that nothing is better settled, than that corporations may institute suits in the courts of other states and countries than those under whose laws they may have been established."

Scammon v. Cline
orig. ed. 3 Ill.456

(Ill. Rep.: Scammon v. Cline 3 Ill.456)
December Term 1840

This is the first case heard by the Illinois Supreme Court in which Lincoln is listed as counsel. It was commenced in a justice of the peace court, and appealed by Lincoln's opponent to a circuit court where the appeal was dismissed. Lincoln proved the court had no jurisdiction to hear the case. This ruling was appealed to the Supreme Court.

Scammon brought an action against Cline before Alexander Heely, a justice of the peace in Boone County. Cline had the cause removed to Hiram Waterman, another justice of the peace of the same county. The report is very short, and doesn't say what the issue was. It also doesn't state why the issue was moved. Obviously Cline thought he had a better chance with J.P. Waterman. Whether he did or not, he won, and a judgment was rendered for him on February 21, 1839.

Scammon appealed to the Circuit Court of Boone County, and filed his appeal bond in the clerk's office, which was approved by the clerk on March 1, 1839. The act fixing the time of holding the Circuit Court of Boone County passed on March 2, 1839; previously the Circuit Court having jurisdiction over that area was the Jo Daviess Circuit Court. The case was continued until April, 1840, when Cline moved to dismiss the appeal because it was taken to the Circuit Court of Boone County before any court was appointed in that county. Judge Dan Stone sustained the motion and dismissed the appeal.

G. Spring and J.Y. Scammon (presumably the plaintiff listed as "Jonathan Y. Scannon") represented Scammon in the appeal, and Lincoln was joined by J.L. Loop in the appeal representing Cline. Chief Justice Wilson wrote the opinion for the supreme court saying the appeal to the circuit court was improperly dismissed. Boone County Court must be considered to be in existence when the clerk was appointed for the court--which was earlier than March 1, 1839. Thus judgment was reversed and cause remanded for trial.

Duncan v. McAfee, assignee of Greathouse
orig. ed. 3 Ill.559

(Ill. Rep.: Duncan v. McAfee 3 Ill.559)
December Term 1840

This is an appeal from an action of debt in the Fayette circuit court before Judge Breese. Duncan executed a note to Greathouse for $200, who assigned it to McAffee. The note is due and McAffee sues. Judgment for McAfee.

The Supreme Court, with Justice Breese writing the opinion, affirmed the judgment. Duncan's defense was he signed the note "J.M. Duncan," but was sued in the name of "James M. Duncan;" and, the form of the written promise was not in sufficient form to be actionable. Judge Breese had presided at the trial, and had solved these issues against Duncan, and probably had even less trouble when writing the opinion of the court.

This was subsequently considered at 4 Ill.93.

Rogers v. Hall
orig. ed. 4 Ill.5
(Ill. Rep.: Rogers v. Hall 4 Ill.5)
July Term 1841

Rogers brought an action of slander against Hall, alleging Hall had said that Rogers had attempted to assassinate and murder him. Hall pleaded the words were true, and proved that some unknown person had shot at him. To prove that Rogers had done this he offered in evidence several anonymous letters and advertisements of a threatening and hostile import. Rogers objected, stating there was no evidence these had been written by him. The court overruled this objection, and found a verdict for Hall. Logan represented Rogers on the appeal at least.

The supreme Court, in an opinion written by Justice Ford, affirmed the judgment. The bill of exceptions was inadequate to justify Rogers position that there was no evidence the threatening writings were written by him, because the bill of exceptions simply stated there was no evidence the papers were written by Rogers. Without any additional information, it could be inferred there might have been other evidence connecting Rogers with the writings submitted at the trial. The bill of exceptions is a pleading, and the one who makes it is liable for ambiguity, uncertainty or omission; and like any other pleading ought to be construed most strongly against the party who prepared it. Thus there is nothing stated in the bill of exceptions to make it appear that the evidence was improperly admitted.

Cannon v. Kenney
orig. ed. 4 Ill.9
(Ill Rep.: Cannon v. Kinney 4 Ill.8)
July Term 1841

This was a case of trespass brought in the Sangamon Circuit Court by Cannon against Kenney before Judge Samuel H. Treat. Lincoln represented Cannon on the appeal, and S.T. Logan (who became

Lincoln's law partner in the spring of 1841 after Lincoln and Stuart dissolved their partnership) represented Kenney. Kenney won in the Circuit Court, and upon appeal at the July term, 1841, the judgement was reversed.

Cannon owned a horse that he gratuitously loaned to John Harris to be "rode" by him from Lead Mines to Sangamon County. John Harris rode the horse to Sangamon County, and put the horse in the hands of his brother James, to feed and keep the horse for a fee. James transferred the horse's care to another brother, Robert, who "after feeding and keeping him (the horse) until the grass came, turned him on the prairie with his own horses, occasionally salting him." That's when Kenney took the horse, which was worth sixty-five dollars at the time.

Kenney argued there was no evidence that he took the horse from the possession of Cannon, which position the court sustained and rendered judgment for Kenney, dismissing the case.

This appeal was taken by Cannon, with Lincoln as the sole counsel. Lincoln submitted in his brief a virtual primer on ownership of personal property, including what constitutes possession, constructive possession, bailments of several kinds, liens against personal property, and when trespass or trover is the proper remedy when personal property has been taken. Justice Breese delivered the opinion of the Court, using Lincoln's brief to support the court's reasoning, and reversed the lower court holding that the absolute owner (Cannon) still had absolute ownership despite the Harris to Harris to Harris transfers, and was still entitled to possession. Thus Kenney took the horse from Cannon's possession, and had committed trespass. The judgment was reversed and remanded for a new trial.

Leigh v. Hodges
orig. ed. 4 Ill.15

(Ill. Rep.: Leigh v. Hodges 4 Ill.14)

July Term 1841

This is an action of debt brought by Leigh against Hodges, as surety of one English in an appeal bond. Leigh had sued English in an action of slander, and judgment was rendered for English. Leigh elected to appeal, and Hodges agreed to be surety on the appeal bond. Leigh and English agreed that English would pay the costs and attorneys' fees, if Leigh agreed not to appeal. Testimony supporting this agreement included a statement by Leigh that "he was too good a Virginian to claim more than the costs." English paid at least some of the items promised in the compromise, and left the state. Leigh, apparently having been away from Virginia too long, brought this action against Hodges to recover what if any, English had not paid. Judgment for Hodges, who is represented by Logan on the appeal at least. The case contained several motions, the ruling on which adverse to Leigh; which are the basis of his bringing the appeal.

The supreme court, in an opinion written by Justice Breese, affirmed the judgment. After reciting the procedural facts and certain of the evidence, Justice Breese wrote; "Sitting, as the Circuit Court was, in disposing of this motion for a new trial, we are only to ascertain if , upon the whole case as presented, substantial justice has been done. It does not always follow that a new trial will be granted, even if the jury finds against the weight of evidence, against the instructions of the court, or through misdirection of the court on a point of law, provided the court is satisfied that justice is done." He went on to say in this case, "where a surety is sued, after assurance by the plaintiff (Leigh) that the matter had been adjusted with the principal (English), who had left the country with property," justice had been done.

Justice Scates wrote a short concurring opinion. The majority opinion stated a motion for a new trial based on improper instructions to a jury could not be granted, if the aggrieved party had not excepted to the instruction when given. Justice Scates agreed with the affirmation of the judgment, but stated he did not agree with this statement, and a new trial could be granted on improper instructions to a jury, although not excepted to when given.

Maus v. Worthing
orig. ed. 4 Ill.26

(Ill. Rep.: Maus v. Worthing for use of McCann 4 Ill.26)

December Term 1841

This is an extraordinary case in that the dissenting opinion is reported in by far the greater length. The above matter was appealed from Tazewell Circuit Court, and the attorney for the appellant (Jacob Maus) is not listed in the opinion. Lincoln represented the appellee (Amos Worthing) and made a motion to dismiss the appeal because "the appeal bond appears to have been executed on the part of the surety therein, by an attorney in fact appointed by letter or power of attorney not under seal," and cited two Supreme Court of New York cases which reviewed a number of authorities, both English and American, to support his motion. Justice Lockwood stated the authorities are conclusive on this point in writing the opinion of the court dismissing the appeal, because the power to execute a deed on the part of a surety did not have a seal. A seal historically was a substance put on a document that could be, and was, impressed by some special mark, as it developed it could be replaced by the letters "L.S." or the word "seal." The document here had neither of these. Lincoln did an able job, and won the case for Worthing.

Justice Breese dissented and his articulate reasoning had the power to influence the court in the future. He stated that the rule on the necessity of seals "seems to me to be destitute of any good reason on which to base it, and altogether too technical for this age". A scrawled seal should not have undue importance as a test for validity. "The general tenor of our laws has made great inroads upon many of those technical and refined notions which it was considered at one time heresy to question, and with the improvements made in other respects, it would seem to be time to release such proceedings from the dominion of a rule so arbitrary, so technical, so wholly inapplicable to our condition, and so little calculated to promote justice." Later he wrote further "You may hang a man on his own confession, but yet he shall not pay a debt of twenty dollars evidenced by his note of hand or bond, on the same kind of proof! I cannot consent to yield up my judgment, in any case, because others have decided a point in a particular manner, unless I can see the reason of the decision. Seeing none in this case, and believing that the purposes of justice are not at all subserved by an adherence to such antiquated rules and unmeaning technicalities, I dissent from the opinion." Then he makes a general summary of the court's powers in relation to the powers of the constitution and the legislature. "Several of my brother judges coincide in the views here expressed, but think the rule is the law with which they cannot interfere, it being for the legislative power to change it. I think differently. I am of the opinion that courts are bound to see the propriety and reason of every rule, before it receives their sanction and approbation, in cases wherein there are no statutory provisions applicable; in such cases the will of the legislature, as expressed by them, is the law, however unwise or unreasonable it may be, if no constitutional provision is violated, nor so in other cases--we should know the reason why it is and should be so: and if the alleged reason is absurd, we should not yield our acquiescence."

Warren v. Nexsen et al.
orig. ed. 4 Ill.38
(Ill. Rep.: Warren v. Nexsen et al. 4 Ill.38)
July Term 1841

This was an action of assumpsit tried before Judge Stephen A. Douglass, and appealed with the opinion of the supreme court written by Justice Douglass. The only subject covered in the supreme court decision was the propriety of the judge's rulings on alleged defects in the pleading. Some of Judge Douglass' rulings were deemed incorrect by the supreme court, and it, with Justice Douglass having the privilege of pointing out to Judge Douglass the errors of his ways, reversed the judgment and remanded the cause. Logan represented Nexsen et al. on the appeal at least.

The defendants responded to the complaint with an answer containing two subjects or counts. The plaintiff responded with six pleas, each of which professing to answer but part of each declaration. Since the plaintiff had not pleaded to the entire declaration of the defendants, the defendants moved for a discontinuance; which was granted. The plaintiff had moved for a judgment on the points which were not answered in the declaration, which was not granted.

The court cited common law historical precedents where in similar situations if one party does not answer all of the parts of pleading, the case will be discontinued. However, in some subsequent cases in the interests of doing justice in a case, and in not allowing technical breaches to impede justice, the court said: "We think the authorities cited fully justify the following just and reasonable rule: that the plaintiff may correct his error, upon the payment of costs, at anytime before final judgment, during the term at which the plea or replication is filed." Thus "the court should have sustained the plaintiff's motion, upon the payment of costs, and have rendered judgment accordingly, and for not having done so, the judgment is reversed, and the cause remanded for further proceedings not inconsistent with this decision."

Wilcox v. Woods et al.
orig. ed. 4 Ill.51
(Ill. Rep.: Wilcox v. Woods et al. 4 Ill.51)
July Term 1841

Wilcox made a note to Woods, Christy & Co. for $250.63, which is in default. Woods and the two Christys sue Wilcox, who demurs because they sued as individuals rather than as a partnership. The court overrules the demurrer, and when Wilcox makes no further pleading, awards judgment for Woods et al. Logan represented Wilcox on the appeal at least.

The supreme court, in an opinion written by Justice Treat, affirmed the judgment. Even though Woods and the two Christys sued as individuals, it was clear they were partners and had a proper cause of action. Thus the overruling of the demurrer was proper. Secondly, Wilcox contended there had been no formal joinder of the demurrer, thus the procedure was improper. However, after judgment, the court will presume there was a joinder in the demurrer, or that it was waived by the defendant, especially, as in this case, where no objection appears on the record. Thirdly, under the practice act, the judge had the power to set the damages in the judgment, when judgment is given in default.

These early cases had more rulings on procedural motions, as apposed to substantive law. Perhaps the legal participants were learning the common law procedures by experience rather than research in the limited law libraries available.

Mills et al. v. The County Commissioners of St. Clair County orig. ed. 4 Ill.53

(Ill. Rep.: Mills et al. v. The County Commissioners of St. Clair County 4 Ill.53)
July Term 1841

Mills et al. owned land on the Mississippi River and had been operating a private ferry over the river for some years, but less than twenty. The legislature enacted a law to authorize St. Clair county to establish a ferry across the river, which provided how the ground should be acquired and assessed as to value. The county chose the land owned by Mills et al. condemned it, assessed value; and Mills et al., being unsatisfied with the amount, appealed to the Jackson circuit court, and were awarded $600. At the trial, they sought to have included as evidence the property value of the private ferry they had been operating, which was rejected by Judge Scates. Logan represented Mills et al. on the appeal at least.

The supreme court, in an opinion written by Justice Breeze, affirmed the judgment. It is a principle of common law that ferries are publici jurors (of public right), and can be granted by the sovereign power. Therefore, it follows that riperian (land bordering a river on other body of water) owners are not, because of such ownership, the only ones entitled to a public ferry franchise. The legislative act specifying how the franchise was to be granted, implied the power could be granted to persons other than the owners of the land. Thus Mills et al. had no exclusive right to operate private ferries, and had no property value in their ferry which must be compensated for in the condemnation. Also since they had not operated the ferry for twenty years, there could be no property right acquired under adverse possession.

Palmer v. Logan
orig. ed. 4 Ill.56

(Ill. Rep.: Palmer v. Logan 4 Ill.56)

July Term 1841

Palmer sold Logan two lots in Pittsfield and Logan gave him two notes aggregating $1987. The notes were unpaid, and Palmer brings this action to collect. Unfortunately he cannot find the notes, and contends Logan either has them, or has destroyed them. The circuit court excludes oral testimony, including that of Palmer, of the existence of these notes, and enters judgment for Logan. Richard Logan, the defendant, was represented by Stephen T. Logan on the appeal at least.

The Supreme Court, in an opinion written by Justice Scates, reverses the judgment and remands the cause. Oral evidence including that of the plaintiff, should be sufficient to establish the existence of lost notes, and Scates referenced the law in other states, as follows: "In New York, Pennsylvania and North Carolina, the testimony of the plaintiff is admissible as to the loss of an instrument, so as to lay the foundation for the introduction of inferior proof of its execution and contents, such testimony being addressed to the court solely. Much serious and irreparable injustice might be done to individuals should a different rule prevail. There are many circumstances which might, and most probably would, prevent any other person from knowing the fact of a loss or destruction of a private writing. To deny him the benefit of his own oath would, in many cases, amount to a denial of justice. We think the rule sustained by both reason and justice."

Thompson v. The County Commissioners of Rock Island County

orig. ed. 4 Ill.66

(Ill. Rep.: Thompson v. The County Commissioners of Rock Island County 4 Ill.65)
July Term 1841

A motion was made by the County Commissioners of Rock Island County to quash a **supersedeas** (a writ containing a command to stay the proceedings at law) issued by the circuit court, on the grounds that the record was not complete.

The Supreme Court, in an opinion written by Justice Treat, sustained the motion and quashed the **supersedeas**. The rules state a **supersedeas** shall only be granted if a transcript of the record on which the application is made is complete, and so certified by the clerk of the court below. Treat said: "It is apparent, from a bare inspection of the record, it does not include all the proceedings in the cause."

Bailey v. Cromwell et al., adm. of Cromwell

orig. ed. 4 Ill.71

(Ill. Rep.: Bailey v. Cromwell et al., adm. of Cromwell 4 Ill.70)
December Term 1841

This is another case where Lincoln represents one side (Bailey) and S.T. Logan the other (the administrator for Cromwell). This appeal by Lincoln is from an action in Tazewell County involving non-payment of a note given to purchase a purported slave.

Bailey agreed to purchase a "black or negro girl or woman, named Nance" from Cromwell and gave him a note. Cromwell in turn agreed that before payment would be demanded, he would produce evidence to show the necessary papers and indenture. Cromwell died, and the girl was "in possession of Bailey for about six months, at the expiration of which time she left his service, and never since returned, she asserting and declaring all the time that she was free." Cromwell's administrators brought an action of assumpsit against Bailey, and recovered damages of $431.97.

Upon appeal this decision was reversed at the July term, 1841, with the opinion written by Justice Breese. The court held the note and agreement made at the same time, must be taken together as forming one entire contract. Cromwell did not furnish the evidence of indenture as promised, thus no consideration for the notes.

The court cited an Illinois Supreme Court case, Kinney v. Cook, (4 Ill.232 3 Scam. 232), decided at the December term 1840 which decided the presumption of law was, in Illinois, that every person was free, without regard to color. There was no evidence she had been indentured to Cromwell, and she asserted her freedom "in the only modes she could, by doing as she pleased, making purchases, contracting debts, and controlling her own motions" [proving human nature hasn't changed much since 1841]. Since the sale of a free person is illegal, and that was the consideration for the note, the note was illegal as well.

This is the first Supreme Court case in which Lincoln was involved where precedent from the Illinois Supreme Court was cited as authority. In every other case the citations have been from England, or New York, Pennsylvania, Ohio, Kentucky, and other states which had appellate courts for a longer period of time.

Duncan v. McAfee, assignee of Greathouse
orig. ed. 4 Ill.93

(Ill. Rep.: Duncan v. McAfee 4 Ill.93)
July Term 1841

Stephen T. Logan, representing McAfee, made a motion in the Supreme Court to amend the judgment rendered in the Supreme Court by the transcript from the court below, by erasing "James," and inserting "Isaac," as the christian name of the defendant in error (McAfee), and by adding to the judgment of the court below, the interest due on the judgment in that court, from the time the same was rendered, to the time of the rendition of the judgment in this court.

The motion was allowed and the record accordingly amended. The debt was $200 and the interest was increased from $6.50 to $22.50.

Prior activity in this case reported at 3 Ill.559.

Buckmaster v. Jackson ex dem. Carlin
orig. ed. 4 Ill.104

(Ill. Rep.: Buckmaster et al. v.
Jackson ex dem. Carlin 4 Ill.104)
December Term 1841

This was an action in ejectment brought by Carlin to recover possession of 320 acres of land. Carlin traced his title to Pruitt, the original patentee from the United States, Buckmaster et al. traced his title from Pruitt as well. However, Pruitt had obtained a mortgage from the State Bank of Illinois, which became in default, was foreclosed, and sold to Buckmaster's predecessors in title by judicial sale. In this case, the court refused to hear evidence of this mortgage, because it was unconstitutional for the State Bank of Illinois to loan money on a mortgage; therefore the mortgage and subsequent sale under it, was void. The unconstitutionality of the mortgage was established in a judgment rendered in Illinois that a contract between another person and the State Bank was void, because the contract was in violation of that clause of the Constitution of The United States, which prohibits the states from emitting bills of credit, such bills having been the consideration of that contract. This was the basis of the courts ruling to exclude evidence on the mortgage sale, and consequently judgment was rendered for Carlin.

The supreme court, in an opinion written by Justice Smith, reversed the judgment and remitted the cause. The evidence should have been permitted. If a court has jurisdiction of the persons and the subject matter, as it did in the case of the foreclosure of the mortgage and sale thereunder, no errors or irregularities, which may have been committed during the progress of the cause, can render the judgment void. No question was raised as to the constitutionality of the Bank's actions by the parties to the foreclosure suit, and collateral inquiry by the parties in this suit is improper. The court quoted some pertinent text from Voorheese v. Bank of the United States (1836) in a comparable action for ejectment:

"A judgment, or executions, irreversible by a superior court, cannot be declared a nullity by an authority of law, if it has been rendered by a court of competent jurisdiction of the parties and the subject matter, with authority to use the process it has issued. It must remain the only test of the respective rights of the parties to it. That some sanctity should be given to judicial proceedings, some time limited, beyond which they should not be questioned; some protection afforded to those who purchase at sales by judicial process, and some definitive rules established, by which property thus acquired may become transmissible with security to the possessors, cannot be denied. In this country particularly, where property, which within a few years was but of little value, in a wilderness, is now the site of large and flourishing cities, its enjoyment should be at least as secure as in that country when its value is less progressive. It is among the elementary principles of the common law, that whoever would complain of the proceedings of a court must do it in such time as not to injure his adversary by unnecessarily delay in the assertion of his right."

Weatherford v. Fishback
orig. ed. 4 Ill.170
(Ill. Rep.: Weatherford v. Fishback 4 Ill.170)
December Term 1841

This is an action to recover damages for deceit. Fishback desired to buy certain land owned by Harbard Weatherford, but he did not know its lines or boundaries. Jefferson Weatherford said he knew these, and would show them to Fishback. The two then inspected the land, and Jefferson showed him the lines and boundaries. Fishback bought the land from Harbard for $400, and Jefferson received nothing from the transaction. Fishback brings this action stating Jefferson knowingly deceived him. The land he bought was worth $ 10 an acre, whereas the land Jefferson showed him, and he thought he was buying, was worth much more. Jefferson demurred, in the belief he was the wrong defendant - Harbard received the purchase price, and Jefferson received no benefit. Judgment was rendered for Fishback for $183.40. Logan represented Fishback in the appeal at least.

The supreme court, in an opinion written by Justice Breese, affirmed the judgment. When Jefferson demurred, he admitted that even if all the facts in the complaint were true, the plaintiff is not entitled to a judgment as a matter of law. There was some old common law cases cited stating the servant is not personally liable for any fraud he commits for the benefit of his master. However, this is no longer the law. Only two elements are necessary in an action of deceit - fraud, and knowledge by the wrongdoer that it was fraudulent. Both are present here against Jefferson. The fact he had no personal interest in the fruits of the fraud is immaterial.

Logan, representing Fishback, filed a petition for a rehearing on a technical point. When the action was first brought, defendant (Jefferson) demurred but there was no joinder in it by the plaintiff. The cause was continued, when Jefferson filed a second demurrer, and there was joinder -thus an issue for the judge to decide. Fishback was given permission to amend his declaration, to which Jefferson also demurred; and the demurrer was overruled, as reported in the original case. Logan contended the record did not properly show this, and thus the proceedings were irregular, and should be restored. The court said:

"The practice on the circuit has been, though a loose one, when an amendment to a plea or declaration is granted, for the pleader to interline the original draft, and the clerk, in making up the record, does not usually transcribe that draft, together with the amended declaration, at length." However, the intention of all the parties were clear as to which pleadings were demurred to, and when. No violence was done to anyone, and proceedings were correct.

Capps & Capps v. Smith & Smith
orig. ed. 4 Ill.177

(Ill. Rep.: Capps v. Smith et al. 4 Ill.177)
December Term 1841

John and William Smith brought this action against John Capps to recover $1058.06 due on two notes executed by Jabez and John Capps. The Smiths held a mortgage executed by Jabez Capps, and in consideration of John Capps signing the notes, they promised to transfer the mortgage to him. They had not transferred the mortgage, or even offered to do so, when this suit was commenced. Judgment was rendered by Judge Treat for the Smiths, who were represented by Stephen T. Logan on the appeal at least.

The Supreme Court, in an opinion written by Justice Wilson, reversed the judgment and remanded the cause. The rule is well settled, that where the undertakings of the parties to a contract are mutual, one in consideration of the other, and no time is fixed for their performance, they are to be regarded as dependent contracts, which neither party can enforce, without averring and proving a performance, or at least an offer to perform, on his part.

Hinton et al. v. Husbands
orig. ed. 4 Ill.187

(Ill. Rep.: Hinton et al. v. Husbands 4 Ill.186)
December Term 1841

This was an action of assumpsit on a promissory note. Hinton and others signed a piece of paper and delivered it to Allen, who said he would have a note written on it and then would discount it at a bank. Instead he discounted it with Husbands, who brings this action to collect on the note. Hinton et al. plead the note is invalid because it was used for another purpose than was intended. Husbands demurs to this plea, which is sustained and judgment entered for Husbands for $761.40. Logan represented Husbands on the appeal at least.

The supreme court, in an opinion written by Justice Breese, affirmed the judgment. The only question was whether the demurrer was properly sustained. The circuit court ruled it was, and the supreme court concurs. The opinion only speaks to the adequacy of the various pleas. A demurrer is a pleading which says, in effect, even if all the facts the other party alleges are true, he still can not prevail in the case. The defendants pleaded against an action to collect on a promissory note they had signed, that they signed it in blank. The common law at the time was that anyone who signs a blank note, which is filled in by another party; and transferred to a third party who acts in good faith, the third party prevails. That's what happened here, as the allegations of Hinton et al. were self defeating. The plaintiff's demurrer admitted all the facts defendants alleged, and the true facts they presented negated any possible defense as a matter of law.

Logan v. Dunlap
orig. ed. 4 Ill.188

(Ill. Rep.: Logan v. Dunlap 4 Ill.188)
December Term 1841

The Supreme Court commenced its opinion thusly: "This is professedly a proceeding under the 'Act for the benefit of mechanic's' for the purpose of acquiring a lien upon the mill of the defendant." The petition set out a note wherein Abel Logan offered to pay Dunlap \$166.81 in thirty days with 12% interest. The note also said: "The above sum due for work on my mill." Abel Logan, represented by Stephen T. Logan on the appeal at least, demurred, which was overruled by the court and judgment entered for Dunlap.

The Supreme Court, in an opinion written by Justice Wilson, reversed the judgment. The statute authorizing mechanic's liens is very specific about what must be alleged in a proceeding to enforce the lien. Most of the specified items which must be pleaded, if not all, were absent here. All these omissions are fatal errors, and the demurrer to the petition should have been sustained by the circuit court.

Wells v. Reynolds
orig ed. 4 Ill.191

(Ill. Rep.: Wells v. Reynolds 4 Ill.191)
December Term 1841

This suit was originally commenced before a justice of the peace, in Rock Island county, by Reynolds against Thompson, Wells and Judson, on an account for service as an attorney, for \$66.50. Judgment of nonsuit was rendered against Reynolds, who appealed to the circuit court. Process was served on Thompson and Wells, but not Judson. Thompson made no defense, but Wells defended, and the jury awarded $37.50 against Wells alone. Wells is represented by Stephen T. Logan on the appeal at least.

The supreme court, in an opinion written by Justice Breese, reversed the judgment and remanded the cause. The jury trying the case against Wells, should also have included Thompson. By making no defense, Thompson admitted a cause of action to exist against him, and he should either have been included in the judgment, or the case, as to him, disposed of in some way. Secondly, when two or more are sued in a joint undertaking, the plaintiff must prove a joint contract. If plaintiff can't do this, the suit must be dismissed.

Reynolds, suing for payment for his services as an attorney, showed ineptitude in the lower court case. Perhaps he performed the same way for Thompson, Wells and Judson, which could explain their reluctance to pay him.

Ballentine et al. v. Beall, adm. of Wilson
orig. ed. 4 Ill.203

(Ill. Rep.: Ballentine et al. v.
Beall, adm. of Wilson 4 Ill.203)
December Term 1841

The circuit court case was tried in Wabash County before Hon. William Wilson at the September term, 1841. The action was in chancery brought by Wilson (who died before the proceedings ended, and Beall was appointed administrator) against Ballentine and others to enforce a judgment execution. Lincoln represented Beall, presumably at the trial and on the record at the appeal, and Beall was granted the relief he sought in the chancery court, which was affirmed on appeal.

Taylor was indebted to Wilson, and recovered a judgment in a justice of the peace court. Two executions were issued, and both returned finding no property to attach. Taylor was in debt to many people and had paid purchase money for some land from Correll, and Taylor directed the land be conveyed to Ballentine, in trust for Taylor. Wilson contended this conveyance was made to defraud creditors. This action was brought to set aside the sale, and to sell enough of the property to pay Wilson's debt. Decree entered giving this relief.

Justice Treat wrote the decision affirming this decree at the December term, 1841. Ballentine's attorney cited seven English cases in support of his appeal, and Lincoln cited two sections in Story's Equity Pleadings. The opinion specified six points presented in the appeal, and rebutted each one. We must presume Lincoln's arguments against each one of these points influenced the Court's opinion.

Elkin et al. v. People ex rel. Flemming et al.
orig. ed. 4 Ill.207

(Ill. Rep.: Elkin et al. v. People,
for use of Flemming 4 Ill.207)
December Term 1841

This is an appeal from a cause heard at the November term, 1840, of the Sangamon Circuit Court before Hon. Sidney Breese. The facts are not presented in the Supreme Court opinion at the December term 1841 written by Chief Justice Wilson, but there is enough to infer what happened.

Certain real property was sold under execution of a judgment under an Illinois act concerning judgments and executions. It was bought back by the judgment debtor who paid the sheriff who had executed the judgment, but who was out of office when he received the redemption payment. Apparently he failed to do the proper thing with the money, because this action is against the Sheriff's sureties, who were "bound for the faithful discharge of all the official acts and duties of the sheriff." They contended since the sheriff was out of office, he had no more responsibility, and thus couldn't commit any official act, including redeeming the property. The trial court held otherwise, and damages of $1,492.83 were awarded.

S. Strong and Lincoln represented the sureties against S.T. Logan, for the appeal of this judgment. Logan cited four cases and a Jacob's Law Dictionary meaning for the word "Execution." Strong and Lincoln cited no authorities. The court upheld the lower court judgment, so we can infer Logan's position had substantially more merit, precedent-wise. The court cited the pertinent statute which states the defendant whose lands are sold under judgment can redeem them within twelve months by paying to the purchaser or "to the sheriff, or other officer who sold the same" the sum of money paid to purchase the property. Thus payment to the sheriff who had executed on the property, even if he was out of office at the time, is proper, and he had a duty to complete whatever business he had began when he was in office.

Perhaps if the facts, especially what the out-of-office sheriff did with the money, were known, the equities for each party in the case would be clear.

Burrass v. Hewett
orig. ed. 4 Ill.224
(Ill. Rep.: Burrass v. Hewett 4 Ill.224)
December Term 1841

Hewett gave a note for $800 to Young, who assigned it to Burrass. The note is due, and Burrass brings this action to collect on the note. Hewett pleaded there was a failure of consideration, and that Burrass was not a bona fide purchaser of the note. Burrass demurred, on the grounds of two distinct matters of defense set up in one plea, and the demurrer was overruled. Burrass was represented by S.T. Logan on the appeal at least.

The supreme court, in an opinion written by Justice Smith, reversed the judgment, and ordered the circuit court to sustain the demurrer, and enter judgment for Burrass. Smith said the demurrer of Burrass "assigned duplicity as the ground of objection, and it seems to be well taken. The plea is in the matter of defense stated both prolix and ambiguous . . . These are clearly two distinct matters of defense set up in this special plea; and there is no doubt, therefore, that it is double." Where two distinct matters of defense are set up in one plea, it is bad for duplicity.

Bledsoe, the attorney for Hewett, petitioned the court for rehearing, citing many cases, and reference to Chitty's Pleadings especially. Petition was disallowed, and another victory on demurrer recorded for Logan.

Lane et al. v. Doe ex dem. Dorman et ux.
orig. ed. 4 Ill.238
(Ill. Rep.: Lane et al. v.
Doe ex dem. Dorman et ux. 4 Ill.237)
December Term 1841

This is an appeal from an action of ejectment brought in the Gallatin circuit court by John Doe, on behalf of Dorman and wife, against Lane and others. Verdict was rendered for Doe, and Lane appeals. Lane was administrator of the estate of Robinson, who died, leaving Mrs. Dorman his only heir. Lane was owed money as administrator of the estate, and in some fashion, he influenced the legislature to pass "an act authorizing the sale of lands belonging to the estate of Christopher Robinson, deceased." He then sold the land under this authorization, and paid himself and John Brown, who worked with him, $1008.87. The Dormans brought this action of ejectment against those purchasers, and were successful. Judge Scates ruled the act of the legislature was unconstitutional, and thus did not justify the sale of the land. Judgment for Dorman et ux (wife).

The judgment was affirmed by the Supreme Court, with Justice Scates writing the opinion. The constitution provides for a separation of powers, and the act in this case was clearly judicial. He stated: "Whenever it is clear that the legislature has transcended its authority, and that a legislative act is in conflict with the constitution, it is imperatively required of the court to maintain the paramount authority of that instrument, which it is solemnly pledged to support, and to declare the act imperative and void."

See Dorman v. Lane (6 Ill.143) and Dorman et ux. v. Yost (13 Ill.122) for further proceedings in this matter.

Benedict v. Dillehunt
orig. ed. 4 Ill.287

(Ill. Rep.: Benedict v. Dillehunt 4 Ill.287)
December Term 1841

This is an interesting case in which Lincoln's opponent in the appeal argued what seems to be a ridiculous technicality. Justice Breese disposed of it in two short paragraphs in the opinion at the December term, 1841.

Dillehunt (represented by C. Emerson and Lincoln on the appeal) recovered $33.53 from Benedict in a justice of the peace court of Macon County. Benedict appealed to the Circuit Court, and the Hon. Samuel H. Treat affirmed that decision, and in his written opinion he did not state the amount of the judgment. Benedict appealed to the Supreme Court, on the grounds the amount of the judgment was uncertain. However, the appeal bond he posted recited the $33.53 judgment against him.

Justice Breese said there was no uncertainty, since the reference of the amount recited in the appeal bond makes the amount in the Circuit Court certain. He dignified it by quoting a Latin phrase found in Blackstone's Commentaries (2 Fl. Comm. 143; 1 Bl. Comm. 78) "id certum est, quod certum reddi potest"--that is certain which can be made certain.

Abrams & Klein v. Camp
orig. ed. 4 Ill.290
(Ill. Rep.: Abrams & Klein v. Camp 4 Ill.289)
April Term 1841

Klein obtained a judgment against Camp for $191.43 on a note made by Camp to Abrams, and assigned by him to Klein. Camp files a bill in chancery to set aside the judgment on the grounds the note had been for a gambling debt from a card game between Camp and Abrams, and the statute to restrain gaming declares all notes given in consideration of money won in play void and of no effect, whether in the hands of a payee or an assignee. At the action at law for the debt Camp called Abrams as a witness to the game, but Abrams refused to testify on the grounds he would incriminate himself. He was excused from testifying, and Camp offered no other evidence. The equity court awarded the injunction, and Abrams and Klein appealed, represented by Logan and Lincoln.

Justice Treat reverses the injunction. The general rule in equity is, it will not relieve against a judgment at law, on the ground of its being contrary to equity, unless the defendant in the action at law was ignorant of the facts constituting his defense, while the suit was pending, or they could not have been received as a defense at law. Neither exception was applicable here. Camp had a good defense if it were truly a gambling debt. He set up his defense in the court of law, but he failed to prove it due to his own neglect or want of preparation. His only remedy was to appeal the decision of the court of law. There is a well established principle that the decision of a court of competent jurisdiction is conclusive upon all courts of concurrent powers.

Logan and Lincoln cited English cases and a reference in Story's Equity which Justice Treat relied on in his opinion. The mystery is why <u>Justice</u> Treat states the decree of the Circuit Court (presided over by <u>Judge</u> Treat) "was clearly erroneous." Perhaps Logan and Lincoln did not represent Abrams and Klein there, since the precedents cited on appeal couldn't have been presented at the equity proceeding. <u>Judge</u> Treat could have ruled otherwise, and not granted the injunction.

Nichols v. Ruckells
orig. ed. 4 Ill.298
(Ill. Rep.: Nichols v. Ruckells 4 Ill.298)
December Term 1841

Ruckells rented a mill from Nichols. As part of the agreement Nichols was to "dig out the dirt from the wheel, within one month, so that the shaft would be clear, and erect works to keep the banks from washing under the mill, and furnish blocks for underpinnings, and pries to raise the mill." Apparently he didn't do this, because in this action for rent before a justice of the peace in Sangamon County, Ruckells pleaded he had been damaged as follows, "hired two hands, three months, and were unemployed in consequence of disappointment, at $1.00 per day, 150 days - $150." Nichols objected to this attempted offset, because it was unliquidated, and thus not certain enough to be used as an offset; plus the fact the justice of peace only had jurisdiction to hear matters involving $100 or less. The court ruled Nichols was entitled to recover $50.23 1/2, and also Ruckells offset was allowed; so judgment was rendered for Ruckells for $61.14. This was affirmed by the Sangamon circuit court on appeal.

The supreme court, in an opinion written by Justice Browne, affirmed the judgment. It was established in Edwards et al. v. Todd, 2 Ill.162, that unliquidated damages arising out of a contract can be set off. Also the $100 limit in a justice of the peace court applies only to the amount of the judgment. The justice of the peace may render a judgment for less than $100, even though the account in question was for more than that amount, Browne concluded: "The law abhors a multiplicity of suits, and by this mode of proceeding it will unquestionably be avoided."

Hanckock et al. v. Hodgson, exec of Milnor
orig. ed. 4 Ill.329

(Ill. Rep.: Hanckock et al. v.
Hodgson, exec of Milnor 4 Ill.329)
December Term 1841

This is an appeal from an action in assumpsit brought in Tazwell Circuit Court by Hodgson, as excutor of the estate of Milnor, against John Hancock, and his sureties Peter Menard, Benjamin Greely, and Benjamin Briggs. Milnor had sold certain property to Perkins, who gave a mortgage to Milnor. The mortgage was in default and a decree of foreclosure was entered, and sale ordered to pay the sum of $4,644.87 then due on the mortgage. Perkins had sold the property to Hancock, who wanted to have the sale postponed. He executed a note to Hodgson promising to pay $1,000 if the sale would be postponded for four months. The note specified that if the property sold for more than the amount due, the note would be void, and if sold for less, only the amount of a deficiency less than $1,000 would be due. Judgment rendered for Hodgson for $1,017.83.

Lincoln, Logan, and J.B. Stewart represented Hancock on the appeal. Lincoln presented six separate pleas, in essence saying there was no consideration for the note, and in one of the pleas, that the transaction was usurious.

Justice Treat disposed of these arguments quickly, and judgment was affirmed. The forbearance of four months of the sale was adequate consideration. There was no evidence the property had been sold, and if it had been, it was the duty of Hancock to show it, by way of defense. Also the $1,000 was not interest, and thus could not be considered usurious.

Gerard v. The People
orig. ed. 4 Ill.362

(Ill. Rep.: Gerard v. The People 4 Ill.362)

July Term 1842

Gerard was indicted for the murder of one Mayhew. He was tried, found guilty of manslaughter, and sentenced to one year's imprisonment. He then moved to arrest the judgment on the grounds it was faulty, in that the jury had not imposed a fine upon him. This motion was granted, and he was released. However, shortly thereafter he was indicted again for the same act, and brought to trial. He contended that he had already been tried for that act, convicted, and could not be tried again. The People demurred, which was sustained. Gerard then pleaded not guilty, was tried, found guilty of manslaughter, and sentenced to three year's imprisonment.

The supreme court, in an opinion written by Justice Treat, affirmed the judgment. In the first case, the court arrested the judgment for insufficient cause, the imposition of the fine being a duty the law had devolved on the court, and not on the jury. Where a prisoner has been indicted and found guilty, by the verdict of a jury, if the judgment is arrested, even for an insufficient cause, and the defendant discharged, he has not been legally in jeopardy, and he cannot plead the conviction in bar to a subsequent indictment. He cannot claim error when the motion to dismiss the first judgment had been made by him.

Grable v. Margrave
orig. ed. 4 Ill.372
(Ill. Rep.: Grable v. Margrave 4 Ill.372)
July Term 1842

This case is an action of trespass on the case by Margrave against Grable, in the Gallastin Circuit Court before Judge Scates, for the seduction of the daughter of Margrave. At the trial, Judge Scates permitted evidence of the pecuniary ability of each party. This was objected to, and after judgment for Margrave for $300 damages, Grable appeals. Lincoln represented Margrave on the appeal.

Justice Treat wrote the opinion of the court affirming the judgment. He commenced by reciting the common law basis of the action originally given to the master to recover damages for loss of service occasioned by the seduction of his servant. Loss of services is still the basis of the action, and the father was to prove that because of the seduction, his daughter is less able to perform the duties of a servant. However, Lincoln cited English common law cases that stated this rule of damages had been extended to cover more than the mere loss of services. In vindictive actions, like this, juries should be permitted to give damages for the double purpose of setting an example, and of punishing the wrong-doer.

Thus to make certain a wrong-doer is punished, his pecuniary ability is a proper subject of evidence. "A verdict which, as against one individual, would be sufficient for all purposes, would, as against another, be scarcely felt, by reason of the difference in ability to respond in damages." Thus evidence of the defendent's wealth was admissable. As far as evidence of pecuniary ability of the plaintiff, Justice Treat said "This evidence does not go to the jury, as was stated in argument, for the purpose of exciting their prejudices in favor of the plaintiff, because he is a poor man, but to enable them to understand fully the effect of the injury upon him, and to give him such damages as his peculiar condition in life and circumstances entitle him to receive." This last point is not very clear, but it is clear Lincoln relied on the disparate pecuniary positions of each party to influence the jury for Margrave's victory. It also should have influenced Grable to seek out a rich man's daughter if he ever decided to repeat his uncivilized act.

Conklin v. Underhill
orig. ed. 4 Ill.388
(Ill. Rep.: Conkling v. Underhill 4 Ill.388)
December Term 1842

Conkling executed a note to Wood, who assigned it to Underhill for consideration, before it matured. The note is not paid, and Underhill brought this action. Conkling pleads the note was usurious, thus void, and he has no liability. Judgment rendered for Underhill for $625 debt and $93.75 in damages. Logan represented Underhill on the appeal at least.

The supreme court, in an opinion written by Justice Ford, affirmed the judgment. The innocent endorsee (Underhill) of a note, before it becomes due, is not to be prejudiced by the illegality of consideration, as between the maker and the payee, unless the note has been made void by statute. Ford then said: "In England, and in many states of the union, the statutes declare a note taken for usury to be void; thereby making it proper that a usurious note be taken out of the general rule. But in this state, the statute does not declare such a note to be void; on the contrary, it is expressly provided that the plaintiff shall have judgment for a portion of his debt. Therefore, the note in this state not being void, and Underhill being an innocent assignee, he is entitled to recover."

Averill et al. v. Field
orig. ed. 4 Ill.390
(Ill. Rep.: Averill et al. v. Field 4 Ill.389)
September Term 1841

Field owned certain lots and sold one-half of them to Averill and Lowell, and received a promissory note in exchange. The note was due, and an action was brought by Field of assumpsit. Averill and Lowell pleaded a writing under seal had been entered into at the same time as the note was executed, wherein both parties agreed to sell lots and pay to the other one-half of the proceeds if either side made a sale. They said Field's note was to be paid out of the proceeds of sales made by Averill and Lowell. There was no evidence that either party had made any sales. The Tazewell circuit court, Judge Treat presiding, held for Field, and judgment was rendered against Averill and Lowell, who bring this appeal, represented by Logan and Lincoln.

Lincoln cited Bailey and Cromwell, 4 Ill.71, which held the two instruments executed together on the same subject matter, should be considered together. Justice Treat agreed this was the law. Averill and Lowell pleaded they had not made any sales; thus since they could not pay the note from proceeds of sales, Field would just have to wait until sales were made, since the combined writings inferred the note was only to be repaid by such sales. Treat said it was inferred from the two documents, payments of proceeds of sales by Averill and Lowell would be used to pay the note, if they occurred before the note because due. But on its due date, it should have been paid. Judgment affirmed.

This was an early instance where an Illinois case was cited as precedent. However, even though the precedent was agreed to, the interpretation of the two instruments read together did not support Lincoln's contention.

Wilson, adm. of Wilson v. Alexander
orig. ed. 4 Ill.392

(Ill. Rep.: Wilson v. Alexander 4 Ill.392)
December Term 1842

This action of assumpsit was originally heard in the Tazwell Circuit Court before Judge Samuel H. Treat and a jury. The opinion of the Supreme Court reversing the judgment was written by Justice Treat. Lincoln appeared for James Wilson at the appeal, and it is not known whether he was the attorney for James at the trial.

James Wilson was the administrator of Samuel Wilson, deceased, and brought this action on a note made by Alexander to Samuel. Alexander pleaded payment. It was proved that Alexander had paid the note, and part of the payment was a note for $100, purporting to be executed by Samuel to Isaac Kreider, who assigned it to Joseph Allen, who assigned it to Alexander. The note was a forgery, but it was admitted by the parties that Alexander, at the time of the transfer, had no knowledge it was forged. At the instance of Alexander's counsel, Judge Treat instructed the jury that unless they believed Alexander knew the note was forged when he paid Samuel, they must find for Alexander. They did, and James appeals.

The charge to the jury was based upon case law, that a person who appears to be the contracting party to forged negotiable paper, is charged with a knowledge of its genuineness; and acts at his peril, when called upon by an innocent holder for performance of the contract. But as Lincoln pointed out on the appeal, the purported maker of the forged note (Samuel Wilson) was deceased when the forged note was paid to

James Wilson. James cannot be held to have the same knowledge Samuel would have had. Therefore, the question of authenticity is at the risk of the person passing the paper (Alexander). Therefore, the lower court is reversed.

If we assume Lincoln did not represent James at the trial, and the cases Lincoln cited on appeal were not cited at the trial, then Judge Treat's instructions are understandable. When Lincoln argued the appeal, his citations compelled the court (and Justice Treat) to reverse the lower court judgement (which was based on Judge Treat's instructions).

Howell et al. v. Edgar & Forsyth
orig. ed. 4 Ill.417

(Ill. Rep.: Howell et al. v. Edgar et al. 4 Ill.416)
December Term 1842

Edgar and Forsyth sued out a writ of attachment against Shewalter and McCrary, which was served upon Howell, with others, as garnishees, after obtaining a judgment against Shewalter and McCrary for $765.51. Shewalter, who apparently had many creditors, conveyed property to Howell to be held, under certain conditions, for the benefit of his creditors. Justice Scates summarized these conditions thusly: "I will pay some of you all (you are owed) if I have enough; if there be surplus, I will pay the rest of you pro rata, provided you will, within twelve months, release me from all liability for any deficiency." Edgar and Forsyth, being in the second category of creditors, elected not to sign the agreement; and brought a successful suit against Shewalter and McCrary, based on the theory the assignment of assets to Howell was void as fraudulent against creditors. Judgment was rendered for Edgar and Forsyth. Logan represented Edgar and Forsyth on the appeal at least.

The supreme court, in an opinion written by Justice Scates, affirmed the judgment. Scates said, "The right of a failing debtor to prefer a creditor by deed of assignment, is too firmly settled by the authorities to be questioned, if it be fairly made, without onerous conditions to the creditor, or provisions for his own advancement, and there be no bankrupt or attachment laws abridging the right." He then cited many authorities from England and other states, in similar cases, some holding an assignment like in this case was fair, and some fraudulent. Recognizing the inconsistencies, he stated "I think it our duty to lay down the rule that should govern us, at as early a day as possible, that none may be deceived, either in making or trusting to such a title." The court held this assignment was fraudulent. He concluded "It would be extremely difficult to determine that the weight of authority was settled either way, amidst such a number of conflicting decisions. But it is much less difficult to determine that reason and justice incline the scales against such a transaction."

McDonald v. Bacon
orig. ed. 4 Ill.428
(Ill. Rep.: McDonald v. Bacon 4 Ill.428)
December Term 1842

McDonald and Bacon both possessed water mills on Crooked Creek, in McDonough county. Disputes arose between them concerning mill privileges, and damages incurred by each, which they submitted to arbitration. The arbiters awarded damages to McDonald, and also required Bacon, who was down stream from McDonald, to remove eleven inches of planks from his dam to reduce the amount of water backed up to McDonald's dam. McDonald brought this action against Bacon to recover damages for his non-performance of the award. Bacon believed the award was void for uncertainty; so he demurred, which was sustained and judgment awarded for Bacon, Logan represented McDonald on the appeal at least.

The supreme court, in an opinion written by Justice Treat, affirmed the judgment. As a general principle, an award, to be obligatory on the parties must decide all the matters contained in the submission. This award did not do so. It settled the money damages with certainty, but did not adequately solve the problem caused by the backwater from Bacon's dam causing hardship to McDonald. Justice Treat cited the following uncertainty in this solution: "We do not think that it would follow as a necessary consequence from a certain reduction in the height of the dam, that the back water near the upper mill would fall the same distance. There is no general rule by which anything like certainty could be attained, without an actual examination and survey of the stream." This had not been done by the arbiters; hence the uncertainty which rendered the award void.

Reddick v. Smith
orig. ed. 4 Ill.451
(Ill. Rep.: Reddick v. Smith 4 Ill.451)

Smith recovered a judgment against Douglass. Execution was issued on the judgment directed to Reddick, the sheriff of La Salle county. He collected the money from Douglass; and while it was being held by him as garnishee, Smith brought an action of attachment to recover the money. Judgment for Reddick.

The supreme court, in an opinion written by Justice Treat, affirmed the judgment. Money in the hands of a sheriff, collected by him on execution, is not liable to be levied on, and taken by him, by virtue of another execution. It does not become the property of the judgment creditor until it is paid over to him, and consequently can not be levied upon or attached as his.

The facts reported in the opinion give no clue why Reddick didn't pay the money when requested by Smith.

Edwards v. Pope et al.
orig. ed. 4 Ill.465

(Ill. Rep.: Edwards v. Pope et al. 4 Ill.465)
December Term 1842

Edwards bring this action in chancery seeking a perpetual injunction against an action for partition of certain land in Alton instituted by Pope et al. Pope had applied to the Illinois legislature for a special enactment to enable him to petition a circuit court for an order to sell subject land owned by himself, and the heirs of both Whitesides, and Ninian Edwards (from whom complainant Edwards in this suit is descended). The legislature passed the measure, and Pope petitioned the Madison circuit court, who ordered the sale. Three commissioners were appointed, the land was platted including public streets, a special provision of land ceded to Abigail Easton for dower rights; and the land sold with the proceeds to be distributed to the known parties. Edwards brings this action to delay the procedure until all interested people are found, and for them to give consent to the sale. Decree for Pope et al. Logan represented Edwards on the appeal at least.

The supreme court, in a decision written by Justice Scates, affirmed the decree. Edwards action was based on his contention the legislature had assumed judicial powers here, which is unconstitutional. Lane et al. v. Dorman et ux. (3 Ill.238) was referenced as a case wherein the court held the act of the legislature void, on the ground it made a judicial determination empowering Lane to sell land from Robinson's estate to satisfy a debt owed him. Scates said "It is difficult to lay down any general rule distinguishing between legislative and judicial acts . . . By every rule of interpretation applicable to this act (of the legislature), I can not resist the conclusion, that all the proceedings are intended to enhance the interest of the proprietors. The state is not seeking to take private property for public use. It neither needs, asks, or requires a public highway there. The act declares the streets public highways, not because it wants one, but to secure, by this public easement, an increased competition and value to the lots." Also: "This (act), then but empowers the parties to do that for themselves, which they could not do by reason of infancy, their not being known, or being non-residents." He concluded: "Each act of the legislature must depend upon its own peculiar phraseology and provisions. We will look to the particular circumstances of the parties applying for, and to be affected by it as well as their intention and the intention of the legislature, and the object to be accomplished." If from these, it be manifest that the legislature has exercised but a remedial power in enabling the parties to do with their own property, what they had not power before to do, and had not adjudicated that they should do, what they are unwilling to do it seems to me the act would be within legislative competency."

Schlencker et al. v. Risley
orig. ed. 4 Ill.483

(Ill. Rep.: Schlencker et al. v. Risley 4 Ill.483)
December Term 1842

Risley, represented by Lincoln, brought an action of trespass for false imprisonment against several parties, including Wallace and Schlencker who were the only ones found guilty, and the sum of $333 was assessed against them. Wallace, acting as a constable arrested Risley with the assistance of Schlencker, who was recruited as part of a posse. Wallace and Schlencker moved for a new trial on the grounds that there was newly discovered evidence, the verdict was excessive, and the judgment was defective in form. Lincoln defeated each one of these points, and the judgment against Schlencker was appealed.

Schlencker said he was summoned by Wallace to aid him in arresting Risley. Schlencker objected, and offered Wallace one dollar to let him out, who refused it. He also offered new evidence of a witness who confirmed what Wallace and Schlencker had said to each other. Justice Caton, who wrote the opinion, said this new evidence was on a point already established at the trial, thus did not constitute adequate grounds for a new trial. He then stated courts have always manifested a reluctance to disturb verdicts on account of excessive damages, unless it is probable the jury had acted under the influence of prejudice or passion. The damages here were not so high as to induce that belief. Also it was too late to object to the form of the verdict. If objection had been raised at the delivery of the verdict, it could easily have been adjusted then. No harm done to anyone by the form of the verdict. The lower court opinion was affirmed.

Heaton v. Hulbert
orig. ed. 4 Ill.489

(Ill. Rep.: Heaton v. Hulbert 4 Ill.488)

December Term 1842

Reiley executed a promissory note to Bledsoe and Turpin, and Turpin assigned his interest in the note to Bledsoe; who assigned the note to Heaton, who wrote on the back of the note: "For a valuable consideration, I guaranty the payment of the within note," signed it, and assigned it to Hulbert. The note is unpaid, and Hulbert sues Heaton. Judgment for Hulbert for $338.30. Logan represented Heaton on the appeal at least.

The supreme court, in an opinion written by Justice Douglass, affirmed the judgment. Firstly, a guaranty like this one which does not name any person as a party guaranteed, is a valid instrument, and may be enforced by anyone who advances money upon it. Secondly, the guaranty here is absolute and unconditional, that the note will be paid when due. Hulbert did not have to sue Reiley first, or prove his insolvency, because the guarantor's liability does not depend upon the solvency or insolvency of the maker and endorser of the note. Such were not the terms of his contract, or the nature of his undertaking.

Evans v. Merriweather
orig. ed. 4 Ill.492

(Ill. Rep.: Evans v. Merriweather 4 Ill.491)

December Term 1842

Evans owned a steam mill on a stream. Merriweather also owned a steam mill on the same stream, but downstream from Evans'. In 1837 there was a drought, and Evans built a dam across the stream to retain sufficient water to run his mill. Merriweather could not run his, and sued Evans for damages. Judgment rendered for Merriweather. Harden and Logan represented Merriweather on the appeal at least.

The supreme court, in an opinion written by Justice Lockwood, affirmed the judgment. He stated: "The language of all the authorities is, that water flows in its natural course, and should be permitted thus to flow, so that all through whose land it naturally flows, may enjoy the privilege of using it . . . A riparian proprietor, therefore, though he has an undoubted right to use the water for hydraulic or manufacturing purposes, must so use it as to do no injury to any other riparian proprietor." Later on he concluded: "Where all have a right to participate in a common benefit, and none can have an exclusive enjoyment, no rule, from the very nature of the case, can be laid down, as to how much each may use without infringing upon the rights of others. In such cases, the question must be left to the judgment of the jury, whether the party complained of has used, under all the circumstances, more than his just proportion." The jury held damage had been done, so the judgment of the jury was affirmed.

Cushman v. Dement
orig. ed. 4 Ill.497

(Ill. Rep.: Cushman v. Dement 4 Ill.497)

December Term 1842

Dement brought an action of assumpsit against Cushman as an endorser of a promissory note. Eager & Hill gave a promissory note to Dement for $848, to pay for cattle, who refused to take the note without some additional guarantor of payment. Cushman endorsed the note in blank. The note is due. Cushman said he didn't understand his potential liability. Judgment for Dement.

The supreme court, in an opinion written by Justice Douglass, affirmed the judgment. He said: "We have decided at the present term, in the case of Camden et al. v. McKay et al., 4 Ill.437, that a blank endorsement of a promissory note, at the time of its execution, is prima facie evidence of a liability in the capacity of the guarantor, and operates as authority to a bona fide holder to fill up the endorsement, by writing a guaranty over the signature. This legal presumption is liable to be rebutted by parol proof, as has been attempted in this case. But the Circuit Court was of opinion that the whole evidence showed the defendant intended to become responsible for the payment of the note, in case the makers did not pay it, when due; and we think the evidence fully sustains the verdict."

Tiffany, Duvall & Co. v. Breese
orig. ed. 4 Ill.499

(Ill. Rep.: Tiffany et al. v. Breese 4 Ill.499)
December Term 1842

Tiffany, Duvall & Co. brought an action of assumpsit against Afflick and Sidney Breese to recover the amount of a promissory note made by them as partners. Summons was issued for the two defendants, but the sheriff only made a return of service on Afflick. Judgment was rendered in the Sangamon Circuit Court, by Judge Treat, for $1,495.06 against Afflick et al. Two years later Tiffany et al. sued out a summons to make Breese a party to the judgment against Afflick. Breese moved to quash this summons, and judgment by the court to do so.

The supreme court, in an opinion written by Justice Treat, reversed the judgement, and remanded it for further proceedings. Justice Treat stated it might be irregular to have rendered a judgment against Afflick, when there was no return of the process as to his co-defendant. However, if so , it can only be attacked by someone who is injured by it. Breese was not injured, and cannot question the regularity or the judgment.

We assume the Sidney Breese in this action is the same person who later became a justice of the court. We are more certain that Judge Treat in the Sangamon circuit court is Justice Treat who wrote the opinion. Today the court system is more civilized and the justices of the supreme court don't have to consider matters decided by them individually as circuit court judges.

Williams v. Smith
orig. ed. 4 Ill.524

(Ill. Rep.: Williams v. Smith 4 Ill.524)
December Term 1842

Williams made a promissory note to Smith, as part of a real estate transaction wherein Smith sold a house to Williams. The note was for $500 and specified it was payable when William Henry Harrison would be elected president of the United States. Harrison was, but Williams declares the agreement void because it was against public policy and good morals, as a wagering agreement. The court rendered judgment for Smith. Logan represented Smith on the appeal at least.

The supreme court, in an opinion written by Justice Scates, affirmed the judgment. There were no facts to infer the contract grew out of a bet upon the presidential election.

Perhaps the court experienced revulsion when the maker of a note suddenly decides what he did was "against public policy and good morals." We all respect confession of wrongs, but respect it more when the confession is not made to relieve one of a monetary obligation.

Morgan v. Pettit
orig. ed. 4 Ill.529
(Ill. Rep.: Morgan v. Pettit 4 Ill.529)

Powell made a wager with Morgan, wherein Morgan was to pay Powell $50.00 if General Harrison received three thousand more votes in Kentucky than Van Buren in the presidential election. Pettit was the surety for Morgan. Harrison carried Kentucky by more than three thousand votes, and Pettit paid Morgan $50.00, and brings this action of assumpsit to recover the $50.00 from Morgan. Morgan pleads the wager was illegal, either under an Illinois statute which made it illegal to bet on elections, or under English common law. Judgment for Pettit.

The supreme court, in an opinion written by Justice Treat, affirmed the judgment. The Illinois statute only applied to elections in Illinois, and not to those made in Illinois on elections in other states. Treat cited many English cases involving wagers, and summarized as follows: "At common law, all wagers were recoverable but such as were prohibited by statute; such as were against sound policy; and such as tended to a breach of peace, to immorality, or indecency, or injuriously affected the rights of third persons." This situation did not fit any of those exceptions, and was recoverable under common law.

Mason v. Park
orig. ed. 4 Ill.532
(Ill. Rep.: Mason v. Park 4 Ill.532)
December Term 1842

This was an action of debt to recover the penalty given by "An act to prevent trespassing by cutting timber," originally brought before a justice of the peace, by Park, represented by Lincoln and Aaron Shaw, against

Mason. This was appealed to the circuit court of Richland County, tried before a jury and Judge William Wilson, and a verdict returned for Park for $48. At the trial, Park, to prove title to the land on which the trees were cut, called a witness, who testified to a conversation in which Mason admitted to him, that two of the trees were cut on the land of Park. This was all the evidence in relation to the title. Mason appeals, on the grounds this evidence was inadequate. The Supreme Court agreed with Mason, and Justice Treat gives the court's opinion, reversing the circuit court.

There is a long standing rule in common law that the best evidence which the nature of the cause permits, should be furnished in a trial. When title to land is claimed, the best evidence would be his deeds and other documentary evidence of title. These are always presumed to be in his custody, and could be easily produced. The oral testimony of what Mason said about ownership of two trees cut was the weakest kind of evidence, and far from adequate here. Lincoln argued that the admission of a party who has the right to compel his antagonist thus to make out his case, dispenses with the necessity of producing the best evidence of title. Thus Mason's admission, while he had the right to require Park to produce the best evidence of title, excused the necessity of application of the "best evidence" rule. Judge Treat probably said "nice try" and refused to make new law by agreeing with Lincoln's ingenious argument. Incidently, Chief Justice Wilson dissented, so Lincoln persuaded one Jurist that his position was right. He also was the trial judge.

We know Lincoln represented some appellate clients when he hadn't been associated with the case at trial. Presumably this was one, as the "best evidence" rule had been around a long time in 1842, and it still is given credence.

Ryder et al. v. Stevenson
orig. ed. 4 Ill.539

(Ill. Rep.: Ryder et al. v. Stevenson 4 Ill.539)
December Term 1842

Stevenson brought an action against Ryder, Frost, and Gilman as garnishes of one John Anderson, and recovered a judgment for $318.64. Ryder and Frost appealed, and entered into a bond in the amount of $500, with Bowman and Topping as sureties. The bond was filed in due time, executed by Ryder, Gilman, Bowman, and Topping. Stevenson made a motion to dismiss the appeal, because Frost had not executed the appeal bond.

The supreme court dismissed the motion, because Frost, as one of the persons bringing the appeal, should have signed the appeal bond.

Greathouse et al. v. Smith
orig. ed. 4 Ill.541

(Ill. Rep.: Greathouse et al. v. Smith 4 Ill.541)
December Term 1842

Smith, represented by Lincoln on appeal at least, brought an action of debt against Greathouse and Chestnut in the Macoupin Circuit Court at the September Term, 1842. The declaration supporting the action is the record of a judgment recovered in the same court, at the September term 1941 by Smith against Greathouse and Chestnut for $852.02. Defendants contended since the first judgment was in full force, and had not been excuted upon, this action was unnecessary. Also the action was vexatious and instituted to avoid the effect of a law, regulating the sale of property, passed on the 27th of February, 1841. Judgment for Smith, and Greathouse & Chestnut appeal.

Justice Treat writes the opinion in which the judgment is affirmed. He states "No rule of law is better settled than the one, that an action of debt is maintainable on a judgment of a court of record. The judgment is a good cause of action, it being as between the parties, the most conclusive evidence of indebtedness." As for the second point, it was not pleaded in the trial; and the question whether the rights of the parties, under the valuation law, would be changed by the second recovery, could not properly arise until Smith attempted to collect the judgment, without reference to the provisions of the law.

Watkins v. White
orig. ed. 4 Ill.549

(Ill. Rep.: Watkins v. White 4 Ill.548)
December Term 1842

This is an action of replevin brought by Watkins (represented by Lincoln in the appeal) against White, for a certain mare, in the Sangamon Circuit Court before Judge Samuel H. Treat and a jury. Verdict and judgment rendered for the defendant, White, and appealed based on improper instructions by Judge Treat to the jury.

The evidence was Watkins bought the mare when a colt, and sold her to one Ferguson, who kept her six or eight months, and sold her back to Watkins for seventy-five dollars in cash notes, and thirty barrels of corn. Watkins kept the mare in a lot surrounded by a good fence at night, but she was missing one morning, "the fence being laid down as by human hands." Shortly thereafter Watkins son, who was under age and had left home, sold the mare to James Maxcy in Springfield for ten dollars in money, and forty dollars in county orders, some time in the year 1838. Maxey sold her to John Constant, who sold her to White. Subsequently Watkins looked for the horse in livery stables in Springfield where the mare was, but she was not in the stables the particular times Watkins looked for her. There was also testimony that Watkins knew someone had ridden the mare to some races in 1840 that Watkins attended. The jury was instructed that if Watkins knew the mare was in Springfield in possession of other people, who were exercising acts of ownership over her, for more than a reasonable time to claim her; the jury might infer he ratified the sale by his son, and find for the defendant, although the statue of limitations had not expired.

The court, Justice Semple writing the opinion, reversed the circuit court and ordered a new trial on the grounds that the instructions given by Judge Treat to the jury were entirely too general. Lincoln argued that a party is not bound to sue immediately for any injury he may sustain. He may consult his own convenience as to when he will assert his rights, provided he is not barred by the statute of limitations, or such length of time as will amount to presumption of payment, or satisfaction. The court held the jury should have been allowed to make their verdict as to the real ownership of the mare, from the evidence before them; without being instructed that there was any presumption of the ratification of the sale, as the jury was charged in this case.

Reed et al. v. Phillips et al.
orig. ed. 5 Ill.39

(Ill. Rep.: Reed et al. v. Phillips et al. 5 Ill.39)
December Term 1842

Reed et al. agreed to pay Phillips et al. for certain quantities of rock and wood delivered to Reed et al's. place of work. The facts are obscure, but certain rock and wood were delivered, but payment was disputed. Phillips et al. brings an action of debt, and are awarded $153.85. Judge Treat tried the case, and Logan represented Phillips et al. on the appeal at least.

The supreme court, in an opinion written by Justice Wilson, affirmed the judgment. The opinion began as follows: "The record of this case affords a very imperfect knowledge of the proceedings had below, on account of the irregular and confused manner in which they are stated." One major issue was a receipt issued by Phillips et al. stating they had received $120 for rock delivered at the work site. There was no evidence whether this was for all rock delivered to that date, or merely for one shipment. The jury decided Phillips et al. was entitled to more compensation and the supreme court said: "The court very properly left to the jury to determine, under all the circumstances, to what extent the receipt was an acknowledgment of payment. The judgment is affirmed with costs."

Paine & Alexander v. Frazier & Frazier
orig. ed. 5 Ill.55

(Ill. Rep.: Paine et al. v. Frazier et al. 5 Ill.55)
December Term 1842

The Fraziers, represented by Lincoln on appeal, filed a bill in chancery in Vermillion Circuit Court before Judge Harlan alleging they had purchased certain tracts of land from Payne, over which the Northern Cross railroad was located. For damages occasioned by the location of the railroad, Payne had obtained a judgment against the state of Illinois for $150 which Payne had agreed to pay to the Fraziers. This bill sought an injunction restraining the payment to Payne, and also that Alexander (Commissioner of the Board of Public Works) be required to pay the money to the Fraziers. An injunction was granted, and served on Payne and Alexander. Alexander filed his answer acknowledging the recovery of the judgment by Payne, denying all knowledge of the sale by Payne to the Fraziers; and that before he had any knowledge of the pendancy of this suit, he paid Payne $50 in full satisfaction of the judgment, and received from him a relinquishment to the State of the right of way over the land. The Fraziers failed to file a replication (which was a necessary formal pleading to protect their rights against the allegations in Alexander's answer).

The court went on to make the injunction permanent, and ordered Alexander to pay $150 to the Fraziers. This order is the subject of this appeal. The Supreme Court, with Justice Treat writing the opinion, reversed the decree ordering Alexander to pay. The answer of Alexander, if true, furnished a complete defence to the suit. No replication was filed by the Fraziers, putting Alexander's allegations in issue, and in such case, the answer is taken to be true, and rquires no proof to support it. The cause is remanded, with instructions to permit the Fraziers to file their replication to the answer, and proceed with the cause.

The purpose of formal responses in pleadings is to identify and isolate significant issues to be litigated in a particular proceeding. Failure to file a replication here was not simply a legal technicality. It was necessary to reply to a statement made by Alexander which if true closed the case against him. He was entitled to be dismissed from the suit if his answers were true, and if the Fraziers did not believe him it was their duty to say so, and the proper vehicle for that was the replication. We assume Lincoln did not represent Frazier et. al at the trial.

Taylor et al. v. Whitney
orig. ed. 5 Ill.61

(Ill. Rep.: Taylor et al. v. Whitney 5 Ill.61)
December Term 1842

Whitney donated certain land in Springfield to be used by the Northern Cross railroad from Jacksonville to Springfield. He intended the land to be used as a station or turnout, but the railroad chose other sites for these purposes deemed more efficient and less expensive for the project. Whitney brought this action in chancery in Sangamon county before Judge Treat for an injunction to prevent the railroad using land other than that donated by him for a turnout or station. The petition is granted. Logan represented Whitney on the appeal at least.

The supreme court, in an opinion written by Justice Breese, reversed the decree and dissolved the decree. There is nothing in the acts of the legislature requiring the railroad to use donated lands, unless such use would be their most efficient and least expensive for the railroad project.

Fitch et al. v. Pritchard et al.
orig. ed. 5 Ill.69

(Ill. Rep.: Fitch et al. v. Pinckard et al. 5 Ill.69)
December Term 1842

This is a very lengthy opinion, written by Justice Scates, involving an appeal from an action of ejectment brought to recover possession of "all that messuage, tenement, and lot of ground situate, lying and being in the city of Alton, and state of Illinois, etc." The action was denied in the Madison Circuit Court and the petitioners make this appeal.

The appellants (Fitch) were represented by three attorneys and the appellees (Pritchard) by four (including Lincoln). Most of the attorneys submitted trial briefs, and the detailed report of them takes six pages of the opinion. At the end of the trial, the petitioners submitted seven errors, and the defendants eight. Lincoln's brief cited five English common law cases, and specified the reasoning and authorities Justice Scates relied upon, after masterfully disposing of all the other clutter in a ten page opinion.

Fitch and Fay claimed the property by virture of a tax title acquired through a sale of taxes in 1837, and also by virtue of a sale on a judgment and execution. Lincoln pointed out that it was not certain in either sale what premises were sold. To claim land from a tax sale, it is material to have strict compliance with the law governing such sales, which was patently not done here. And in the execution of the judgment, the levy specified as follows: "Levied this execution, May 28th, 1837, on a certain lot situated on the angle of Second and State streets, in the town of Alton, and advertised to be sold July 29th, 1837. N. Buchmaster, Shff. M.C." Justice Scates pointed out several possible lots on the plat that would answer this description, perhaps repeating questions asked by Lincoln in oral arguments, and stated "I am of opinion that it is too uncertain to enable any one to value it so as to bid, or to find and identify it." Thus the whole proceeding was void for uncertainty, and the judgment below was affirmed.

Holdridge v. Bailey
orig. ed. 5 Ill.124

(Ill. Rep.: Holdridge v. Bailey 5 Ill.124)
December Term 1842

Bailey brings an action in Lasalle county against Holdridge, for the specific performance of a contract to convey a tract of land; alleging Holdridge agreed in writing to convey certain land to Bailey, if he paid him $250 at a certain time. Bailey alleged he paid the money, but Holdridge did not convey the land. Holdridge replied he remembered the agreement in general, but could not remember the details; and it was not included in Bailey's court documents. Decree entered for Bailey.

The Supreme Court, in an opinion written by Justice Treat, reversed the decree. Where a bill in chancery alleges the execution of a document to convey land if certain conditions are met, and the answer denies, or does not admit its execution; it is incumbent upon the complainant (Bailey) to produce or file it as an exhibit in the cause, and prove its genuineness; or, if lost, make the necessary proof, by parol, of its genuineness and contents.

Mason, for use of Mason v. Wait et al.
orig. ed. 5 Ill.127

(Ill. Rep.: Mason, for use of Mason v. Wait et al. 5 Ill.127)
December Term 1842

This is an action of debt on a promissory note. Mason, through her guardian, agreed to sell land to Wait et al., who gave the promissory note, with the land to be conveyed when the note was paid. The guardian derived power to sell the land through two special acts of the legislature. Wait contends the laws are unconstitutional, and pleaded seven special pleas. The decisions against Mason overruling demurrers to some of the pleas is the basis of the appeal.

The supreme court, in an opinion written by Justice Scates, affirmed the judgment, and remanded the cause for further proceedings. Guardians have no power to sell real estate of their wards, unless authorized by the courts, or perhaps by the legislature. In these legislative acts she was authorized to sell the property, under the direction and sanction of the judge of probate. Justice Scates referenced Lane et al. v. Dorman et ux., 4 Ill.238 in defining "judicial powers" under the constitution. The legislature acted properly in conferring this power to sell the land on the guardian. The power of the legislature is limited and defined by the constitutions of the state and the United States. He then said: "And in my view of the law-making power of these state governments is , that they can do any legislative act not prohibited by the constitutions; and without and beyond these limitations and restrictions they are as absolute, omnipotent, and uncontrollable as parliament."

Edwards et al. v. Helm
orig. ed. 5 Ill.142

(Ill. Rep.: Edwards et al. v. Helm 5 Ill.142)
December Term 1842

This is a complicated set of facts involving several personal loans and mortgages on land. Justice Scates resolves the case by admitting the pleadings do not support any equitable solution for either side, and reverses a decree which had been rendered against Lincoln's clients, with leave to allow the other side to make additional findings. The case was retried later, appealed and reported in 6 Ill.220.

The facts, as best made out from the opinion, are: Ware sold land to Edwards, who, with Helm and Gray as sureties, executed a note to Ware for six thousand dollars. Ware assigned the note to Craig and Warner. Edwards was indebted to Helm for seven thousand dollars, and gave him a note and mortgage for that amount. Edwards note to Ware is in default, and Craig and Warner bring suit against Edwards, Helm, and Gray. They obtained a judgment against Edwards, on whom alone process was served, and the land (including that in his mortgage to Helm) was sold under execution to Craig and Warner. Helm, whose note from Edwards is in default, brings this action against Edwards, and Craig and Warner as judgment creditors of Edwards. A decree was entered in the Madison Circuit Court by Judge Sidney Breese for Helm in the amount of $12,224.30 and costs of the suit. This decree is reversed because the equitable remedy is not readily apparent.

Lincoln was persistent, and persuaded Justice Scates to reverse the unfavorable decision in the lower court, since the equities on either side, especially Helm's who won in the lower court, were not clear enough to justify a favorable decree for either party.

Grubb v. Crane
orig. ed. 5 Ill.153

(Ill. Rep.: Grubb v. Crane 5 Ill.153)
December Term 1842

This case in the Sangamon Circuit Court before Judge Treat involves an action to enforce a note. Under common law, the particular debt could have been enforced several ways. The real issue in the case was whether the payee of the note sought the proper remedy. Lincoln and Logan defended Crane on the appeal, which affirmed a decree for Crane in the lower court.

Crane sold land to Grubb, and received two notes, one for $800 and one for $1,000. Title to land was to be transferred when the notes were paid. Grubb paid the first note and a small portion of the second. Crane brought an action in chancery for the balance. Execution was issued, and when no property of Grubb was found to pay the debt, Crane asked the court to order the contracted land sold to pay the debt. Grubb was served, but he did not appear. The subject premises were then sold under the decree. Grubb then appears, and moves to set aside the report. Grubb then filed this motion, called a bill of review. Crane appeared and demurred (this is a pleading by a defendant which even if the facts in the motion are true, they are insufficient to oblige the defendant to answer). The demurer was sustained (agreed to) by the court, and the motion dismissed. Grubb makes this appeal to the Supreme Court.

Justice Douglass, writing the opinion for the court, in affirming the decision, stated that even though Crane had several remedies, the one employed here did equity to both parties. Another choice would have been to convey the land, to Grubb, and then levy his execution against it. In either choice the land would be sold, and if for more than the balance of the note due, Grubb would be entitled to any excess. Substantial justice was done, and there is no reason to reverse the decree.

Reece v. Darby et al.
orig. ed. 5 Ill.159

(Ill. Rep.: 5 Ill.160)
December Term 1842

Reece was doing business as a merchant, and bought goods from McGill and Darby. The accounts were paid at various times, and the pleadings indicated the parties disagreed how much, if any, was still owed. Reece had given a mortgage as security, and this was assigned to James Mason. Reece alleged this assignment was fraudulent, and brings this action in chancery for an injunction against all the defendants and that an account be stated between McGill and him. The defendants all appeared, and filed separate answers. The action was commenced in 1834, and with the matter still pending, the defendants made a motion to dissolve the injunction and dismiss the bill. This was granted, Logan represented Reece on the appeal at least.

The supreme court, in an opinion written by Justice Scates, affirmed the decree. The motion was nothing more than a hearing on the pleadings. Since the answers denied the whole equity of the bill, without any contrary proof the answers must be taken as true, and the bill was properly dismissed.

Higby v. People ex rel. Fishbourne
orig. ed. 5 Ill.165

(Ill. Rep.: Higby v. People ex rel. Fishbourne 5 Ill.166)
December Term 1843

This action was brought in the name of "the people on the complaint of Abraham S. Fishbourne" to recover the penalty of fifty dollars provided for in legislation pertaining to the mode of granting licenses to clock peddlers, and requiring such clock peddlers to exhibit the license when conducting their business. Judgment was rendered against Higby, with half the money to be paid to the informer, Fishbourne, and half to the county. Logan represented Higby on the appeal at least.

The supreme court, in an opinion written by Justice Treat, reversed the judgment. The state had no interest in the recovery, and it was improper to bring it in the name of the people. It should have been brought either in the name of the informer, or in that of the county.

Laswell v. Hickox & Hickox
orig. ed. 5 Ill.181

(Ill. Rep.: Laswell v. Hickox et. al. 5 Ill.182)
December Term 1843

Laswell instituted an action before the mayor of Springfield against Horace and A. Hickox, and was successful. The defendants appealed to the Sangamon circuit court, before Judge Treat, on the ground the mayor did not have jurisdiction in this case. It was admitted by the parties that the cause did not arise within the city, and that both Hickox were served with a summons outside the limits of the city. Judgment rendered for Hickox et al. who were represented by Logan on the appeal at least.

The supreme court, in an opinion written by Justice Treat, affirmed the judgment. The mayor of the city of Springfield is a local officer, and can exercise only such powers as are clearly conferred on him by law. In the exercise of civil jurisdiction, he is confined to cases in which the cause of action arises within the city, and to cases where the parties to be summoned before him are served with process in the city. Neither was present here.

Ogden et al. v. Bowen
orig. ed. 5 Ill.301
(Ill. Rep.: Ogden et al. v. Bowen 5 Ill.301)
December Term 1843

Bowen sued five people as makers of a promissory note. Only three were served, a trial was had, and judgment rendered against all five. On appeal the judgment was reversed and the cause remanded, with directions to the circuit court to render judgment only against the three who were served (3 Ill.33). The three who were thus liable for the judgment then offered certain pleas to absolve themselves from liability. The pleas were stricken, and judgment entered against all three. Logan and two of the three judgment debtors, who were also lawyers, represented Ogden et al. on the appeal at least.

The supreme court, in an opinion written by Justice Treat, affirmed the judgment. Where a cause is remanded to the circuit court, with instructions to enter a particular judgment therein, the circuit court cannot disregard the mandate of the supreme court; its only duty consists in entering the judgment. In such case the pleading cannot be opened, and the pleas were properly stricken.

State Bank by Johnson v. People
orig. ed. 5 Ill.303
(Ill. Rep.: State Bank of Illinois v. The People 5 Ill.304)
December Term 1843

The State Bank of Illinois owned considerable real estate in the county of Cook, which was assessed for taxation for county and state purposes, for the year 1840. The People brought this action for an order to sell the bank's land for taxes. The bank said it was exempt from these taxes, but the court rendered judgment for the People and ordered the land sold.

The supreme court, in an opinion written by Justice Lockwood, reversed the judgment. The legislative act creating the bank specified the bank should pay one-half per cent on the amount of capital stock actually paid in by individuals, "in lieu of all taxes and impositions whatever." Justice Lockwood said "To divest the legislature of the inherent right of taxation upon every species of property, the language of the statute relied on must be clear and explicit. In this section, the legislature, for an ample consideration, have, by words not liable to doubt or uncertainly, expressly exempted the bank from all taxes and impositions whatever. Whether this was a wise provision is not a question for this court to decide. The legislature had the power to make this contract with the bank. Such contracts have frequently been made, and their validity not doubted." The court then quoted as authority a New Jersey case in point.

Pentecost v. Magahee
orig. ed. 5 Ill.326
(Ill. Rep.: Pentecost et al. v. Magahee 5 Ill.326)
December Term 1843

Magahee, represented by Lincoln, recovered a judgment at law against Pentecost and Pickering, who brought an action in chancery for an injunction to stay proceedings on the judgment. The court dismissed the injunction, and Pentecost et al. brought this appeal. Judge Treat, writing the opinion for the Supreme Court, dismissed the appeal.

Lincoln presented an Illinois case (Cornelius v. Coons, 1 Ill.15) which held that an appeal does not lie from an order of a court dismissing an injunction. He also cited a U.S. Supreme Court case, Young v. Coundy, 6 Cranch 51, which held the dismissal of an injunction is an interlocutory, and not a final decree. The cause must be finally disposed of in the circuit court before either party can appeal it.

There are no facts cited in the case to even allow an inference as to why Pentecost et al. tried to appeal the dismissal of the injunction. Obviously Lincoln knew the applicable precedents, and the Supreme Court dismissed the appeal in an opinion of less words than this summary of the opinion.

Robinson v. Chesseldine & Nye
orig. ed. 5 Ill.332
(Ill. Rep.: Robinson v. Chesseldine et al. 5 Ill.332)
December Term 1843

Robinson executed a note to Chesseldine for $680.85 payable in one year. The note was in default, and Chesseldine recovered a judgment under the note against Robinson. Execution was issued, and levied upon the lands of Robinson. The land was advertised for sale, without having it appraised according to the provisions of the act of 27th of February 1942. Robinson seeks to avoid this sale since the applicable statute hadn't been complied with, by bringing an action in chancery to prevent the sale in the Brown Circuit Court before Judge Stephen A. Douglass. Judge Douglass dismissed the bill.

The Supreme Court in an opinion written by Justice Scates affirmed the circuit court ruling, Lincoln and S.T. Logan represented Chesseldine, and presented the winning arguments. First, the court said that notwithstanding the circuit courts are invested with equity (chancery) as well as common law jurisdiction, they are distinctly separated in their administration, as if vested in different courts. However, courts of common law have a general supervisory power over their process, either mesne (intermediate) or final; and, according to the settled practice, may prevent or correct any abuse of it. Thus Robinson could have interceded with the circuit court that issued the execution on his land directly, if he had proper cause to have the sale delayed. He did not need to bring an action in chancery to obtain any appropriate relief.

Courts of chancery were invented in England when it was determined that the formal common law actions did not always produce the fairest results, recognizing the relative equities of each party. Care was always taken to make certain the rules of the chancery courts did not infringe upon the common law courts, even though the courts and judges were the same for both law and equity. This case affirms this, in an opinion well written by Justice Scates, in about the same number of words as this summary.

Wright v. Kirkpatrick
orig. ed. 5 Ill.339

(Ill. Rep.: Wright v. Kirkpatrick 5 Ill.340)
December Term 1843

Wright brought an action against Kirkpatrick in the Jo Daviess circuit court, and won a verdict. After several motions, the court awarded a change of venue to Adams county. The clerk of the Jo Daviess circuit court sent copies of the proceedings to Adams county, but they were not certified as the statute required. Kirkpatrick moved the Adams circuit court to strike the case from the docket, which was granted. Logan represented Wright on the appeal at least.

The supreme court, in an opinion written by Justice Treat, affirmed the judgment. The statute provided what constitutes a valid transcript of the record of the prior proceedings to the new court, when a change of revue is ordered. This was not done here, because the papers presented as the transcript were not certified, as the statute required. Justice Treat closed the opinion as follows: "Under such circumstances, and the cause, being so imperfectly before the court, it decided correctly in refusing to take cognizance of the cause and in dismissing it from the docket."

Swiggart et al. v. Harber et al.
orig. ed. 5 Ill.364

(Ill. Rep.: Swiggart et al. v. Harber et al. 5 Ill.364)
December Term 1843

This is an action of ejectment brought by Swiggart et al. against Harber et al. Both parties claimed title under Joseph Cornelius; Swiggart from deeds from Cornelius' heirs, and Harber through the foreclosure of a mortgage Cornelius gave to the State Bank of Illinois. The mortgage foreclosure had some irregularities to which Cornelius or his heirs could have objected, but they did not. Judgment was rendered for Harber et al. Logan represented Swiggart et al. on the appeal at least.

The supreme court, in an opinion written by Justice Thomas, affirmed the judgment. Although a judgment may have been erroneous, and an execution issued thereon so irregular that it would have been quashed, if a motion had been made by the defendant therein, they cannot now be attacked and declared invalid by strangers to that action.

Bledsoe v. Graves
orig. ed. 5 Ill.383

(Ill. Rep.: Bledsoe v. Graves 5 Ill.383)
December Term 1843

Riley made a note to Turpin and Bledsoe, which was assigned by Turpin to Bledsoe, without recourse. Bledsoe assigned it to Graves who held it for two years after the note became due, and sued Riley. Riley apparently was insolvent when the note became due, and was, for sure, when Graves sued him. Graves then brings this action against Bledsoe, his assignor. The court, Judge Lockwood presiding, awarded $356.50 to Graves, A.T. Bledsoe and Logan represented M.O. Bledsoe on the appeal.

The Supreme Court, in an opinion written by Justice Caton, reversed the circuit court and remanded the cause for further proceedings, based on erroneous rulings of the judge. Justice Lockwood dissented. Under the statute in relation to promissory notes there are three contingencies when an assignor may be found liable: first, when an assignee has used due diligence to collect the money, by prosecuting a suit against the maker; second, if the maker left the state or otherwise absconded when the note was due; and, third, if suit against the maker would have been unavailing. Here Graves waited too long to sue Riley, and did not use due diligence.

Lockwood in his dissent says the statute provides that if the maker of a promissory note is insolvent when the note becomes due, the assignee may sue the assignor. Waiting two years to sue the maker does not negate the right to sue the assignor, if the maker can't pay for one of the stated reasons.

Gregory & Swallow v. Scott
orig. ed. 5 Ill.392

(Ill. Rep.: Gregory et al. v. Scott 5 Ill.392)
December Term 1843

Gregory and Swallow promised to pay Beeman $500 on or before January 1, 1838. Beeman promised to convey certain land to Gregory and Swallow on February 1, 1838. Beeman assigned the note to Scott, and Gregory and Swallow refused to pay the note when due because they believed Beeman did not have title to the land. Scott sued on the note, and Gregory and Swallow pleaded failure of consideration. Scott demurred to this, which was sustained, and damages awarded to Scott.

The supreme court, in an opinion written by Justice Scates, reversed the judgment and remanded the cause. Failure of consideration would be a good defense. The matter should be tried. Even though Beeman did not have title on January 1, he might have acquired it by February 1. Even so, Gregory and Swallow should not have had to pay the note, when a month later Beeman would not have been able to deliver the property. Scates said "It is said the law does not require a useless thing, that it abhors a multiplicity of actions." Therefore "it seems to savor more of technicality, harshness, nay injustice, than of reason or equity, to say to them, because you agreed to pay a month before you were entitled to a conveyance, that you must now pay the money, and sue upon your covenant, although you are ready and able to show that the covenantors are not able to convey the estate which they agreed to convey in 1838."

Justice Young wrote a concurring and dissenting opinion. Defendant should be able to plead no consideration for failure of title when the note falls due.

Hall v. O'Brien et al.
orig. ed. 5 Ill.405
(Ill. Rep.: Hall v. O'Brien et al. 5 Ill.406)
December Term 1843

The O'Briens recovered a judgment against Hall for $350 and costs. Hall appealed on the grounds that the judge was absent from the court house for a short time, during the trial, and placed another person "on the bench with the consent of both parties," who decided upon the questions as they were presented, in the progress of the cause. The appeal was dismissed for want of prosecution. Hall now seeks to reinstate the appeal because his attorney was away on other business when the appeal was heard. His attorney had arranged for Logan and Lincoln to represent Hall on the appeal, but Logan reviewed the record, decided there were no grounds for appeal, and did not appear.

The supreme court, in an opinion written by Justice Thomas, denied the motion to reinstate the appeal. The substitution of someone else on the bench during the trial, with consent of both parties, does not constitute grounds for appeal. Thus even though the absence of Hall's attorney was caused by "the inclement weather, the bad state of the roads and streams, and a very severe soreness of the eyes," which could have been adequate excuse to justify reinstating the appeal, there were no grounds for doing so.

Subsequently Hall's attorney solicited the supreme court for an injunction. The court decided it had no jurisdiction to grant an injunction, stating that the application should have been made to one of the justices of the court. Three justices dissented.

Lazell v. Francis
orig. ed. 5 Ill.421
(Ill. Rep.: Lazell v. Francis 5 Ill.421)
December Term 1843

Francis, represented by Lincoln and Logan on appeal, executed a note for $202.06 to John A. Lazell, who assigned the note after its maturity, to George A.B. Lazell, the plaintiff (and appellant) in this action. George said the note was not paid when due, and he sues Francis. Francis pleads that he had an understanding with John that, since John owned the firm of Collins and Hannay, Francis could discharge the note by paying Collins and Hannay. Francis paid that firm on behalf of John, and pleads the note has thusly been discharged. Judge Treat in the Sangamon Circuit Court rules for Francis. The Supreme Court affirmed this in an opinion written by Justice Thomas.

The court allowed the oral argeement between John and Francis to be taken together with the written note to be the entire contract, Bailey v. Cromwell, 4 Ill.71, as authority for this position. The court held that since the note was assigned after its maturity, Francis is allowed by law to make the same defence against the assignee (George), that might have been made against the payee (John).

Spear v. Campbell & Dabney
orig. ed. 5 Ill.424

(Ill. Rep.: Spear v. Campbell et al. 5 Ill.424)
December Term 1843

Lincoln and Logan represented Campbell and Dabney, who brought a bill in chancery to set aside an alleged fraudulent conveyance of land. Isaac P. Spear was indebted to them, and judgments were obtained against him. But before the judgments could be executed, Isaac conveyed land he owned to David Spear. The Sangamon circuit court judge, Samuel H. Treat, held for the complainants (Campbell and Dabney) and ordered the conveyance of land to be set aside as fraudulent. David Spear appeals, stating that Isaac should have been a party to the action, but hadn't been included. Lincoln and Logan submitted many authorities, acknowledging the authority of the chancery court to add necessary parties, but said Isaac wasn't necessary.

The Supreme Court, with the opinion written by Justice Samuel H. Treat, reversed the lower court, said Isaac was a necessary party, and told the complainants (Campbell and Dabney) to start over if they wished, but if so, make sure to include Isaac.

All agreed that in a court of equity all persons should be made parties to a suit if they have any substantial, legal, or beneficial interest in the subject matter of the litigation, and who may be materially affected by the decree which may be pronounced. It is a favorite objective of a court of equity to do full and complete justice, and thus to avoid a multiplicity of actions. Common law courts and procedures did not have enough flexibility to accomplish this in all cases. Lincoln knew this was the law, but said Isaac's absence should have been brought up in the circuit court, and not for the first time at the appeal. Justice Treat said it is so important that all the necessary parties be included, introducing an essential missing party could be done this late in the proceedings.

Bruce v. Truett
orig. ed. 5 Ill.454
(Ill. Rep.: Bruce v. Truett 5 Ill.454)
December Term 1843

Truett sued Bruce in Jo Daviess circuit court before Judge Brown for a debt of $452, and recovered a judgment. Bruce requested a new trial on the basis that he believed that he could prove that $300 of the debt had been paid to Truett by O. Ellers on behalf of Bruce. Also shortly before the suit Ellers had left "the country" and Bruce had just found him in Delaware, having made a diligent search for him before the trial.

Lincoln and Logan represented Truett at the appeal at least, and Justice Wilson, writing for the supreme court affirmed the judgment. The general rule is that the law intends everyone should have a fair trial; and if by any misfortune or accident, without any fault on his part, a party has been unable to present the merits of his case before a jury, as a general rule the court will allow him another hearing or such terms as may be decided equitable. This principle was enunciated in Schlencher v. Risley, 4 Ill.483, by Justice Caton. Lincoln was the attorney for Risley, and successfully argued in that case although this is the law, the error in the case is damnum absque injuria (wrong without injury). Thus the other parties had not been harmed by the error. While Justice Wilson did not state Lincoln used the same Latin phrase in this case, the result was the same. Lincoln's client prevailed because Bruce could not prove he was so injured by the unavailability of Ellers that he should be granted a new trial. Bruce could not prove Eller's evidence, even if he would have been available and believed by the court, would have changed the decision. It also seemed strange that Bruce discovered on the same day as the verdict was rendered, that Ellers was indeed alive and living in Delaware.

England v. Clark
orig. ed. 5 Ill.486
(Ill. Rep.: England v. Clark 5 Ill.487)
December Term 1843

England purchased a horse from a constable, who sold it by the execution of a judgment obtained by Clark against a third party. The constable believed the horse belonged to that third party. Apparently Clark received the money from the sale. However, the real owner of the horse brought an action against England for the horse, and he had to give it up. England sues Clark to recover the purchase price, in the Menard ciruit court before Judge Samuel H. Treat. The court held for Clark.

Lincoln represented England in the appeal and based his request for reversal of the lower court on a precedent from the English common law of "ex aequo et bono" first pronounced by Lord Mansfield in Moses v. M'Ferlan v. Burr. 101 r. This case held that if a plaintiff is better entitled to have a thing, than the defendant is to withhold it from him, he has a remedy to recover it. Justice Scates, writing for the court, stated the rule of "caveat emptor" (let the buyer beware) applies to all judicial sales, as long as the representative of the court making the sale had proper authority. The buyer acquires only whatever title the judgment debtor had, without any additional warranties. The lower court judgment was affirmed.

Chief Justice Wilson wrote a concurring opinion, apparently because he wanted to state clearly what he thought of the Moses v. M'Ferlan case, and the "ex aequo et bono" sale. He stated "this is a most comprehensive rule, but I believe it has never been recognized in any subsequent case, to the extent its terms would seem to imply, and does not, conceive, apply to this case."

The impression is that Lincoln made an ingenious argument to seek a victory for his client. Clark had a valid judgment against the third party, and was entitled to have it executed against any property owned by the third party. The constable thought Clark owned the horse, probably because the horse was in his possession, and levied the execution. England really learned what "caveat emptor" meant, and perhaps he had a better entitlement to the purchase price than Clark, but the court didn't agree.

Johnston v. Weedman
orig. ed. 5 Ill.495

(Ill. Rep.: Johnson v. Weedman 5 Ill.495)

December Term 1843

Lincoln represented Weedman in an appeal from an action in DeWitt circuit court before Judge Samuel Treat. Weedman won in that action, and Lincoln's citations obviously influenced the court to affirm the judgment.

Justice Scates wrote the opinion, and if all the opinions were written as succinctly, the time required to write these observations about Lincoln's cases would have been reduced by at least one-third. He started the opinion as follows: "Trover, for a horse: issue not guilty: trial and verdict not guilty. The plaintiff moved for a new trial, which the court denied, and rendered a judgment for costs. The agreed case shows the following facts; that the plaintiff bailed a horse to the defendant to be agisted and fed, for a valuable consideration; that while the horse was so in defendant's possession, he rode the horse fifteen miles; that the horse died within a few hours afterwards, but not in consequence of the riding. And the cause is submitted for the opinion of the court upon two questions: First; is the plaintiff entitled to recover upon the facts stated? and Secondly; ought a new trial to have been granted?"

Justice Scates answered both questions "No." Firstly, Johnston tried to recover the value of the horse, since it could not be returned. Lincoln argued the riding of the horse was not an unlawful conversion. Failing in that, he cited an English case, Murray v. Barling 10 Johns 176, arguing that "if the riding was a conversion, the injury done by the riding, and not the value of the horse, is the measure of damages." The cited case said "as if a man takes my horse to ride, and leaves it at an inn, that is a conversion; for though I may have him by sending for him, and paying for his keeping, yet it brings a charge upon me. It is this charge that is to regulate the damages." Johnston was only entitled to nominal damages, which he can't recover in this form of action. Secondly, since a new trial cannot be awarded to seek only nominal damages, the motion for same was properly dismissed.

Lincoln's opponent brought the wrong form of action, and recovered nothing. This type of inflexibility of the common law resulted in the establishment of courts of chancery (equity) where relative merits of each side of the case could be adjusted during the trial.

Hall v. Perkins
orig. ed. 5 Ill.548

(Ill. Rep.: Hall v. Perkins 5 Ill.549)
December Term 1843

Hall gave certain notes to Perkins, who agreed to convey certain land to Hall. The notes were due, although Perkins had not conveyed the land. Perkins sues on the notes in the Tazwell circuit court before Judge Treat, and was awarded a judgment for $564.

Lincoln, W.H. Leonard, and M. Bragman represented Perkins in the appeal. The supreme court reversed the judgment, despite whatever authorities cited and entreaties made by Lincoln. The note and the agreement to convey the land were one agreement, and Perkins had to make the conveyance of land before he could collect on the notes. This principle was decided in the case of Duncan et al. v. Charles 5 Ill.561 made at the same term of this court.

The case had much pleading, which is not germane here because it did not effect the decision. Perhaps Lincoln's attempt was to obfuscate the issues. The Duncan decision is one of the few citations of an Illinois supreme court case that has influenced the decisions in a case to date in which Lincoln was involved. And in this instance the Duncan case was such a recent decision, the report book for the term hadn't been published. The court knew of these for sure, and possibly the attorneys. However, there is no indication the attorneys for Hull were aware of the Duncan case.

Another interesting side-light: We have seen cases where the trial judge has also been on the supreme court, and in several has written the opinion. Here's a case where it is noted that Justice Thomas gave no opinion in the supreme court's deliberations, because he had been of counsel in the trial. Lawyers in those days wore many hats, including the stove pipe variety.

Lockridge v. Foster et al.
orig. ed. 5 Ill.569

(Ill. Rep.: Lockridge v. Foster et al. 5 Ill.569)
December Term 1843

In 1836 George Foster sold two hundred and forty acres of land plus an interest of seven-elevenths in another tract of land containing one hundred and twenty-eight acres, for $2,400 to John Lockridge warranting he had full title to both of these interests. Lockridge agreed to pay $1,200 in May 1837, and $1,200 in December, 1837. Lockridge paid the first amount, moved onto the land, and built a house. He didn't make the second payment, because he suspected George, who died in mid-1937, did not leave a proper title. Peyton Foster, as administrator, sued Lockridge for the second payment in 1842, and recovered a judgment. Lockridge brought an action in equity to clarify the situation and to enjoin the collection of the judgment pending final determination in the Sangamon circuit court, before Judge Samuel H. Treat. The judge decided Lockridge owed the $1,200 minus $200 computed to offset a proven defect in the title.

Lockridge appealed, and Lincoln and Logan represented Foster. The opinion of the court was written by Justice Treat, and affirmed the opinion of the lower court. Contracts must be executed in good faith, with both parties knowing all the pertinent facts. A false representation by a vendor, or intentional concealment of material facts will vitiate a contract. Lockridge could have had the contract voided back in 1837, but he acted like he wanted to ratify the contract when he moved onto the land and built a house. He waited too long to revoke the contract, but the court did equity to all, by computing a pro-rata adjustment in the price to offset the flawed part of the land title.

We assume Lincoln represented Foster in the circuit court proceeding and thus was able to convince Judge Treat, and Justice Treat and his associates in the propriety of his client's position.

Dorman et ux. v. Lane, admr. of Robinson
orig. ed. 6 Ill.143

(Ill. Rep.: Dorman et ux. v.
Lane, admr. of Robinson 6 Ill.143)
December Term 1844

Lincoln represented Dorman and his wife (indicated as "ux." in the title) in the appeal of this action before Judge Walter B. Scates in the Gallatin circuit court. Lane, as administrator of the estate of Christopher Robinson, files a petition in the circuit court for an order to sell real estate of the intestate (Robinson) to pay the sum of $1,008.87 adjudged to be due Lane as an individual by order of the probate court in 1826 (15 years before). Dorman and wife are the only heirs and object due to the time delay, and also that Lane had lived on the land and had received the profits from it all that time. Judgment entered for Lane.

The supreme court in an opinion written by Justice Shields reversed the decree, and remanded the case to be reheard in the circuit court. Based on the cases cited by Lincoln that the lapse of time should bar this recovery, the court commented, "It would be extremely hazardous for this court to sanction such gross negligence, and particularly in a case where the same person was both administrator and creditor." The cases cited had different periods of time between when suit could be brought to sell assets of an estate to pay a claim, and when the claim became due. Illinois had no statutory or case authority on it, so the court stated that by analogy to the rule established in Maine and Massachusetts, the general rule of the state will be that one year would be the limit, unless there be such a peculiar case that it would be the duty of a court of equity to depart from the rule.

Justice Scates wrote a separate opinion concurring with the decision but stating it is impractical for the circuit court to sort out whether Lane needed to sell any land to pay himself the $1008.87. The probate court would be the proper forum since it had knowledge of the total financial situation during that 15 year period. Scates had tried the case, and had attempted to do the impractical.

Lincoln won a case for his clients in the supreme court, and strongly influenced a rule of law in Illinois to apply to comparable situations in the future.

This case also appears as Dorman et al. v. Tost, 13 Ill.128. See also Lane v. Dorman (4 Ill.238) for previous proceedings in this matter.

Graves et al. v. Bruen et al.
orig. ed. 6 Ill.167

(Ill. Rep.: Graves et al. v. Bruen et al. 6 Ill.167)
December Term 1844

Bruen brought an action of ejectment in the Adams circuit court for certain land possessed by Graves, and to which Bruen had an auditor's deed. This deed had never been acknowledged or recorded. Graves offered in defense copies of land records indicating the subject land wasn't listed. He claims he had bought the land without knowing Bruen had received an auditor's deed. Judgment for Bruen.

The Supreme Court, with the opinion written by Justice Shields, affirmed the lower court. An auditor's deed, whether given by a state or the United States, does not have to be registered as required in the registry acts. The evidence offered to defeat the auditor's deed of a diagram copied from a book, and a deposition by the principal clerk in the registry office that the land included in the deed was not duly listed according to the law, was loose and indefinite, and calculated to mislead the jury. It was properly rejected by the circuit court.

Davis, adm. of Hains v. Harkness
orig. ed. 6 Ill.173

(Ill. Rep.: Davis, adm. of Hains v. Harkness et al. 6 Ill.173)
December Term 1844

This is an action in equity in McLean circuit court before Judge Samuel H. Treat, brought by the heirs of Samuel Harkness to recover payment from the estate of Thomas Haines. Lincoln and Logan represented the heirs. The judge awarded $1,292.50 to the heirs.

Samuel Harkness died in 1822 in Ohio, leaving a widow and two children. The widow was appointed administrator, and she had $1,000 in her control which had been left specifically for the children. She married Haines, and they all moved to Illinois. Haines supported the family, and voluntarily brought up the children, "they doing service in his family as is common in such cases." Haines died, and there were not enough assets to pay all the claims. The children bring this action to be paid the estate ($1,000) left them by their father, and to have priority in this claim against other creditors. They succeeded, and the decision was affirmed by the Supreme Court.

Justice Caton in his opinion stated the general rule that the expenses of a ward should be paid from the income from the estate, and not the principal. While the children were technically not wards, with Haines as their guardian appointed formally, his obligation was to protect the principal for the children--even more than if he had been officially appointed, because then the court would have supervised his stewardship.

The statute of wills was enacted by the Illinois legislature to formalize the disposition of estates. The 110th section provides for the priority of claims--1) funeral expense; 2) expenses of administrators; 3) assets received in a representative capacity as guardian, etc.; 4) all other debts. The court of equity had the power to treat the status of Haines in relation to the inheritances of the children, as being one of formal guardianship. Thus the assets were properly in the third class. Payment to the heirs was a proper priority over other creditors.

The opinion stated that "courts of equity are not bound down by the literal expressions of the statute, but where a case is found to be within the equity of the provision, it is held to be within the provision itself." This case, and others involving Lincoln's practice of law, could indicate Lincoln had a sense of fairness which was expressed in the principles of equity courts. At least he convinced Judge Treat on numerous occasions of this.

Martin & Warfield v. Dryden et al.
orig. ed. 6 Ill.187

(Ill. Rep.: Martin & Warfield v. Dryden et al. 6 Ill.187)

December Term 1844

In 1836 Dryden et al., totalling 28 citizens of Baltimore, Maryland, entered into articles of co-partnership, by the name of "Baltimore and Western Land Association" for the purpose of buying and selling, and speculating in lands in the state of Illinois and elsewhere, with a capital of $20,000. They employed Warfield as their agent, who purchased the lands in controversy in 1836 and 1837, in his own name. He conveyed these lands to three members of the company, Dryden, Gasnell and Wood (the latter two are the "et al.") on March 11, 1840, which deed was recorded in Madison County, Illinois on December 20, 1840. Meantime, Martin sued out an attachment against Warfield on July 14, 1840, and on the same day it was levied upon the lands in controversy. Warfield denied the debt, but in September, 1841, judgment was rendered for $1,666.35, and in October an execution was issued on the judgment, under which the lands were sold to Martin. Dryden et al. bring this action in equity to enjoin Martin from proceeding, and to remove his lien on the land. The Madison circuit court, Judge James Semble presiding, granted the relief.

Martin appealed, and Lincoln and Krum represented Dryden. The opinion of the court cites extensive arguments on each side, including a seven printed page brief on behalf of Dryden which is identified as follows: "A. LINCOLN and J.M. KRUM, for the appellees. The following is a portion of a printed argument, presented by JOHN M. KRUM, Esq. who contended, 1. that the decree etc." The lower court was reversed in the opinion written by Justice Scates, meaning Dryden et al. lost, and perhaps the results would have been different if Lincoln had argued the case.

The heart of the case was the timing of the filing of the deed from Warfield (December 1840) and when Martin filed the levy under his action on debt against Warfield (July 1840). The statutes governing filing of liens on land had been in force for ten years to the time of this trial but the definitions of a "creditor" under the law, having right to file a lien, had not been defined. Justice Scates examined the cases from various states, discarding those of Kentucky and New York as being opposite extremes and not acceptable. He chose Massachusetts as the model for Illinois stating the time of levy in an action on debt is the proper date, and it becomes binding when, and if, judgment is rendered, but at the date of the levy. Under this newly minted definition "of a creditor," the lien of Martin was established before he had constructive notice of the interests of Dryden et al. Martin had no actual notice of this interest, and since the deed wasn't filed until December of that year, his claim was prior and prevailed.

Warner & Craig v. Helm et al.
orig. ed. 6 Ill.220
(Ill. Rep.: Warner et al. v. Helm et al. 6 Ill.220)
December Term 1844

This is the retrial of the issues between the same parties in Edwards et al. v. Helm 5 Ill.142. Justice Scates again drew the duty to write the opinion.

The facts in the combined situations are: Ware sold land to Edwards, who, with Helm and Gray as sureties, executed a note to Ware for six thousand dollars. Ware assigned the note to Craig and Warner. Edwards was indebted to Helm for seven thousand dollars, and gave him a note and mortgage for that amount to secure the loan and his potential liability as a surety. The Edwards note to Ware is in default, and Craig and Warner bring suit against Edwards, Helm and Gray. They obtain a judgment against Edwards, on whom alone process was served, and land (including that which was mortgaged to Helm) was sold under execution to Craig and Warner. Helm, whose note from Edwards is in default, brought the former action (Edwards v. Helm) against Edwards, and Craig and Warner as judgment creditors of Edwards. Helm was awarded a decree for $12,224.30, which was reversed, and cause remanded giving leave to Craig and Warner to file a cross bill. This was done, and dismissed in the Madison circuit court by Judge James Shields, who also granted a foreclosure for Helm. Thus this appeal.

Lincoln and N.D. Strong represented Craig and Warner, and obtained a reversal of the lower court's decree. Justice Scates stated the mortgage by Edwards to Helm had proper priority to Craig and Warner's judgment, and the subject property should be foreclosed and sold. However, any surplus would belong to Craig and Warner, and the judgment obtained against Edwards is reinstated so other properties owned by Edwards could be levied against.

Both of these supreme court cases applied general rules of equity, and arrived at an equitable solution for both Helm, Craig, and Warner. Most of the opinion is spent on sorting out the facts. Lincoln was persistent in both cases, and finally prevailed.

McDonald v. Fithian et al.
orig. ed. 6 Ill.269
(Ill. Rep.: McDonald v. Fithian et al. 6 Ill.269)
December Term 1846

Fithian purchased a lot in Milwaukee, Wisconsin territory, from Juneau, who also sold a lot to John H. Murphy. Juneau was unable to convey title to either one. Later Fithian and three others (one being the agent for McDonald and another being Hezekial Cunningham who was the complainant in a subsequent case) journey to Milwaukee to buy land. Fithian volunteered to talk to Juneau alone, since he knew him, and the others agreed. Juneau agreed to sell land to them, but wanted to do business through Fithian, who would arrange for the others to pay him. This was agreed to, and the land was transferred. Later McDonald thinks he had paid too much, and thinks Fithian had defrauded him. He brings this action in equity to rescind and to get his money back. Judge William Wilson in the Vermilion circuit court dismissed complainant's bill.

Lincoln, Logan, and Edward D. Baker represent Fithian on the appeal. The opinion has omitted their names, but a subsequent case, Cunningham (another of the four investors) v. Fithian (7 Ill.650) states they appeared in the McDonald case reported here. Justice Scates wrote the opinion of the court after listing eighteen pages of summations of testimony and depositions from the trial. He cites the rule of agency an agent must disclose all relevant facts. However, since the arrangement amoung Fithian and the others was verbal, there can be no formal agency since this involves real estate. However, "Fraud is odious, and will not be tolerated under the guise of friendship or gratuitous service," and if fraud is proven all the consequences should follow, "whether as agent or friend, and with or without compensation for the trouble."

The testimony was bountiful and confusing. We assume Lincoln represented Fithian also in the lower court, and that his mastery of inquiry and confrontation of witnesses earned the win. Among other indications of possible fraud by Fithian was two sets of notes covering the same part of the transaction, with the higher one, which obligated McDonald and the others to pay more, used. Murphy who had earlier dealings with Juneau believed he had been ill used, and that Fithian had withheld information from him. The court states some evidence on this as follows: "In 1838, Fithian was a candidate, and was charged with fraud in the matter by John H. Murphy, and in a hand-bill, when Fithian said he would not explain the two sets of notes if his election depended upon it." This also establishes negative campaigning did not commence with the Presidential election of 1988. Justice Scates reasons from this question of the two notes, that this was a private matter involving Juneau asking Fithian to conceal information from Murphy, which had no bearing on this case. Scates wrote "It seems to me to be unfortunate for him (Fithian), that he assumed an obligation of secrecy, that prevented him from answering the legitimate inquiries of those concerned; and it should be an admonition, from its consequences, of that truth, that open confession is good for soul." The decree was affirmed.

The case presents more evidence by way of summary of testimony and depositions than any case noted here to date. Most of it seems negative to Fithian, which prompts the observation Lincoln must have dominated the trial.

Justices Treat, Shields, and Thomas dissented from the opinion, which is further indication there was a lot of evidence unfavorable to Fithian.

See Cunningham v. Fithian (7 Ill.650) for another case about this same transaction.

Draper et al. v. McFarland
orig. ed. 6 Ill.310

(Ill. Rep.: Draper et al. v. McFarland 6 Ill.310)
December Term 1844

Draper held title to premises in trust for McFarland. He fraudulently conveyed the property to the four infant children of Barnhart. Since that transfer and up to the time of this suit, the guardian for the four infant children of Barnhart received $173.25 as rents and profits from the land. McFarland brought this action to recover the land, and the $173.25 from the heirs of Draper, who had died, because Draper had committed the fraud. Decree was entered in his favor, and the heirs of Barnhart bring this appeal.

The supreme court, in an opinion written by Justice Caton, reversed the decree as it pertained to the four heirs of Barnhart. Any fraud committed by Draper died with him, since the heirs did not receive any property tainted by fraud. They never pretended to have any interest in the land, and they did not receive any rents or profits. Thus the decree to repay the $173.25 was improper.

Favor et al. v. Marlett
orig. ed. 6 Ill.385

(Ill. Rep.: Favor et al. v. Marlett 6 Ill.385)
December Term 1844

This is an appeal from a trial in the Kane circuit court before Judge John D. Caton, which was appealed, and in an opinion written by Justice Caton, the court reversed the decision. Lincoln and T.L. Dickey represented the appellant (Favor) in the Supreme Court.

Favor owned a shop in Aurora, Illinois, and Grant was his tenant. The rent was overdue, and Favor distrained certain furniture of Grant, and had it sold to pay the rent. However, Marlett was owed money by Grant, and had taken an assignment on the same property as security for that debt. Marlett sues Favor, and recovers $92. Grant was allowed to testify as to the value of the furniture and Favor objected to his testimony on the grounds Grant was interested in enhancing the value of the damages. The court overruled this objection, and this is the basis of the appeal.

Caton starts out his opinion as follows: "In this case I have no doubt but I improperly admitted Grant, as a witness to testify as to the value of the property, for the taking of which this suit was brought." Grand had a greater interest in having Marlett prevail, because he would have received any balance left after the furniture was sold and Marlett paid off. Favor took the property, sold it, and kept the balance. Caton said he relied on a New York case, Alexander v. Mahon, 11 Johns 185, which held a person in a comparable situation had interests in each side that were equally balanced. However, Lincoln submitted a case in arguing the appeal, also from New York (Graves v. Delaplaine, 14 Johns 148,160) which held that a witness is incompetent to create or enhance a fund from which he is to be benefitted, either by receiving money or having his own debts paid. Caton said this case controls because Grant did not have balanced interests for either side, and thus his evidence should have been received.

Obviously the Graves case was not submitted in the trial, as Caton states he would have ruled differently if it had been. The logical explanation is that Lincoln did not go to Aurora to try the case but was involved in the appeal; submitted the ruling case there, and his client prevailed.

Parker v. Smith et al.
orig. ed. 6 Ill.411

(Ill. Rep.: Parker v. Smith et al. 6 Ill.412)
December Term 1844

Smith brought an action for debt against Parker before a justice of peace, Allen. The action was tried before a jury, who returned a verdict for Smith for $14.12 1/2, and the justice added his costs of $19.61 1/4. Execution of the verdict was issued, and Warren, a constable, levied the execution on two steers. Parker contends the judgment was irregular because he was not present, and the execution was a trespass. He brings this action against Smith, Allen and Warren for trespass before Judge

Caton in the La Salle circuit court. The defendants denied this, and Smith pleads Warren knew of the alleged irregularities. Warren demurs, which is sustained, and this appeal results. A demurrer was a special form of pleading at common law. It says in effect that even if the facts as stated in the pleading are correct, they are insufficient to constitute a cause of action. Thus the other party does not have to defend the action any further.

Lincoln and T.L. Dickey represented Parker on the appeal and argued that final judgment, in bar of the whole cause of action, should not be rendered upon demurrers to a position on the pleadings only. Justice Scates writing the opinion for the court agrees, and reversed the judgment, with the cause remanded to the circuit court. Justice Thomas wrote a concurring opinion adding that Warren served a notice that was good upon its face, and that he could properly rely on its propriety.

The demurrer, as a form of pleading, was instituted to forestall the necessity of an elaborate trial when one party believes his opponents' issues, even if the facts sustaining them are true, are not sufficient to justify a cause of action. This would have been successful here, based on the Justices' opinions that the execution against the oxen was proper, but there was no copy for the Supreme Court to know all the other issues had been settled. So the case is sent back to consider other issues, if any. Smith thus had an opportunity to bring an action again, if he thought he could win, or to drop the matter. There is no record in the Supreme Court of his having done either one.

J. Charles Stickney & Co. v. Cassell
orig. ed. 6 Ill.418

(Ill. Rep.: Stickney et al. v. Cassell 6 Ill.418)
December Term 1844

This is an appeal from an action in assumpsit (a common law action which lies for the non-performance of the contract) brought by Cassell against Stickney and others in the Gallatin circuit court before Judge Walter B. Scates and a jury. Cassell agreed to "put all his hands upon Stickney's building at $2.50 per day and then to put all his hands at work to complete any carpenter's work that said Stickney and company wishes" etc. Cassell did work on the building, was paid, but dismissed from the job before it was completed. He brings this action to recover damages he believed he sustained because he was not allowed to work on the building to help finish it. Verdict and judgment for Cassell. Stickney moved for a new trial, which was denied, and he appeals. Lincoln represented Cassell.

The supreme court held for Stickney in reversing the lower court. Justice Wilson wrote the opinion, and a footnote states "Scates, J. gave no opinion, having presided at the trial below." Lincoln cited four Illinois Supreme Court cases holding "so far as it appears, the motion for a new trial was not improperly overruled, the bill of exceptions not averring that it contains all the evidence." Justice Wilson said "it was certainly true, as a general rule, that when the overruling of a motion for a new trial on the ground of the verdict being contrary to the evidence is assigned for error, that it should appear to this court, that all the evidence given on the trial below is preserved for this consideration." However, all the court requires is to be satisfied that it has before it all the testimony upon which its judgment is to be predicated. It had all the evidence it needed here to reverse the decision of Judge Scates to deny the new trial. Also there was nothing in the contract to require Stickney to give Cassell any more work on the building. Thus the judgment was reversed, and a new trial awarded. In view of the opinion on the merits of Cassell's claim, it is unlikely he went to the trouble and expense of a new trial. The only question Lincoln raised in his brief to support the lower court decision was that the appeal documents did not contain the entire evidence. He lost on this point, and since he had no supporting authority to allow Cassell to recover for breach of contract, he probably did not recommend a new trial.

Kimball et al. v. Cook
orig. ed. 6 Ill.423

(Ill. Rep.: Kimball et al. v. Cook 6 Ill.423)
December Term 1844

Cook filed his bill in the La Salle circuit court, under the act of 1839, for the purpose of enforcing a mechanic's lien. Cook had a contract with Kimball by which Cook was to do millwright work of a flouring mill, to be paid $4800 in two installments of $2400, the first during the work and the last when work was completed. Kimball paid the first installment only, and Cook sues him for the balance to enforce a mechanic's lien. The trial was before Judge John D. Caton and a jury, and Cook was awarded $2400. Several exceptions were taken during the trial, and ruled against Kimball. These rulings were basis of the appeals.

Lincoln, O. Peters, and T.L. Dickey represented Cook on the appeal. Justice Caton wrote the opinion for the Supreme Court. Lincoln was able to support all Judge Caton's rulings on behalf of his client, except one, and this error in ruling was sufficient to cause the court to reverse the judgment. That particular ruling was the refusal of Judge Caton to allow Kimball to read, as evidence to the jury, that portion of his answer which was responsive to the bill of complaint. In a court of law a defendant's answer was not admissible as evidence, but in a court of equity it could be. Caton examined the enabling statute of the law of 1839 establishing mechanic's liens, and concluded the language prescribing the procedures necessary to perfect the mechanic's lien were much more consistent with the principles of equity than of law. Thus he concluded on this point: "I have no doubt but I decided wrong in the court below, and that the answer of the defendant, so far as it was responsive to the bill, should have been read to the jury as evidence."

Justice Young dissented on this point, and was the only Justice Lincoln convinced this time.

There have been several Lincoln cases to date when the Justice writing the opinion also was the trial judge. Caton gave an elaborate review of the 1839 act before, in effect, reversing himself. He had one prior authority on this subject he could have used to support his new opinion (Turney v. Saunders, 4 Scam. 533), which held the enforcement was a chancery proceeding, but "as that was not the direct question before the court, and as that remark was incidentally made in attempting to illustrate another question, we do not consider ourselves bound by its authority. Hence we shall proceed to examine this question as a new one before the court."

Wren v. Moss et al.
orig. ed. 6 Ill.560

(Ill. Rep.: Wren v. Moss et al. 6 Ill.560)
December Term 1844

Aquilla Wren filed a bill for a divorce from his wife, Clarissa, a divorce was decreed, and the question of alimony was continued to the next term of the court. Before the next term of the court Aquilla made a will leaving his property to people other than his wife, and died. Clarissa on motion had the question of alimony abated (quashed). She now, with Lincoln and E.N. Powell, as her attorneys, makes this motion to the Supreme Court for a writ of scire facias (to show cause why a judgment should not be amended) and for a writ of error, so as to revise the decree of divorce.

Lincoln contended that a question of property (the right of dower or alimony) is involved, as the decree a vinculo (a term descriptive of a kind of divorce, which effects a complete dissolution of the marriage contract) bars her divorce; and by abating the suit as to the pending motion, she is cut off from alimony; therefore the action survives on account of the nature of the interests involved.

The motion was allowed, with an order of publication of the motion to the non-resident defendants. Publication of this decision would constitute notice to non-residents of the state, so in a subsequent action a court would have jurisdiction over them as if they had made a personal appearance. Subsequent activity in this case is recorded at 7 Ill.72, and Lincoln, continuing his representation of Clarissa won the case for her.

Morgan v. Griffin
orig. ed. 6 Ill.565

(Ill. Rep.: Morgan v. Griffin 6 Ill.565)
December Term 1844

Griffin recovered a judgment against Gunn and Fox. An execution was issued thereon, and levied on certain property claimed by Morgan. The right of property was tried before the sheriff, and found against Morgan. Morgan appealed to the Scott circuit court where a motion was made to dismiss the appeal. The appeal was dismissed, and judgment was rendered against Morgan for costs. The only evidence presented on the appeal was an uncontradicted affidavit by the sheriff that the property was sold after the trial, but before the dismissal of the appeal. He also affirmed the matter in dispute had been settled by the parties at the same time. Morgan appeals the alleged errors made in dismissing the appeal and the rendering of costs against him. Lincoln and D.A. Smith represent Griffin in the appeal.

The Supreme Court, with the opinion written by Justice Treat, agree the circuit court properly dismissed the appeal because the matter had been settled, and thus shouldn't have been brought. Apparently Morgan changed his mind after the settlement, or he wouldn't have pursued the appeal. Morgan did win on the other point, as the costs assessed against him were reversed. When a case is compromised each party bears his own costs.

Cook v. Hall
orig. ed. 6 Ill.575
(Ill. Rep.: Cook v. Hall 6 Ill.575)
December Term 1844

Cook brought an action of ejectment in the Richland circuit court before Judge William Wilson, against Hall to recover possession of certain real estate in Clay county. Both parties claimed title through Jacob Slentz.

Cook, who was represented by Lincoln and C.H. Constable on the appeal, recovered a judgment against Slentz in the Clay count circuit court on October 8, 1840. Execution was issued and premises were sold to Cook.

Hall acquired his claim to title as follows: Slentz conveyed the property to Anderson and Flanders on October 3, 1840, and the deed was taken to the county clerk's office to be filed on October 5, 1840. The deed was misplaced in the office, and was put on the records on December 20, 1840 when it surfaced. Anderson and Flanders conveyed the property to Hall in March 1841.

The circuit court held for Hall because the deed to his grantors, Anderson and Flanders, was rendered (October 3) before the recovery of the judgment by Cook on October 8. Lincoln argued on appeal that the deed had been recorded in December rather than on October 3.

The Supreme Court, with the opinion written by Justice Treat, held that the deed takes effect as being officially recorded from the time of its filing, and not from the time it is actually recorded. Thus the lower court judgement was affirmed. The big winner here was Slentz, who not only had a judgment against him satisfied by having the property levied upon and sold, but also sold it to Anderson and Flanders.

Field et al. v. Rawlings
orig ed. 6 Ill.581
(Ill. Rep.: Field et al. v. Rawlings 6 Ill.581)
December 1844

Alexander A. Field, as Secretary of State, presented to Moses M. Rawlings, as Fund Commissioner, an account claiming seventy-five cents per bond for affixing the seal of state to 1000 state bonds. Rawlings paid the bill and took a bond executed by Field as principle, and his sureties, conditioned that Field should return the money with interest, in case it should be decided by the Legislature or the Supreme Court that the fees were not legally chargeable. Rawlings brought an action for debt in the

Gallatin circuit court before Judge Scates, contending that Field should have had the matter decided by the Supreme Court or the Legislature, but he had not done so. Also the Legislature, by the Senate, had decided the fees were not legally chargeable. Judgment rendered for Rawlings for $1,040.25.

Lincoln and H. Eddy represented Field and the sureties on the appeal. Justice Shields wrote the opinion reversing the judgment. Firstly, the stipulation in the bond that a decision must be made by the Legislature or Supreme Court is express, and the guarantors are not chargeable unless either happens, and Fields does not have an obligation to seek either one. The sureties did not stipulate that Field obtain a decision. The court cannot add additional stipulation by implication. Lincoln cited Miller v. Stewart, 9 Wheat 680, and the court agreed it was decisive on this point: "Nothing can be clearer, both upon principle and authority, than the doctrine that the liability of the surety, is not to be extended by implication, beyond the terms of the contract." Secondly, a decision by only one branch of the legislature is not sufficient. Field is liable to repay the money, with interest, if he received the money without authority of law, but his sureties stand on an entirely different footing, and are only liable according to the strict terms of their bond. Thus the judgment is reversed, and the cause remanded, with leave to amend the proceedings.

Broadwell et al., for use of Thompson et ux. v. Broadwell orig. ed. 6 Ill.599

(Ill. Rep.: Broadwell et al., for use of Thompson et ux. v. Broadwell 6 Ill.599)
December Term 1844

John B. Broadwell executed an instrument stating he would transfer specific portions of his land to several people. The husband of one of the grantees, Mary Jane Thompson, and his wife, bring this action for specific performance of the portion of the instrument giving her certain land. The instrument promised to give Mary Jane and William Broadwell each an equal half of described land if either lived to lawful age. This was given under the penalty of $1000. Mary Jane lived to a lawful age, but John B. Broadwell decided to give her $500 rather than half the land. The Sangamon circuit court by Judge Treat decreed that John B. could satisfy his obligation by giving Mary Jane $500.

Lincoln represented John B. Broadwell on the appeal, and the court ruled against him, reversing the lower court. There were many authorities cited on each side, and Justice Caton wrote a very thorough opinion, commenting on most of the authorities cited. He cited a general rule of construction of written instruments: "While the rule of law is inflexible, that a written instrument cannot be altered by parol proof, yet the court of chancery will never hesitate to rectify mistakes in fact, which have occurred in drawing up the paper, when a proper case is presented and clearly proved, and then carry into effect the instrument when thus corrected, as if it had been written as the parties supposed it was at the time." However, Justice Caton said only the writing itself can be looked at to ascertain the intent of the parties, and the writing here indicated the express purpose was to convey the land. He stated "Whenever the courts shall establish it, as a general rule, that they will go out of the instrument, and inquire what construction each or both parties put upon it at the time it was made they will be starting upon a path which will lead to interminable labyrinths, and will present an inducement to perjury which will be alarming in its consequences."

What this meant was - if Mary Jane wanted the land rather than $500, she should have been allowed to have it.

Rogers v. Dickey
orig. ed. 6 Ill.636

(Ill. Rep.: Rogers v. Dickey 6 Ill.637)
December Term 1844

Dickey rented a house to Betts, and on May 1, 1842 Dickey caused certain personal property of Betts to be distrained by a constable for unpaid back rent, and recovered a judgment against Betts at the July Term 1842. Rogers obtained a judgment against Betts, and on May 26, 1842, a sheriff levied upon the personal property of Betts in the possession of the constable by virtue of said distress, and took the property out of his possession. This question of who was entitled to the property was submitted as a agreed case in the Sangamon circuit court before Judge Treat, who held for Dickey and ordered the sheriff to re-deliver the property.

Rogers brings this appeal, and is represented by J. Young Scammon. Lincoln and Logan represent Dickey. Justice Young read the briefs submitted by both parties and said "The adjudged cases upon this subject, to which the court has been referred, are numerous and conflicting, and we are, for the first time, called upon to determine which construction we will adopt as best supported by the weight of authority, and as best calculated to subserve the ends of justice." The court concluded that the first execution has priority, even though the goods had been previously distrained, and the first distraint is later reduced to judgment. The judgment of the circuit court was reversed, and the goods should be sold to pay Rogers.

Kelly v. Garrett
orig. ed. 6 Ill.649

(Ill. Rep.: Kelly v. Garrett 6 Ill.649)
December Term 1844

James Kinzie made a note to Garrett payable at the Berren County Bank. Garrett assigned the note to Kelly, who sues Garrett on the assignment because both Kinzie and the bank don't pay the note when due. Apparently the bank is in bankruptcy, and the note was now owned by the bank. Kelly brings this suit as a convenience to the bank, and Garret knew the note belonged to the bank. Garrett wants to offset his obligation to the bank with note obligations of the bank, dated prior to the commencement of the suit by Kelly against him. The Cook circuit court, before Judge Richard M. Young and a jury, held for Garrett, and allowed the offset.

Kelly (and the Barren County Bank) is represented by Lincoln, A.O. Beaumont, and M. Skinner on the appeal, and Garrett is represented by S.T. Logan. The court, with Justice Scates writing the opinion, relied on two precedents cited by Lincoln, one of which being an Illinois case, Peters v. Westlake, 4 Ill.536, requiring proof that the defendant held the bills at the time of the commencement of the suit is necessary before set-off could be allowed. Garrett had not proven he held the bills from the bank when suit was commenced. Lincoln asked the local court to make Garrett prove this, but his request was denied. This was the error in the trial court, and judgment was reversed, with directions to award a new trial.

Since the bank was bankrupt, it would have been easy for Garrett to acquire some deep discount obligations of the bank to offset his debt to the bank at full value. Lincoln prevented him from doing it. Another point of interest here: Lincoln and Logan, although partners, were on opposite sides. They dissolved their partnership in December 1844, which concurs with the term of the Supreme Court in which this decision was rendered.

Wilmans et al. v. State Bank
orig. ed. 6 Ill.667

(Ill. Rep.: Wilmans et al. v. State Bank 6 Ill.667)
December Term 1844

The Bank of Illinois brought an action against Wilmans et al. on a note given to the bank for money loaned in the ordinary course of business, before Judge Walter B. Scates. Judgment was rendered for the bank, and Wilmans et al. appeal on the following issues: (1) renewal of the bank charter in 1835 was unconstitutional (2) bank had violated its charter by its suspension of specie payments (3) the judgment was erroneous, being entered for an aggregate amount of debt and damages, without distinguishing the amount of each.

The supreme court, in an opinion written by Justice Wilson, reversed the judgment, and restated it with an award of $595 for debt and $155.69 for damages and costs in the court below. Wilson reiterated the three points on appeal and concluded: (1) the constitutionality of the bank was clearly established by another case, People ex rel. Stickney v. Marshall 6 Ill.672 (2) violation of the bank's charter cannot be attacked in this collateral way (3) a judgment rendered in an aggregate sum is wrong, and for this reason the judgment is reversed. The supreme court has the power to decide what the judgment should have been, and since it has adequate information from the trial to do so, it did so in this case.

Regnier v. Cabot et al.
orig. ed. 7 Ill.34

(Ill. Rep.: Regnier v. Cabot et al. 7 Ill.34)
December Term 1845

Eliza Cabot and Elijah Taylor brought an action of slander against Regnier, who stated Eliza had engaged in fornication with Elijah. They denied it. The action was originally brought in Menard county, and a verdict of $12 was awarded. Cabot moved to set aside the verdict, and it was not only set aside, but the cause was removed to the Morgan circuit court. Here the outcome was the same, but the award was $1600. Lockwood was the judge. Regnier appealed based on erroneous exclusion of certain evidence he introduced concerning Eliza and Elijah being seen in her bedroom late at night, when Eliza was wearing her night clothes, and evidence of her bad character.

The supreme court, in an opinion written by Justice Purple, and in which Justice Lockwood did not hear the evidence, and thus did not vote, affirmed the judgment. Purple said there had been some conflict about how much evidence a defendant in a slander case can offer to cast guilt on the plaintiff. He stated the rule is now clear - he can only offer proof of the bad character of the plaintiff to mitigate damages or to show absence of malice. Neither was applicable here, so Regnier's evidence was properly excluded. The witness who offered to prove Eliza's bad character only knew of three people who believed that, as apposed to proving a general bad reputation. Purple said "In my judgment, character is too valuable to permit it, in a court of justice to be destroyed, or even sullied by a report derived from a majority of three persons only. It is general, and not partial reputation in the neighborhood where the party resides which, in legal contemplation, establishes character for good or evil."

The record doesn't indicate how Eliza had the first verdict for $12 overturned when it was in her favor. Giving up an award of $12 for one of $1600 was a wise gamble on her part, and the size of the award should have made anyone careful of impuning her character in public.

McGoon v. Little et al.
orig. ed. 7 Ill.42

(Ill. Rep.: McGoon v. Little et al. 7 Ill.42)

December Term 1845

Little brought an action against McGoon in the Jo Davies circuit court before Judge Thomas C. Browne. McGoon filed a petition for a change of venue stating "he entertained serious and well grounded fears, that he would not receive a fair and impartial trial in that court, on account of the prejudices, that he believed existed in the mind of the presiding judge of that court, then on the bench; and that he believed these prejudices so great against him, that he would be unsafe in submitting to a trial before him." Petition was denied, the case tried before a jury, and a verdict rendered for plaintiffs (Little et al.) for $306.28.

McGoon brings this appeal, represented by T. Campbell identified in the record, and Lincoln, who was not identified in the case record but subsequent information uncovered indicates he participated. J. Young Scammon represented Little et al. Justice Scates, writing for the court, reversed the judgment, and remanded the cause. He concluded "As the subsequent orders, and judgments of the court, in this case, are avoided by the reversal of this judgment, upon this ground, it is unnecessary to decide any other point presented by the assignment of errors."

McCall et al. v. Lesher et al.
orig. ed. 7 Ill.46
(Ill. Rep.: McCall et al. v. Lesher et al. 7 Ill.46)

McCall et al.v. Lesher et al.
orig. ed. 7 Ill.47
(Ill. Rep.: McCall et al. v. Lesher et al. 7 Ill.47)
December Term 1845

These two cases before the Supreme Court are part of the same proceedings. In both cases Lincoln represent Lesher and S.T. Logan the McCalls. The action in chancery was before the Wabash circuit court before Judge Harlin. Justice Treat wrote both opinions for the Supreme Court.

The first proceeding was an attempt by Lincoln to dismiss the appeal. His client had been successful in the chancery action. After the decree, the appeal was taken by McCall and the joinder (concurrence) of the errors to be appealed was stipulated by the court. The grounds for the motion to dismiss was that the appeal bond was executed by only part of the appellants. Justice Treat, for the court, dismissed the motion, saying it was too late, commenting "By joining in the error, the defendants submit the case to the judgment of the court, and waive all irregularities in the mode of bringing it here."

The bill in chancery involved here was brought by Lesher and Hinde against the heirs at law of Henry Vanderberg to compel the conveyance of four hundred acres of land lying at the Grand Rapids in Wabash county. Judge Treat states "All of the defendants approved and answered the bill. A replication was filed, and a mass of testimony taken. Subsequently, the death of Julia McCall and Ferdinand Vanderberg, two of the defendants was suggested; and on motion of the complainants, William McCall," and it goes on to name other additional heirs to be made defendants to the suit. "No process was ever issued against these defendants, nor was their appearance ever entered." The cause was heard, and a decree entered for Lesher and Hinde requiring conveyance of the land to them.

The decree was reversed because the decree should not have been rendered when all the defendants were not properly before the court.

"The record ought distinctly to show the service of process on the defendants, or their voluntary appearance to the action. It must not be left to inference or conjecture." Judge Treat said he would not comment on the merits of the case because all the parties materially interested did not have an opportunity to assert defenses any of them might have had. Decree reversed, and the cause remanded for further proceedings.

Perhaps Lincoln believed that since his side asked the court to add these additional heirs after the deaths of Julia and Ferdinand was "suggested," that was all he had to do. Why he neglected to bring these necessary additional parties to court through serving them with process, or by publication is unknown. An interesting possibility in the motion to dismiss the appeal on the grounds all the defendants had not signed the appeal bond, is that it could have been these un-served defendants were the ones who didn't sign the appeal bond. Further, this is another case where Lincoln and Logan were on opposite sides. They had dissolved their law firm by mutual agreement in December 1844.

Wren v. Moss et al.
orig. ed. 7 Ill.72

(Ill. Rep.: Wren v. Moss et al. 7 Ill.72)

December Term 1845

In 6 Ill.560 these same parties appeared, and Clarissa Wren, was represented by Lincoln and E.N. Powell. Aquilla Wren had obtained a divorce from his wife, Clarissa, based on her misconduct. The question of alimony was postponed until the next term. Before that time, Aquilla died, leaving a will leaving his property, after paying his debts, to certain parties (other than Clarissa), naming them. An executor was appointed and took office. He sold land to Moss and Frye, in which Clarissa had not relinquished her right of dower. Clarissa sought a writ of error to revise the decree of divorce. This was granted, making all these persons party defendants. At the next term of the Supreme Court, this application is made for a rule upon the defendants to join in error, and the application was resisted on the ground that a writ of error did not lie in this case.

The Supreme Court, with Justice Scates writing the opinion, granted the motion. He stated the general rule is that a writ of error does not lie against any, but him who, is party, or privy to the first judgment, his heirs, executors or administrators. However, there are exceptions. Some of the parties defendant here do not meet the general definition, but they all have interests which could be influenced if the original decree of divorce were altered. Scates states Clarissa believes she had been injured by an erroneous decree. Her only two remedies are appeal or writ of error. She can't appeal because the judgment against her was not $20 or more. There was no money involved in it, so her only remedy is a writ of error. Thus a writ of error is granted, which in reality entitles her to a new trial, and all the interests of the various defendants must be included to protect their rights. Justice Young dissented, and Justice Purple did not sit in this case, because he had been one of the attorneys for Moss et al. in the first proceeding.

There is no record in the Supreme Court decisions of any subsequent activities between these parties. There apparently was enough property involved to justify these two proceedings, and Lincoln's client prevailed after suffering an initial setback of having been the defendant in a successful divorce action based on her misconduct.

Rysinger & Nye v. Cheney
orig. ed. 7 Ill.84

(Ill. Rep.: Risinger et al. v. Cheney 7 Ill.84)
December Term 1845

Cheney brought an action of assumpsit against Risinger and Nye in the McLean circuit court before Judge Treat. Judgment was rendered for them for $101.25. Lincoln represented Risinger and Nye in the appeal.

Cheney, and Risinger and Nye, entered into an elaborate agreement wherein Cheney agree that Risinger and Nye could remove a stream mill, and all the machinery pertaining to it, place it on land owned by Risinger and Nye near Pekin, and pay for it over a several year period. The purchasers gave Cheney a note for $100 payable if they did not comply with the contract. However, one Thompson was successful in an action against Cheney in which Cheney "and any purchaser or purchasers, agents, attorneys or workmen under them, were perpetually enjoined from the tearing down, or removal of said mill, machinery etc. until the decree made in said chancery suit could be complied with by the said owner and Thomas Cheney."

On the appeal Lincoln argued the injunction issued was sufficient excuse to excuse Risinger and Nye's failure to perform, so as to save the forfeiture of the note. The court, with Justice Young writing the opinion agreed, and reversed the lower court. Both parties were prevented from performing their undertakings because of the injunction, and by Cheney permitting the continuance of the injunction so as to prevent the removal of the mill. The consideration of the note failed. and Cheney ought not be permitted to recover upon it. When there are mutual conditions to be performed, and one of the parties has incapacitated himself from performance on his part, which condition was the consideration of the promise to be performed by the other, that such incapacity will dispense with the performance, or an offer to perform, by the other party to the contract.

Ramsdell et al. v. Sigerson & Harrison
orig. ed. 7 Ill.78

(Ill. Rep.: Ramsdell et al. v. Sigerson et al. 7 Ill.77)
December Term 1845

This was an action to determine the right to certain property by Sigerson and Harrison, which was in the possession of them. Ramsdell et al. had obtained a judgment against Gerry and Weller, and Ramsdell et al. claimed subject property had been fraudulently assigned by them to defraud creditors, especially Ramsdell et al. Gerry and Weller had entered into an agreement with three other people to act as assignees of their property to pay creditors, and these assignees had transferred the property to Sigerson and Harrison to discharge a debt of $6,136.95 that Gerry and Weller owed them. Ramsdell et al. seek to have the judgment enforced against the subject property. Judgment was rendered for Sigerson et al.

The supreme court, in an opinion written by Justice Young, reversed the judgment and remanded the cause with instructions to enter judgment for Ramsdell et al. One creditor can be preferred by an assignment, as long as there is no fraud. Here Ramsdell et al. were not parties to the agreement, and were defrauded.

The question as to whether or not Sigerson and Harrison were properly preferred creditors, or whether they should have been protected as purchasers in good faith was not considered in the circuit court, and thus could not be considered on appeal.

Eldridge v. Rowe
orig. ed. 7 Ill.91

(Ill. Rep.: Eldridge v. Rowe 7 Ill.91)
December Term 1845

Rowe agreed to work for Eldridge on his farm for a term of eight months, for the sum of $90, and Rowe left after four months, without the consent and without any fault of Eldridge. Rowe brings an action before a justice of the peace of Kendall county, who awards him $30. Eldridge appealed to the circuit court before Judge Caton and a jury, who reduced the amount to $26.75. Eldridge had an offset of $3.25, which he proved. Eldridge appeals to the Supreme Court. Lincoln represents Rowe.

The Supreme Court reverses the decision, and with Justice Young writing the opinion, remands the cause. Lincoln argued for a quantum meruit (as much as he deserves) theory, which means Rowe should be paid something because he did a lot of work which had benefit to Eldridge, and cited one New Hampshire case. This was ignored by Young in his opinion, who held basically that if a party promises to do a thing, and abandons his work before it is finished, he shouldn't be paid anything. Quantum meruit applies in some special cases, but not this.

Justice Young writes: "The general rules which govern in ordinary contracts for work and labor, are simple and easily understood, but often difficult in their application to many of the cases which arise in the country, and are constantly presented in our courts for adjudication. The loose manner in which parties frequently express themselves in making verbal agreements, and not infrequently when the contracts are in writing, often obscures the intention, and necessarily involves the proper construction to be given to them by courts and juries, in much doubt and perplexity." Further: "When an agreement is fairly entered into, and upon a good and valid consideration, it should be faithfully performed, and neither party is at a liberty to disregard it, or to perform it otherwise than according to his engagement; and the rule is well established, that where one has the precedent condition in his favor, that he is not liable to an action until the other has performed." Further: "And it is our duty to discountenance any departure from this rule, which will allow a party to abandon his undertaking at pleasure and resort to a quantum meruit, where a part of the agreement only has been performed." He wrote some basic truths still in fashion about the difficulty of understanding oral, and even written agreements, and about the necessity of performing a contract once one has agreed to it.

Doe ex dem. Frisby et al. v. Ballance & Staller
orig. ed. 7 Ill.141

(Ill. Rep.: Doe ex dem. Frisby et al. v.
Ballance et al. 7 Ill.141)
December Term 1845

This is an appeal from an action of ejectment in the Peoria circuit court before Judge Caton. Powell, Williams, Johnson, and Lincoln represented

Frisby et al. The first three attorneys filed an extensve brief citing pertinent cases, and the opinion then states: "A. Lincoln concluded the argument in behalf of the plaintiffs in error." This is an example of attorneys from distant circuits seeking the assistance of the experienced supreme court pleader, Lincoln, to bolster their side, and they won the case.

Bogardus conveyed certain real property to Underhill in 1834 by a deed, which contained sufficient language to constitute a transfer, but did not contain the proper language to validate a technical transfer of a fee simple absolute (this is the common law precedent where a title is conveyed with no limitations or conditions, and belongs to a man, his heirs and assigns forever). Subsequently (1838) Bogardus acquired a patent from the United States for the same property. Whatever interest Frisby et al. have in the title flows from Underhill. In the action of ejectment, the plaintiffs were not allowed to show proof of the deed of 1834, and the jury found for the defendants, ejectment not being granted.

Justice Scates, writing for the court, reversed this judgment, and remanded the case for a new trial. He reversed the precedents cited, and stated that when a person conveys property, and the document shows clear intent to do so (and he doesn't have clear title at the time), if he subsequently acquires title to the same property, this interest passes to the original grantees.

The transfer of title to land was dealt with with much formality originating in the English common law, and continued in our country. Deeds contain certain words and phrases which impart clear and precise meanings, tested by courts over the years. This particular decision was specifically overruled in Frink v. Dorst, 14 Ill.304.

Hall v. Irwin et al.
orig. ed. 7 Ill.176

(Ill. Rep.: Hall v. Irwin et al. 7 Ill.176)
December Term 1845

This is an action of ejectment brought in the Sangamon circuit court before Judge Treat and a jury, by the heirs of Thomas Payne, and who were represented by Lincoln and W. Thomas on appeal.

Payne made a will leaving his estate to be divided amoung his children, with stipulation that the land should not be sold for a price less than eight dollars an acre. He did not appoint an executor. Payne died, and Gatten was appointed administrator. He believed he had the power to convey the real estate, and did so to Hall. Payne's heirs contend he did not have this power, and want Hall off their land. The court holds for the heirs, and Hall appeals.

The supreme court, in an opinion written by Justice Koerner, agrees with Lincoln and affirms the judgment, holding that while it is true an executor would have the power to sell the land, an administrator does not. Justice Koerner cites the English common law precedents concerning the relative rights of executors and administrators. When dealing with personal property, the rights are the same, not so with the real property. The Illinois legislature enacted statutes pertaining to estates, which did not give administrators more power than the common law. A statute changing the course of common law in derogation of it must be strictly construed, and when it appears doubtful from the phraseology used, whether the legislature intended to make such a change, the presumption is, that such was not their intent.

Justice Young dissents resting his opinion on "a reasonable and proper construction of our statute of wills, and not upon decisions predicated upon the common or statute law of England, or the statute laws of our sister states, differing in a more or less degree from our own." Hall paid valuable consideration (over 8 dollars an acre) for the land in good faith, and should be entitled to it.

Justice Scates also dissented. He stated "In England, with a view of sustaining a landed aristocracy, great restraints upon alienation of land remain to this day. In most of the states, and particularly here, all restraints are removed." Real estate should be treated the same as personal poperty in the proper administration of estates.

Springfield v. Hickox et al.
orig. ed. 7 Ill.241

(Ill. Rep.: Springfield v. Hickox et al. 7 Ill.241)
December Term 1845

This was originally an action brought before the mayor of the city of Springfield to recover twelve dollars from Hickox et al. for a debt incurred as a penalty under an ordinance of the city requiring licenses to be taken out by merchants etc. The case was taken by appeal into the Sangamon circuit court before Judge Treat. Hickox et al. had a city order (an order drawn by the mayor to the treasurer to pay city funds to a named person[s]) for fifty dollars, which was introduced as an offset, and judgment was rendered for Hickox et al. for thirty-eight dollars. Lincoln and W.I. Fergason represented the city of Springfield in the appeal to the supreme court, and contended the offset was not an effective claim where the lawsuit was concerned, because there had been no demand on the city to pay the order. Hickox et al. had made a claim on the city for the fifty dollars after the lawsuit was instituted, but payment was refused, "there being no funds in the treasurey, and proved by the city treasurer that there was not then, and had not been for some time previous, any funds in the treasurey, either appropriated or otherwise." Lincoln cited two Illinois supreme court cases as precedent.

Justice Purple, writing for the court, affirmed the lower court judgment. He distinguished this case from Lincoln's citations, because the city was involved, and the order was a valid obligation without any demand for payment being made. He concluded by saying: "Mutual demands in equity extinguish each other; and unless we hold the doctrine, that political corporations of this sort are not liable to be sued upon their contracts and obligations thus issued,--unless we allow them the privilege of collecting debts due them, and compel the holder of their papers to await the tardy operation of an assessment and collection of taxes for the payment of his claim, without the privilege of a set off, I can see no just reason why the judgment in this case should not be affirmed."

Ross et al. v. Nesbit
orig. ed. 7 Ill.252

(Ill. Rep.: Ross et al. v. Nesbit 7 Ill.252)
December Term 1845

Nesbit sued Ross et al. in the DeKalb circuit court before Judge Caton and a jury in an action of quare clausum fregit (whereas he broke the close [land boundary]). Ross et al. made five pleas in answer and the issue was joined on the first two, and Lincoln, who represented Nesbit, demurred to the last three, which were sustained by the court. Judgment for Nesbit for $9. Ross et al. appeal to the supreme court to overrule the decision on the demurrers, since they believe they had good defenses to their action in those pleas.

A demurrer in pleading is in effect a statement that even if the facts in the pleading to which the objections are taken are true, the legal consequences of them are not sufficient to raise a proper legal cause. Lincoln cited a New York case to support his position, in addition to his oral arguments, and Justice Koerner, writing for the court, affirmed the lower court opinion--the demurrers were properly sustained by the court, and the three pleas involved were inadequate to support a defense, even if true. In the report of Lincoln's appeal brief it says "the court will consider these pleas, and examine the authorities of the plaintiffs in error (Ross et al.), and if the court can then decide that they are good pleas in trespass, we will cheerfully submit."

Simpson v. Ranlett
orig. ed. 7 Ill.312
(Ill. Rep.: Simpson v. Ranlett 7 Ill.312)
December Term 1845

Simpson made a promissory note to Burnett for $323.64, who assigned it to Ranlett. The note is due and Ranlett brings an action in assumpsit against Simpson (who is represented by Lincoln) before Judge Caton in the Putnam circuit court. The declaration of Ranlett in the pleading after stating the making of the note by Simpson to Burnett in the usual form, contains this averment (offer to prove a pleading) as the endorsement: "and the said Isaac Burnett then and there indorsed the same to said plaintiff (Ranlett), whereof the said defendant (Simpson) then and there had notice, etc." The court then states: "This averment of the indorsement, the counsel for the appellant, Simpson, insists, does not set forth such an assignment of the note, as is required to be made by our statute, and consequently the appellee, Ranlett, cannot maintain this action against him in his own name as indorsee." Ranlett was awarded $391.64 on one count, but Lincoln demurred to the other count claiming the assignment was not sufficient to justify the pleading, which was overruled.

The supreme court, with Justice Young writing the opinion, affirmed the ruling. Young held the declaration about the assignment was good, and that Simpson's demurrer for the want of a sufficient averment in the endorsement was properly overruled. In his comments on the history of promissory notes, he states they were not transferable by indorsement and made negotiable as bills of exchange until an act of parliament, which allowed the transfer and also gave the right to the assignee to bring an action in his own name. His reliance on precedents is well stated as follows: "The language of the English act of parliament, so far as the assignment is concerned, is almost identical with that contained in our own statute, and the rules of pleading, therefore, ought not in practice to vary in any essential particular; uniformity in precedent and decision being always an important desideratum in our courts of justice, unless very strong reasons should render it proper and necessary that the role should be changed, which should always be done with reluctance. It is necessary then to ascertain what that practice is, and to conform our opinion to the well established precedents upon the subject of averment, in cases in all respects similar to one now under consideration."

Klein et al. v. Mather
orig. ed. 7 Ill.317

(Ill. Rep.: Klein et al. v. Mather 7 Ill.318)
December Term 1845

The legislature of the State of Illinois passed a bill on February 25th, 1837, stating the seat of government for the State would be Springfield, if the sum of $50,000 should be donated by individuals, payable as the governor should direct. Fifty-one private individuals agreed to these terms, including Samuel H. Treat, Ninian W. Edwards, John T. Stewart, Elijah Iles, and many other names remembered by present day Springfieldians. The money was to be paid in 3 installments, and the first two were paid. When number three became due, some of the 51 had died, and others became insolvent. Mather, one of the 51, was sued by the state for the whole amount due ($16,666.66 2/3), and judgment was recovered against him. The legislature passed an act authorizing this debt to be discharged in State indebtedness. Mather paid the judgment in these obligations, which he bought at 80 cents on the dollar. Twenty-six of the other obligers paid Mather some proportion based on an agreement among themselves. Mather computed he was still due $4,607.55, and brought this action to recover this amount form the 11 remaining solvent obligers in the Morgan circuit court before Judge Lockwood. Judgment for Mather, who is represented by Logan on the appeal.

The supreme court, in an opinion written by Justice Purple, affirmed the judgment. Justice Purple did vary the amount each obligor owed from $351.55 found by the circuit court to $354.89, after giving a good detailed explanation as to how this sum was determined item by item. The law was clear as to the obligation of the co-obligers. Purple said: "No doctrine is better settled, than that a co-obligor or surety, who advances money for his co-obligers or co-sureties, shall be indemnified to the extent of his advances." The court noted: "Treat, J., being a party to the suit of Klein v. Mather, did not sit in the case."

Murphy v. Summerville
orig. ed. 7 Ill.360

(Ill. Rep.: Murphy v. Summerville 7 Ill.361)
December Term 1845

This is an appeal from an action of debt upon a bail bond brought by Summerville against Murphy before Judge Treat in the Degar Circuit court. Murphy was represented by Lincoln, who demurred to the declaration, which was overruled, and judgment rendered against Murphy for $250, the penalty of the bond, to be discharged on payment of $150.62 1/2. Lincoln appeals that the declaration was insufficient to support this cause of action (the reason for the demurrer). The supreme court agreed, and reversed the judgment, remanding the cause, with leave for Summerville to amend his declaration.

Justice Scates, in writing the opinion for the court, agreed the declaration was defective. Certainty is one of the common, general rules of pleading, and it requires, in setting forth the cause of action, that every fact necessary to support the action must be averred. One failure of the declaration was it did not show with certainty that a judgment was ever rendered against the principal, which was essential to support a cause of action.

The other missing element in the declaration was that it did not aver that a capias ad satisfaciendum was ever issued. This is a writ of execution which commands the sheriff to take the party named, and keep him safely, so that he may have his body before the court on a certain day, to satisfy the damages, if any, assessed in the proceedings. Summervile's attorneys pointed out this did not have to be averred in the English precedents. Scates agreed this is what the English authorities held, but said they were not applicable, because of the Illinois constitution Art. 8, Section 15, which states "no person shall be imprisoned for debt, unless upon refusal to deliver up his estate for the benefit of his creditors, in such manner as shall be prescribed by law, or in cases where there is strong presumptions to be found." Scates then said: "But under a constitution so jealous of liberty of the citizen, we are of the opinion the plaintiff ought to aver the fact" that the principal was liable to be deprived of his liberty, before he can show cause of action in his non-surrender.

Law dictionaries state this writ, called "ca. sa" for short, was a very common form of execution of judgments, but its efficiency has been destroyed by statutes.

Trailor v. Hill
orig. ed. 7 Ill.364
(Ill. Rep.: Trailor v. Hill 7 Ill.364)
December Term 1845

This is an appeal from a bill in equity for specific performance of a contract purporting to require Hill to convey certain land to Trailor. The bill was dismissed by Judge Treat in the Sangamon circuit court. Lincoln and Logan represent Hill on the appeal, and the decree was affirmed. The contract had a detailed description of the land to be conveyed. However, Lincoln disputed the description of the land as being what both parties intended. Several witnesses further confused the issue.

Justice Purple, writing the opinion for the court, held Hill did not have to convey the land. To award a decree of specific performance the propriety of the award must be proven incontrovertically. Such was not the case here. The land was described, and a single map was included, which did not have "north" indicated. He said "It is urged by the complaint's counsel that inasmuch as all scientific men make the top of a map north, that we are therefore bound to infer that the parties, in this instance, have been guided by the lights of science. A base glance at the contract itself, it seems to me, would sufficiently prove, without the aid of experience in matters of the sort, that this would be a somewhat strained, and by no means a safe interpretation. If the parties possessed sufficient knowledge and intelligence to make a perfect plat of the sixteenth section, and did so, treating the top thereof as north, it is difficult to understand why they could not describe the land correctly in the contract."

Chase v. DeBolt
orig. ed. 7 Ill.371
(Ill. Rep.: Chase v. Debolt 7 Ill.371)
December Term 1845

DeBolt sued Chase in a justice of the peace court in Peoria to recover payment for work done by DeBolt on Jubilee College. DeBolt was awarded $75.93 3/4, and Chase appealed to the circuit court before Judge Caton and a jury, and the verdict and judgment were rendered for DeBolt for the same amount. Chase had testified in the justice of the peace court that he had hired DeBolt on behalf of Bishop Chase for Jubilee College but although he had not told DeBolt he was an agent rather than a principal, DeBolt knew it from other sources. Chase appeals to the

Supreme Court, and in this matter DeBolt is represented by Lincoln and H.O. Merriman.

Justice Scates, writing for the court, reverses the judgment, and remands the case for a new trial. Lincoln objected to the inclusion of testimony in the circuit court by the justice of the peace that Chase testified he hired DeBolt, and DeBolt knew he was an agent from other sources. He said this was hearsay, and not admissible. Scates held that Chase's testimony was an admission, and thus proper as evidence. The two lower courts had said Chase was liable to pay because DeBolt believed him to be a principal, and not an agent. An agent is liable as a principal if he does not disclose this; but if the other party knows the agency status from other sources, he is not. New trials can be awarded if there is a strong preponderance of testimony that the judgment was improper, especially where apparent injustice has been done. Chase was not a principal and should not have been found liable as one. He was an agent, and DeBolt knew it.

We don't know when Lincoln joined this case, and presume it was only for the appeal. By this time in his career his services were frequently sought for appeals to the supreme court, when he had not been involved in the trials. He argued every positive point he could, and cited pertinent cases and treatises on English common law to support his points. Once it was clear to the court that Chase was but an agent, there was no way to affirm lower court opinions that he had been a principal.

Ripley v. Morris
orig. ed. 7 Ill.381

(Ill. Rep.: Ripley v. Morris 7 Ill.381)
December Term 1845

Ripley lost a case in The Cook Circuit Court to Morris, and sought a writ of error, (This is an order issued by the supreme court to a circuit court to require it to submit the record of a case to the supreme court, so it can determine whether or not alleged errors were made during the trial). Morris made a motion to dismiss the writ of error, because no bond for costs was filed. Ripley was a non-resident, and as such, should have posted a bond. Ripley contended the application for the writ of error was merely a continuation of the original suit, and not a new suit which would require him to post a bond. The writ of error was dismissed.

The supreme court, in an opinion written by Justice Lockwood, affirmed the lower court. A writ of error is a new action. The statute relative to costs requires the court to dismiss the suit whenever a non-resident commences an action, either in the circuit or Supreme court, without filing security for the costs.

Smith & Smith v. Byrd
orig. ed. 7 Ill.412

(Ill. Rep.: Smith et al. v. Byrd 7 Ill.412)
December Term 1845

Joseph H. Smith and Byrd entered into a written agreement to submit all matters in controversy between them to arbitrators. However, Byrd sued Joseph H. Smith before a justice of the peace and was awarded $100. Joe appealed to the Jo Daviess' circuit court. The two parties then submitted the case to arbitration, with the award to be extended as a judgment of the court. The award was, that Joseph H. Smith and George F. Smith pay Byrd the sum of $40. The circuit court rendered a judgment on the award against the Smiths. They appeal to the supreme court, and Lincoln represents Byrd.

The supreme court, with Judge Treat writing the opinion, reversed the judgment, and remanded the case for further proceedings. The judgment was clearly unauthorized against George, since he was not originally a party to the case. He did not become one later, and the court had no jurisdiction over his person. "Although the award may be binding between the original parties, it is a mere nullity as to him (George). The judgment is a unit, and must be reversed as to both Smiths."

This opinion didn't state any other facts. In fact, this summary is about the same length as the report. Byrd seems to have had his initial advantage in the justice of peace court steadily reduced.

Morgan v. Ladd et al.
orig. ed. 7 Ill.414

(Ill. Rep.: Morgan v. Ladd et al. 7 Ill.414)
December Term 1845

Ladd and others brought a bill in chancery in the Scott circuit court against Morgan for an injunction, and other remedies. A decree was rendered directing, among other things, payment to Morgan of $92.54. After receiving the money, Morgan, believing there had been errors in the proceeding (and he should have received more) tried to return the money to the court, brings this appeal to reverse the decree.

The Supreme Court, in an opinion written by Judge Treat, dismissed the appeal, and the decree in the chancery court was thus affirmed. The acceptance of the money operated as a release of errors, if any. A person who voluntarily receives the benefit of a decree, should not be allowed to allege that it was erroneous. The errors are released by his voluntary act; when thus waived, he cannot again assert them.

Moore v. Hamilton
orig. ed. 7 Ill.429

(Ill. Rep.: Moore v. Hamilton 7 Ill.429)
December Term 1845

Hamilton brought an action of assumpsit against Moore in the Hancock circuit court before Judge Norman H. Purple. There was not personal service against Moore, as he couldn't be found. Hamilton then sued out an attachment authorized by new legislation called "act concerning attachments," and following the procedure therein described, served notice on Moore by publication, with again no personal service on Moore. He did not appear, and Hamilton was awarded $145.74, and order made for the attached assets to be sold to pay the judgment. Moore, represented by Lincoln, appeals.

The supreme court, with Justice Treat writing the opinion, reversed and remanded the case. Lincoln argued personal service was necessary and constructive notice (through publication) was not sufficient. In agreeing Justice Treat stated that the action of assumpsit and the attachment were not distinct proceedings, as argued by Hamilton. They constitute but one case, as the attachment is but an adjunct of the original case. Justice Treat stated how this new statute should be interpreted, and went on to say: "The remedies by attachment are in derogation of the common law, and ought not to be extended by implication."

Here is a good case where Lincoln argued successfully on a matter not previously adjudicated, and Justice Treat demonstrated a proper respect for the common law as precedent.

McNamara v. King
orig. ed. 7 Ill.432

(Ill. Rep.: McNamara v. King 7 Ill.432)
December Term 1845

This is an appeal from an action of trespass, assault and battery brought by King against McNamara in the Kane circuit court before Judge Caton and a jury. Verdict and judgment rendered for King for $650. During the trial the court allowed King to prove he was a poor man with a large family, and that McNamara was a wealthy man, with no children, and but a small family. Lincoln and J.B. Thomas represented McNamara on the appeal, contending that judgment was excessive and the evidence about the relative economic status of the parties had been improperly admitted.

Justice Treat, writing for the supreme court, affirmed the judgment. He stated, "The evidence is voluminous and will not be here particularly stated. It has been carefully examined and considered. In the opinion of the court, it shows an aggravated case of assault and battery, without any attending circumstances to justify or excuse it." He did not believe the damages high enough to draw a conclusion that they were excessive. "It must be apparent at first blush that the damages are glaringly excessive," and that is not the case here. He also stated it is proper that the jury should be influenced by the pecuniary resources of the defendant. The more affluent, the more able he is to remunerate the party he has wantonly injured. It is appropriate to punish the defendant.

This was obviously a tough case for Lincoln, with adverse factors of a wealthy assaulter of a poor man, and an aggravated case of assault and battery. Lincoln represented a poor man suing a rich man for rape of his daughter in Grable v. Margrave 4 Ill.372, and was successful in obtaining a higher verdict because of the "poor man injured by rich man" relationship. So he probably wasn't too surprised the judgment here was affirmed but he had to make the appeal to fully serve his client.

Ellis v. Locke
orig. ed. 7 Ill.459

(Ill. Rep.: Ellis v. Locke 7 Ill.459)
December Term 1845

Ellis gave a promissory note, secured by a mortgage to Locke. The note was in default and Locke sues to foreclose the mortgage, in Cook circuit court before Judge Dickey. Ellis' only defense is a plea of usury nullifying the contract. Judge Dickey awards Locke $361.65, and Ellis appeals, represented by Lincoln and J.B. Thomas.

The court, with Judge Treat writing the opinion, affirmed the judgment for Locke in the lower court. During the trial each party testified on his own behalf, and Justice Treat said that each gave testimony, that if believed, his side would have prevailed. There was only one other witness, named Haddock, who testified to the same facts as Locke. Treat said: "His (Locke's) testimony was corroborated by the witness, Haddock, who was cognizant of all the transactions between the parties respecting the note and mortgage. The scale of evidence, therefore, strongly inclined to the plaintiff's side, and the court was not only authorized but required, to find the issues against the defendant."

This opinion summarizes the briefs of the attorneys. S.T. Logan represented Locke, and presented a brief with eleven cases cited on several points, one of them from Illinois. Lincoln and Thomas had no citations, indicating the law was clear supporting Locke. The case thus was argued on the truthfulness of the witnesses, and Treat took the easy way out, and justified the verdict on relative number of bodies testifying--two to one.

Rhinehart v. Schuyler et al.
orig. ed. 7 Ill.473

(Ill. Rep.: Rhinehart v. Schuyler et al. 7 Ill.473)
December Term 1845

Schuyler et al. brought an action of ejectment against Rhinehart to recover possession of certain property in which Schuyler acquired title from Munn. He had acquired the title originally by an auditor's deed in 1831, when the land was seized for unpaid taxes in 1830, and sold to satisfy the tax obligation. Rhinehart had been living on the land, with no notice of adverse claims, for some time. His attorneys contended the revenue laws of the state were unconstitutional; the auditors deed did not comply with the necessary procedure and form for a valid deed; and a statute of limitations of seven years had been enacted by the legislature in 1835, which was a defense against any other claim of title. The court rejected those claims, and rendered judgment for Schuyler et al.

The supreme court, in an opinion written by Justice Young, affirmed the judgment. The majority opinion, which was thirty four pages, cited many precedents justifying the taxation, including the Magna Charta in the original Latin language (English translation also furnished), and concluded the various taxing statutes referred to were constitutional. Secondly, the registry laws prescribing how land titles had to be conveyed between private individuals, did not apply to deeds emanating directly from a state. Thirdly, the seven years statute of limitations, which specified any person who held possession of land for seven years, with no knowledge of any adverse title, had a valid defense against anyone else who claimed title. Rhinehart had lived on the land for over seven years, but some of these were before 1835, and the only time allowed to justify adverse possession was that after the passage of the legislation.

Justice Caton dissented in a ten page opinion contending the method of assessment prescribed in the revenue acts which specified land would be divided into three valuation classes (the first class would be valued at four dollars and taxed at two cents per acre, the second class valued at three dollars an acre and taxed at one and one-half cents, and the third class valued at two dollars an acre and taxed at one cent) did not meet the constitutional requirement that property taxed must be valued so each person would pay a tax in proportion to the value of his property. The method prescribed was too arbitrary and excluded town lots and improvements to the land. Justice Treat stated simply he dissented and concurred in Justice Scates opinion.

This case includes six briefs, three by attorneys on each side. S.T. Logan, representing Schuyler et al. who claimed title though Munn, who had bought the land at a tax sale, started his brief with the following observation. "The substance of the argument seems to be that if the court can in any way destroy tax titles, it should do so. Now, whatever may be the nature of the contest about tax titles in other states and counties, in this state it is a mere contest between speculators; speculators in tax titles on one side, and speculators in tax titles on the other."

Justice Young recognized the importance of the issue commenting as follows: "This case throughout, has been treated as it deserves to be, on all sides, as one of very great importance; not on account of the value of the property involved in the result of the present controversy, but of settling principles of the first magnitude, which, in their effects as precedents, are to control and determine the relative rights of numerous individuals, to a very large class of some of the most valuable property in the country."

Bryan et al. v. Wash et al.
orig. ed. 7 Ill.557
(Ill. Rep.: Bryan et al. v. Wash et al. 7 Ill.557)
December Term 1845

George Bryan executed a deed of certain premises to his granddaughter, a minor, who was afterwards married to Wash. The deed was placed in the hand of her father, Nicholas Bryan, to be retained by him for her until she should arrive at sufficient discretion to take care of it. Nicholas occupied and improved the land. Wash obtained possession of the deed, recorded it, and mortgaged the property. Nicholas brought his action to have the deed ruled to not have been properly delivered to his daughter (and Wash) by George and to restore the deed to Nicholas. The action was dismissed. Lincoln and Logan represented Wash et al. on the appeal at least.

The supreme court, in an opinion written by Justice Caton, affirmed the decision. A delivery is essential to the validity of every deed, and to constitute a complete delivery, it is necessary that there should be an acceptance by, or on behalf of, the grantee. If effective, the grantor loses all control of it. Here the intention was that the son's pleasure was not to be exercised in regard as to whether the title should rest in the infant grantee or not, but only as to the proper time when the evidence of that title should be delivered to her. The presumption of the law is in favor of the delivery being proper.

Wright for use of Davidson v. Bennett & Bennett
orig. ed. 7 Ill.587
(Ill. Rep.: Wright v. Bennett et al. 7 Ill.587)
December Term 1845

Richard E. Bennett was convicted of being the father of an illegitimate child by one Jane Davidson, and was adjudged by the court to pay the sum of forty dollars annually for seven years to support the child. Pursuant to an act of the legislature entitled an "act to provide for the maintenance of illegitimate children," he entered into a bond with John Bennett as surety. Richard demanded the possession and control of the child, under the statute insisting if she did not give over custody, his obligation under the bond was discharged. Ms. Davidson insists a second bond is required under the statute before she must give up custody. Judge Treat in the Menard circuit court held for Bennett, and that no second bond was required. Wright, the Probate Justice of Menard county, for the use of the child, appealed. Lincoln represented the Bennetts.

The court, with Justice Purple writing the opinion, agreed and affirmed the judgment; albeit reluctantly. Justice Purple, in commenting on the lack of necessity of a second bond said: "I regret that, upon a careful and attentive consideration of the law, I can find nothing in its various provisions to warrant this constriction, and am reluctantly compelled to admit that, if the reputed father of an illegitimate child, under the law as it existed at the time of the commencement of this suit, will have the inhumanity, in its helpless and dependent infancy, to demand its surrender by the mother, the law, upon her refusal, imposes upon him no further obligation to aid in its maintenance and support, at least so long as she persists in her refusal." By the common law, the reputed father was not entitled to custody of his illegitimate children. But this statute changed that; however if he does take custody his obligation to the child does not end after the seven years stipulated in the statute. Judge Purple concluded: "and that the legislature did not intend that, when he had once so chosen to demand it of the mother, that his duties toward it should cease at the expiration of seven years, the time limited in the bond for its support, and then be at liberty to thrust it forth upon the world's charity, friendless and unprotected."

Kincaid v. Turner
orig. ed. 7 Ill.618

(Ill. Rep.: Kincaid v. Turner 7 Ill.618)

December Term 1845

Turner sued Kincaid in the Menard circuit court before Judge Treat and a jury for trespass on the case for setting a fire on the prairie, and so negligently watching the same, that it had run over on his premises and destroyed Turner's property. Kincaid proved that previous to this suit, he and Turner had submitted this question to three arbitrators. They could not all agree, but reported to the parties that two of them agreed on a position (deemed favorable to Kincaid), and asked the parties what to do. Both were silent. Kincaid pleads this award was binding because silence gives consent, and constitutes a defense in this suit. The jury disagrees, and awards $150 to Turner. Kincaid appeals, and Lincoln and T.L. Harris represented Turner.

The court, with Justice Caton writing the opinion, concurred. S.W. Robbins, attorney for Kincaid, in arguing the award of the arbitrators was binding, offered an ingenious argument, without citing any legal precedent for it: "Silence gives consent, for instance, the marriage ceremony. If a man bawled out 'aye!' when his assent was asked for by the minister, he would be considered as caring nothing about it. It is the silence that gives consent."

Lincoln cited several authorities including two prior Illinois cases, stating that when questions of fact are submitted to a jury, they are the sole judges. Caton, agreeing there was evidence for the defendant, said: "Although we would have been entirely satisfied and perhaps better satisfied with the verdict, had they found the other way, yet we cannot say that the verdict is so palpably against the evidence, or acted from prejudice or partiality, which should be the case before the court would be authorized to set aside the verdict." Later: "This silence, when this remark was made (by the arbitrators), and immediately after the award of the majority was published, we do not doubt could have been sufficient to have authorized to have found that way, but it, as clearly, did not constrain them so to find." Then: "When a question is fairly and intelligently submitted to a jury, their determination ought not be set aside without the most substantial reasons."

This case, and the one preceding it (Wright v. Bennett 7Ill.587) are two cases where Lincoln successfully litigated positions when the supreme court at least, believed the opposite side had the superior merit.

Cunningham v. Fithian et al.
orig. ed. 7 Ill.650

(Ill. Rep.: Cunningham v. Fithian et al. 7 Ill.650)
December Term 1845

This case involves the same facts as McDonald v. Fithian et al. (6 Ill.269). Cunningham seeks injunctive relief from the same land purchase deal involved in the former case. Lincoln, S.T. Logan, and E.D. Baker represented Fithian et al. here as well, on the appeal, and the supreme court again upheld the lower court decision denying the requested relief.

Justice Lockwood, writing for the court, said "the questions have been very ably reargued at this term, and this court has been called on to review the former decision and pronounce in this case a different judgment. We have accordingly given important questions involved in the controversy between these parties a careful re-examination, but have been unable to discover any good reasons why the decision in the former case should be adhered to." This statement is awkward and misleading. The court held the same way in this case as the McDonald v. Fithian case. To use a double negative, if that's what Lockwood intended, he should have said "have been unable to discover any good reasons why the decision in the former case should not be adhered to."

The court added an additional reason why the complainant in this case, Cunningham, should not be granted relief. He waited five years after suspecting he had been wronged, and he did not pay taxes for three of these years. Also the value of the land had declined, which obviously influenced his decision to try to get out of the deal. "It is a well settled rule of equity that where a party seeks to rescind a contract for fraud, he must ask the aid of the court in a reasonable time, and be in a situation to restore to the opposite party whatever he may have received from him." Here Cunningham waited too long, and could not restore the property as he received it because of the tax liens.

Treat dissented again, this time he was joined by Koerner, and deserted by Justices Shields and Thomas who dissented in the McDonald case. Obviously a close case at each trial, and the effect of oral arguments (by Lincoln and possibly others on his side) again carried the day.

Wilson et al. v. VanWinkle
orig. ed. 7 Ill.684

(Ill. Rep.: Wilson et al. v. VanWinkle 7 Ill.684)
December Term 1845

In 1816 Eller made a promissory note to Thomas Wilson in consideration of the purchase of land from Wilson. Wilson assigned the note to VanWinkle in 1818. In 1819 VanWinkle sued Eller on the note, which was in default, and recovered a judgment. During the same term of the court, Eller filed a bill in chancery against VanWinkle and Wilson saying Wilson did not have title to the land; thus the note was bad, and the collection of the judgment by VanWinkle should be enjoined. Eller obtained an injunction staying proceedings on the judgment, which became perpetual in 1835. VanWinkle brings this action against the estate of Wilson in 1842, proving he was a assignee in good faith. Judge William Wilson (presumable not related to Thomas Wilson, deceased) rendered a judgment for VanWinkle for $1,015.15. Wilson's executor appeals, arguing too long a time has elapsed for VanWinkle to bring this action. Lincoln, J.J. Hardin, and D.A. Smith represented VanWinkle.

The supreme court, with Justice Treat writing the opinion, affirmed the judgment. Justice Treat said "The failure to collect the note was occasioned by the act of Wilson, in selling land to which he had not title. This was made manifest by the decision of the chancery case. The note was successfully impeached in a proceeding against Wilson, which he contested for many years. In good faith he ought long since to have refunded to VanWinkle, the amount be paid for the note with legal interest." It was also insisted the claim was barred by the statute of limitations. However, this defense was not suggested in the lower court, and cannot be used as a defense on appeal, if not pleaded in the circuit court.

There were no citations of cases on either side in the record, and none cited in the opinion. Presumable oral arguments at the appeal carried the day, and Lincoln's side won.

Thomas, adm. of Duncan v. Negus & Robbins
orig. ed. 7 Ill.700

(Ill. Rep.: Thomas, adm. of Duncan v. Negus et al. 7 Ill.700)
December Term 1845

Pinckard leased certain lots to Marsh, Hankinson and Company in Alton, at an annual rent of $800. On January 5, 1837, Pinckard executed a mortgage on lots to Duncan, to secure the payment of $9,641.83. On January 25, 1837, Negus and Robbins conveyed the lots to Pinckard, and at the same time took a mortgage from him for $4,143.75. In February, 1840, several suits were commenced by Duncan and others against Marsh et al. to recover rents due them. Marsh etc. paid the rent money into court, offered to pay them as the court directed, and obtained an injunction staying the action against them in the court of law. In May, 1843, Negus and Robbins filed a bill against Duncan, Pinckard and others to foreclose the mortgage made to them by Pinckard, insisting their mortgage was prior to Duncan's. In July, 1843, the suits were combined, and a decree was entered directing the rents to be paid to Duncan, and declaring the mortgage of Negus to be the prior lien. Duncan received the accrued rent of $1,531.11. Then: "Duncan has departed this life, and his administrator now prosecutes a writ of error. He assigns for error, that so much of the decree as gives to Negus and Robbins a priority in the payment of their mortgages is erroneous."

The Supreme Court, in a majority opinion written by Justice Treat, dismisses the writ, thus affirming the decree of the lower court. The receipt of the money by Duncan, under the circumstances of the case, necessarily operated as a release of errors. A party ought not to receive the benefit of a decree, and then complain it was erroneous. Justice Treat then referred to a New York case cited by Thomas, Clowes v. Dickinson, 8 Cowen 328, which held a party who received money in a decree, could still appeal the decree claiming he was entitled to more. Justice Treat said, "We have maturely considered that case, and cannot concur in the opinion there expressed."

Justice Caton wrote a dissenting opinion, also based upon mature reasoning. He started as follows: "After the most mature reflection in connection with the authorities adduced on the argument, my mind has been brought to the conclusion that the receipt by Duncan, of the money awarded him by the decree, did not operate as a release of the errors which may have been committed against him in other parts of the decree." At the conclusion of the opinion he commented on the Clowes case in New York, indicating a knowledge of, and respect for, the New York court: "In that case, Chancellor Jones and Senators Spencer and Colden all delivered opinions on the same side, and I may truly say that they are amount the brightest ornaments that have ever adorned the legal profession in that state."

In addition to his opinion on Clowes being a precedent, he also stated the action could be severed into independent parts, and appeal would be made on one part, without disturbing the others.

The mortgage to Duncan by Pinckard was executed twenty days before Pinckard's mortgage to Negus and Robbins, and on that fact alone Duncan's mortgage should have had priority. However, the opinion stated Negus and Robbins transferred title to these same lots when they received the mortgage. So we wonder if Pinckard really had title when he leased the property to Marsh et., and when he gave the mortgage to Duncan. The case is silent as to what Duncan's administrator deemed as errors in the case. The prior date of the mortgage seems a logical claim of error.

Patterson et ux. v. Edwards et al.
orig. ed. 7 Ill.720

(Ill. Rep.: Patterson et ux. v. Edwards et al. 7 Ill.720)
December Term 1845

This is an action of slander, brought by Edward and wife against Patterson and wife in the Mason circuit court, before Judge Treat and a jury. The declaration stated Mrs. Patterson said "Mrs. Edwards had raised a family of children by a negro, and I can prove it." Judgment rendered for the Edwards for $220. Pattersons' appeal was the proof did not sustain the allegations in the declaration. The statute supporting the action of slander specified that words falsely published, which in their common application shall amount to charge any person with having been guilty of fornication or adultery, shall be actionable. The words spoken by Ms. Patterson did not necessarily imply fornication or adultery. Lincoln and M. McConnell represented the Edwards on the appeal.

The Supreme Court, with Justice Koerner writing the opinion, reversed the lower court and rewarded the cause with leave to the plaintiff's (Edwards et al.) to amend pleadings. We assume Lincoln was called in for the appeal, after McConnell botched the case with defective pleadings. Koerner wrote "As the pleader has it in his power to state his own case, he must negative all inferences which may reasonably be drawn, and which, according to the rule of pleadings will always be intended strongly against him." Also: "The proof did not sustain the allegations in the declaration. Though all the words used need not be proved as laid, yet so much thereof as in sufficient to sustain the cause of action must be proved, and it will not do to prove equivalent words of slander. The rule, as here stated is a relaxation of the strictness once required by the courts in Great Britain, which held the slightest omission or addition to be fatal. To go further would be destroying the fundamental principles of correct pleading. For a recognition of this rule by this court, I refer to the case of Slocum v. Kuykendall, 1 Scam. 189, and authorities there cited."

The English common law was litigated under very strict rules of pleading. This case indicates some relaxation in Illinois which McConnell relied upon too much. The Slocum case is an example of the evolving reliance on Illinois cases; of interest is that Pattersons' counsel (W.A. Minshall), although citing many authorities in his brief, did not include the Slocum case which was the only one mentioned by the court.

Griggs et al. v. Gear
orig. ed. 8 Ill.2

(Ill. Rep.: Griggs et al. v. Gear 8 Ill.3)
December Term 1845

Harback et al. v. Gear
orig. ed. 8 Ill.18

(Ill. Rep.: Harback, impleaded with Griggs et al. v. Gear 8 Ill.18)
December Term 1845

Griggs and Weld entered into a partnership with Gear, wherein they were to furnish capital to Gear to manufacture lead at Galena, Illinois, and ship it to Boston to be sold by Griggs and Weld. Griggs et al. sued Gear for over $13,000 for goods furnished to him. Gear filed a bill to dissolve this suit, but no process was served on Griggs and Weld. The attorney for Griggs et al. (identified as Cowles and Krum) took it upon themselves to seek to enjoin Gear's action, which failed, and the final result was a finding by a master in equity that Gear had suffered a loss of $50,000 because Griggs et al. had failed to fulfill their part of the contract. The award for Gear was $50,000 minus $13,791.98, the amount of goods furnished by Griggs et al., leaving a balance due of $36,208.02. Harback, who was a partner with Griggs and Weld, but had nothing to do with this business, had been joined by Gear in his action. Griggs and Weld bring an action in Jo Daviess circuit court to review and reverse the former decree. Gear files a demurrer, which was sustained, and the bill dismissed.

Griggs et al. are represented by Lincoln and J.W. Chickering on the appeal. The opinion first states the attorney's briefs, with a multitude of authorities cited, none of them Illinois cases, with a large number of Story's Equity Pleadings references. Story's works on English equity pleadings was the oft quoted authority in Illinois cases. Chickering had a full page of statements and citations, and on the other side, J.J. Hardin and D.A. Smith had almost four pages and on the same side was J. Butterfield, who had about one page of statements and citations. Then is stated: "A. Lincoln, for the appellants replied at length to the arguments of the counsel for the appellee (Gear)."

The Supreme Court, with Justice Caton writing the opinion, reversed the decree of the court below, and remamded the cause for further proceeding. Caton cited one case in support of his opinion, but mostly relied on his interpretation of the rules of equity pleadings, and how the facts related. This is obviously a case where oral arguments were very influential, and Lincoln "replying at length to the arguments" of opposing counsel, carried the day. Lincoln's clients were awarded a reversal of the unfavorable ruling in the circuit court, because Caton said they had not given their previous attorneys in the action against Gear authority to appear for them in the equity matter, and they were never personally served. Caton wrote some impressive prose on this, possibly he was taking notes when Lincoln argued or had a very retentive memory for eloquence, as follows: "It further appears, that those attorneys are irresponsible. Can it be tolerated for a moment that parties are to be bound by a decree to pay more than $36,000 which is entered up behind their backs, and without even an implied knowledge of the existence of the suit, and without their having an adequate remedy against anyone? Can it be said, that the arm of equity is too short to reach such a flagrant case of injustice as this? Neither the law nor good conscience can tolerate such a conclusion. We cannot consent to attach such a sanctity to the character and conduct of a solution that he may bind strangers without their privity or consent in proceedings which may be utterly ruinous to them, and without their being able to respond for the damages which they may occasion, no matter how honest may be their motives. If the fortunes of all our citizens are held by so frail a tenure as this--if they may be utterly ruined without redress, either by their carelessness, the ignorance or dishonesty of every one who may get a license to practice law in a country where there are so many facilities for obtaining a license as in this, it is quite time that everyone should know it." He went on in this vein, leaving Cowles and Krum wishing malpractice insurance had been invented.

The second case references, Harback v. Griggs is a short "per curiam" report sayings it's the same facts, and thus the same decision. Harback had not been named as an appellant in the earlier appeal.

The first case is Griggs et al. v. Gear.

Gear v. Clark
orig. ed. 8 Ill.64

(Ill. Rep.: Gear v. Clark 8 Ill.65)

December Term 1846

This is an action of debt on a bail bond issued by Gear to Clark. Gear surrendered the principle debtor to the sheriff, after the due date of the process, and the debtor was taken into custody. The only question in this case is whether that surrender was too late. Clark contended the debtor should have been surrendered before the date the process was returnable: and since he wasn't, Gear was liable to pay the amount of the bail bond. The court agreed, and entered a judgment against Gear.

The Supreme Court, in an opinion written by Justice Caton, affirmed the judgment. At common law, the principle debtor was supposed to be surrendered before the return of process date. But in view of the hardships on the bail, the court adopted rules by which the principal might be surrendered afterwards. However, this was changed specifically by the Illinois legislature. Granted "at the first reading of this statute, it would seem to be almost unintelligible, or at least somewhat inconsistent, etc.," the statute is construed as to mean the principle must surrender himself, or for the bail to surrender him, at any time **before** the return date of the process sued out against the bail.

Edgar County v. Mayo
orig. ed. 8 Ill.82

(Ill. Rep.: Edgar County v. Mayo 8 Ill.82)
December Term 1846

This case was submitted as an agreed case in the Edgar circuit court and the parties having agreed on the facts, presented the matter to Judge Treat for his decision. Mayo, the clerk of the Edgar circuit court, sued out of his office a scire facias upon a forfeited recognizance against Andrew J. Hanks (a writ compelling Hanks to appear for a legal proceeding, as he agreed to do when the recognizance was granted by the court). The fee for this is $7.93 payable to Mayo for his work, and to be paid through recovery of a judgment and costs from Hanks. Nothing was recovered, and Mayo wants the county to pay him. The county resists, and this law suit results. Treat holds for Mayo. Lincoln represents Mayo on the appeal at least.

Judge Koerner, writing for the court,reverses the lower court. Lincoln argued: "By the common law, the defendant in error (Mayo) is entitled to remuneration for his services. The county called upon him to perform those services, and he has performed them. There is no law of this state which contravenes the common law." To support his argument, he cited several cases, including one from Illinois. Koerner did not agree, stating: "In order to settle this question, it is only necessary to refer to the 105th section of the Criminal Code, Rev. Stat. page 101, which provides "that all recognizance, having any relationship to criminal matters, shall be taken to the people of this state." By virtue of this law, the people of Illinois are the plaintiffs in a suit of such a recognizance, and if any recovery is had, it enures to the benefit of the state treasury. Hence it follows that in a suit of this kind the county can under no circumstances be made responsible for the cost. It cannot be said that services have been rendered to the county for the prosecution of a suit, from the result of which it can derive no benefit. The rule, therefore, which the counsel for Mayo has insisted upon, that each party ought to pay the costs made by their request, as being one founded in natural justice and recognized in the common law, can find no application here."

Lincoln convinced Judge Treat in the circuit court, at least, but not in the Supreme Court. Also it has been written in many histories that Lincoln did not charge high enough fees. However, here's a case where Mayo sought to recover $7.93 which required a trial in the circuit court and an appeal. What is a proper fee in this situation? And did Mayo's suit against his employer effect his continued employment?

Roney v. Monaghan
orig. ed. 8 Ill.85
(Ill. Rep.: Roney v. Monaghan 8 Ill.86)
December Term 1846

Monaghan sued Roney in the Lake circuit court before Judge Hugh T. Dickey, judge of the Cook county court, and a jury, in a case of criminal conversation. Evidence was presented that a criminal intercouse existed between Roney and the wife of Monaghan. Verdict and judgment rendered for Monaghan for $225 damages. Lincoln, G. Spring, and G. Goodrich represented Monaghan in the appeal brought by Roney, who contends a new trial should be awarded as the verdict was against the weight of the evidence.

Justice Purple, writing for the court, stated simply that the evidence was of a character to warrant the inference which the jury had drawn. "In such cases, a court will never disturb the verdict of a jury. The judgment of the circuit court is affirmed with costs."

The opinion covered one page in the report. The reader might have looked for more "purple prose" due to the subject matter, but the Justice was succinct and supported Lincoln's position.

People ex rel. Harris et al. v. Browne
orig. ed. 8 Ill.87
(Ill. Rep.: People ex rel. Harris et al. v. Browne 8 Ill.87)
December Term 1846

This is not an appeal, but a direct motion made to the supreme court for the peremptory mandamus (a final order for an official to perform an act he is required by law to perform) to require Honorable Thomas C. Browne, one of the associate justices of the Supreme Court, and presiding justice in the Jo Daviess circuit court, to sign and seal of bill of exceptions taken during the trial of a cause before him. Harris et al. were the plaintiffs in that cause, and John Roundtree and others were the defendants. The transcript of the record of that trial indicates a jury was impaneled, and that, upon the rulings of the court, the plaintiffs took a voluntary nonsuit (termination of the action with no adjudication of the issues on their merits). Harris et al. want to appeal the case, and need this requested action of Judge Browne to have appeal documents acceptable to the Supreme Court, for an appeal to be granted.

Lincoln represents Judge Browne in this matter, and cites definitions of "non-suits" from several sources. The court agreed with Lincoln and stated that "if a plaintiff voluntarily quits a case he brings before a court, he can't call upon the supreme court to reverse a judgment against him, whether the court committed errors in the proceedings previous to the nonsuit or not. Plaintiff has waived his exceptions, and cannot compel the judge to sign the bill."

Respect for Lincoln's abilities before the Supreme Court can be confirmed by his having been chosen by one of the justices to represent him.

Munsell v. Temple
orig. ed. 8 Ill.93

(Ill. Rep.: Munsell v. Temple 8 Ill.93)
December Term 1846

The commissioners' court of McLean county granted Parke a license to keep a grocery or bar in the town of Bloomington, in the Bloomington Hotel, and Parke gave a note for twenty-five dollars a few months later. Parke transferred his license to Munsell, which was approved by the commissioners and who gave a note to Temple, treasurer of the court for $21.38. Temple wants to collect on this note. The parties submitted the case by agreement to the McLean circuit before Judge Treat. Judgment was rendered for Temple for $24.68. Lincoln represents Munsell in the appeal.

The court, with Justice Koerner writing the opinion, reverses the lower court. The state statute giving authority to grant licenses to sell spirits provides a payment to the county treasurer of no less than twenty-five dollars. The license was personal to Parke, and could not be transferred. Thus the payment of $25 by Parke could not be pro-rated, which apparently was attempted when Munsell only paid $21.38. The license issued to Munsell was against the express provisions of the law, and thus void.

The court said "The policy of our legislature has always been to restrain the selling of spirituous liquors by retail. The section referred to is conceived in this spirit, and prohibits, in language not to be misunderstood, the county commissioners from issuing a license unless the conditions presented by the law have been previously coupled with." This was the spirit of the law pertaining to spirits Lincoln presented, and he was successful.

Buckmaster v. Beames
orig. ed. 8 Ill.97

(Ill. Rep.: Buckmaster v. Beames 8 Ill.97)
December Term, 1846

The original action was brought in the circuit court by Buckmaster, the nominal plaintiff, for the exclusive benefit of Denham, the beneficial plaintiff, against Beames. Beames won this case, and Denham files this appeal in the name of Buckmaster. Buckmaster is concerned about paying costs in relation to the appeal, and brings a motion to compel Denham to post an adequate bond to insure Buckmaster against payment of costs. Buckmaster is concerned because Denham resides outside the state and is insolvent.

The motion is allowed by the supreme court in an opinion written by Justice Treat. Denham is bound to give good security for costs. He must prove the security is adequate, since he has knowledge of the pecuniary circumstances of his surety.

The first appeal in this matter is reported as Beames and Archer v. Denham and Buckmaster (3 Ill.58).

Fell & Perry v. Price & Edwards
orig. ed. 8 Ill.186

(Ill. Rep.: Fell et al. v. Price et al. 8 Ill.186)
December Term 1846

Low obtained a judgment and execution against Fell for $220.81, which was levied on certain parcels of land. The land was sold by the sheriff, and Low took the land in satisfaction of the judgment. Fell had a right to redeem the property within fifteen months by paying the judgment, costs and interest. Shortly before this time expired, Fell, who wanted to reacquire interest in the land, made an arrangement with Low. He conveyed the land by a deed absolute on its face, and also an additional tract of land to Low, in exchange for an extension of the time for the redemption. Fell was not able to pay on time, and with Fell's assent, Low sold the two tracts to Perry, who in turn sold the land to Fell, who made $1000 improvement to the land which was valued at $100. Price recovered a judgment against Fell, which was levied on the subject land, and was in the process of being sold. Fell brings this action in chancery in the McLean circuit court before Judge Treat to enjoin the sheriff from selling the land under this execution. The court granted a temporary injunction, which would be made perpetual if Fell paid Price $100. Lincoln represented Fell in the appeal.

The Supreme Court, with the opinion written by Justice Koerner, reversed the decree, and made the injunction permanent without Fell paying $100 to Price. The court said Price acquired no rights to the land by his judgment. Low could at anytime obtain a sheriff's deed for the land, and if he did so, his title would be effective on the date of the first judgment; thus being prior to Price's judgment. Low had not renounced that right.

The facts are rather obscure as explained in Koerner's opinion, but he did state "But the matter is perfectly explained by complainants' bill, which states what the intentions of the parties were." This bill was drafted by Lincoln, and resulted in his client's victory.

Brown v. Pease et al.
orig. ed. 8 Ill.191

(Ill. Rep.: Brown v. Pease et al. 8 Ill.191)
December Term 1846

Taylor, Hunt and Co. executed three promissory notes to Brown, each for $133.33 and payable on the first days of September, October, and November, 1837. Before maturity, these notes were assigned by Brown to Pease et al. In January 1838, Pease et al. brought an action in the Cook county circuit court against the makers of the notes (Taylor, Hunt), obtained a judgment on the notes, but execution of the judgment against Taylor, Hunt revealed there were no assets to be found. Pease et al. then brought this action against Brown, as the endorser of the notes, who pleaded Pease et al. had not acted with due diligence to collect the notes from the maker, since the municipal court of Chicago met in November 1837, and it had jurisdiction over this subject matter. Judgment was rendered against Brown for only one of the notes (the one due on November 1), and not on the other two, since the default on the notes due on September 1, and October 1, should have been sued upon in the November term of the municipal court of Chicago. There wasn't reasonable time to sue after the November 1 note defaulted, so Pease et al. could recover on this.

The supreme court, in an opinion written by Justice Treat, affirmed the judgment. Pease et al. had an obligation to use due diligence in bringing an action on the notes after default. The trial court decided properly that due diligence had not been used when the first two notes were in default, but did do so for the third (the November 1 note).

Wright v. Taylor
orig. ed. 8 Ill.193

(Ill. Rep.: Wright v. Taylor 8 Ill.193)
December Term 1846

Wright gave a note to Taylor, secured by a mortgage, promising to pay $672.08 payable at the State Bank of Illinois. The note was assigned to the bank by Taylor in payment of a debt he owed the bank. After this, the paper of the bank depreciated, so that it was worth about $.26 on the dollar. Taylor then paid the note to the bank at this depreciated value, without any authorization of Wright. Taylor brings this action in chancery to seek recovery on the note, now past due, for the full amount of the note, and if not paid, to foreclose. The remedy was sought in the Menard circuit court before Judge Treat, who issued a decree in favor of Taylor. Lincoln represents Taylor on the appeal.

The Supreme Court, in an opinion written by Judge Purple, reversed the circuit court, and orders Wright to pay the depreciated value of the note $141.74, rather than $672.08. Taylor only succeeded to the rights of the bank when he paid the note, and could not, by his voluntary act, have any better right or superior equity. Wright could have paid the bank in depreciated currency when Taylor did.

Justice Purple, writing the decision for the court, said: "The case, I think, is plain and easy of solution. The general doctrine of the law relative to the transfer, and indorsement of promissory notes, has necessarily but little application to the question, and the controversy may be settled equitably and legally without the slightest interference with any known or established principle." Judge Treat, in the circuit court didn't see the case as being that "plain and easy of solution;" or if he did, his "plain and easy solution" was the exact opposite of the Supreme Court's. Perhaps Lincoln represented Taylor in the circuit court, and used persuasive argument to convince the judge.

Welch et al. v. Sykes
orig. ed. 8 Ill.197

(Ill. Rep.: Welch et al.v. Sykes 8 Ill.197)
December Term 1846

Sykes brought an action of debt to collect on a judgment of a court in Maryland, in the Clark circuit court before Judge Wilson; against Welch and others. Watson, one of the defendants, was the only one served with process in this action. Watson appeared and entered several pleas, indicating he had been in Ohio at the time, and never appeared in the case in Maryland; thus since the court had no jurisdiction over him, that judgment was not binding, and thus could not be enforced against him in Illinois. Sykes demurred to these pleas, which were sustained by the court, and judgment was entered against Watson for the amount of the Maryland judgment, $340 plus interest. He is represented by Lincoln on the appeal.

The court, in an opinion written by Justice Treat, reversed the judgment on the grounds the court erred in sustaining several of the pleas, and remanded the case. A judgment, fairly and duly obtained in one state, is conclusive between the parties, when sued in another state. However, if that judgment was obtained through fraud, or that the court in pronouncing it had no jurisdiction of the defendant's person, or the subject matter, the judgment is entitled to no credit. Watson pleaded the court had no jurisdiction over him, and since the demurrers were sustained, he had no opportunity to prove it.

The court did observe from the record submitted by the parties, that an attorney purported to represent Watson in Maryland. This was not part of the record of the case, but would be admissible in a new trial. Probably an oversight in the lower court on the part of Sykes' attorney, who lost the case on appeal, and then was gratuitously shown a way to win the remanded case--if the attorney had authority to represent Watson in Maryland.

Hawks v. Landes
orig. ed. 8 Ill.227
(Ill. Rep. Hawks v. Lands 8 Ill.227)
December Term 1846

Landes brought an action in assumpsit against Hawks in the McLean Circut Court before Judge Treat, and judgment was rendered for Landes for $419.48. Lincoln represented Hawks on the appeal, relying on his belief Judge Treat had ruled incorrectly on three questions. Two of these were procedural, and one on Treat's disallowance of a proposed set off since Landes had conveyed certain real estate to Hawks for $1,200, and did not have clear title as guaranteed.

The Supreme Court, with Judge Purple writing the opinion, affirmed the judgment. He rejected Lincoln's two procedural questions, and as to the third part, he said the set-off was not allowable because it was not definite: "Unliquidated damages arising out of covenants, contracts, or torts totally disconnected with the subject matter of the plaintiff's claim, are not such 'claims or demands' as constitute the subject matter of set-off under our act of assembly. To give this construction to the statute would invest justices of the peace with full jurisdiction over questions involving the title to and covenants concerning real estate, compel parties to litigate all their rights, or whatever nature or kind, in one action, and result in irremediable injustice and endless confusion."

Justice Thomas took no part in this decision, since he had been the counsel opposing Lincoln on the appeal.

Garrett v. Stevenson & Wardwell
orig. ed. 8 Ill.261

(Ill. Rep.: Garrett v. Stevenson et al. 8 Ill.261)
December Term 1846

Stevenson and Wardell contracted to perform certain mechanic's labor for Garrett from March 3, 1840 to July 1, 1840. The labor was performed, but no payment was made. A petition was filed to enforce a lien against the property in October, 1841. Under the 1833 law creating mechanic's liens, action had to be commenced within three months of the time that payment should have been made. Garrett contends the suit was brought too late, and in any event, disputes the method of computing how much he might owe. Decree entered for Stevenson et al. for $2,079.44.

The Supreme Court, in an opinion written by Justice Thomas, held the action was properly brought, but modified the decree after reviewing much detailed evidence of particular parts of the awarded amount, and awarded $1,284.06. The 1833 law was amended by an act of the legislature which became law on December 12, 1839, and stipulated no limit as to when an action could be brought.

Henderson v. Welch
orig. ed. 8 Ill.340

(Ill. Rep.: Henderson v. Welch 8 Ill.340)
December Term 1846

Welch assigned a chose in action (a right to recover a debt or money - the exact nature of which in this case is not disclosed) to Henderson. Henderson sued Samuel and Daniel Shaw in Welch's name, on this chose in action, and the suit was dismissed. Welch was assessed damages for bringing the suit of $14.87 1/2 and the sheriff recovered it from him. Welch now brings this action in the McHenry circuit court against Henderson to recover his costs, and the court awarded him $95.34 for the amount of the costs of the case, the execution by the sheriff, and interest. Probably Henderson should have paid the original $14.87 1/2.

The Supreme Court, in an opinion written by Judge Treat, affirmed the judgment. The equitable assignee of a chose in action may sue upon it in the name of the party having the legal title, but he is bound to indemnify such party against the payment of costs.

Passfield v. The People
orig. ed. 8 Ill.406
(Ill. Rep.: Passfield v. The People 8 Ill.406)
December Term 1846

Cornwell, as principal, and Passfield and Shepherd, as sureties, entered into a joint and several recognizance to the people of the state of Illinois, promising to pay $800 if Cornwell did not appear in court to answer to a larceny charge. Cornwell failed to appear. An order to pay the $800 was served on each of the three. Cornwell could not be found, but the other two were served. Judgment by default for $800 was entered against Passfield alone. Logan represented Passfield on the appeal at least.

The supreme court, in an opinion written by Justice Purple, affirmed the judgment. The recognizance was joint and several, and each is liable for the entire amount, even though judgment could have been rendered against the other two.

Cowls v. Cowls
orig. ed. 8 Ill.435
(Ill. Rep.: Cowls v. Cowls 8 Ill.435)
December Term 1846

This is an action brought by Ms. Cowls against her husband in chancery for an increase of alimony, the custody of two infant children, and an allowance for their maintenance. In a former suit, Ms. Cowls had obtained a divorce, but no provision had been made in relation to the children. The children lived with their father, who "had lived in a state of fornication with a woman, until within a few weeks of the time when this bill was filed, when he marred her." He also neglected them, and that "he is in the habitual use of profane, indecent, immoral and vulgar language, as well in the presence of the children as elsewhere." The court gave custody of the children to Ms. Cowls, and awarded her thirty dollars per child a year, for five years, to maintain them. Lincoln represented Mr. Cowls on the appeal at least, so he must have had some redeeming qualities.

The supreme court, in an opinion written by Justice Caton, affirmed the decree, saying: "The power of the court of chancery to interfere with and control, not only the estates but the persons and custody of all minors within the limits of its jurisdiction, is of very ancient origin, and can not now be questioned. This is a power which must necessarily exist somewhere, in every well regulated society, and more especially in a republican government, where each man should be reared and educated under such influences that he may be qualified to exercise the rights of a freeman and take part in the government of the country. It is a duty, then, which the country owes as well to itself, as to the infant, to see that he is not abused, defrauded or neglected, and the infant has a right to this protection. While a father conducts himself as not to violate this right, the court will not, ordinarily, interfere with his parental control. If, however, by his neglect or abuse, he shows himself devoid of that affection, which is supposed to qualify him better than any other to take charge of his own offspring, the court may interfere, and take the infant under its own charge, and remove it from the control of the parent, and place it in custody of a proper person to act as guardian, who may be a stranger." He then referenced similar statements by Judge Story in his treatise on equity jurisprudence, and after reviewing the facts presented by Ms. Cowls, he wrote: "Here we have grouped together into one disgusting and revolting picture, those features of a father's character who has become unworthy of the charge of his own offspring, and any one of which, as we have seen it laid down by Mr. Justice Story, will authorize the court in its discretion, to interfere and remove the child without the influence of such a polluted atmosphere." Also the lower court made a proper decision in awarding custody to the mother, and thirty dollars a year is not too much for the support of each child, although counsel for Mr. Cowls did not agree.

Wilcoxon v. Roby
orig. ed. 8 Ill.475

(Ill. Rep.: Wilcoxon v. Roby 8 Ill.475)
December Term 1846

Roby sued Wilcoxon in an action of debt upon a penal bond executed by the parties, in which they mutually bound themselves that each would desist from all interference with a certain tract of government land to which both had previously set up a claim, until the merits of their respective claims could be settled and adjusted. Roby was awarded damages of $400. Lincoln, and Campbell and Johnson, represented Wilcoxon on the appeal.

The Supreme Court, in an opinion written by Justice Purple, reversed the judgment, and remanded the cause. The court said the finding of the jury and judgment of the court were not responsive to the issues made. "There can be no assessment of damages unless the debt be first found."

There is very little additional detail in this case to elucidate why either court held as it did. Justice Purple indicated the pleadings were defective, and the record rendered it difficult to determine what issues were really submitted to the jury. Obviously this was Lincoln's successful argument on appeal. It is noted Justice Thomas, having been of counsel in the circuit court, took no part in the decision in this case. He probably knew the most about the case, but the Supreme Court did not have the authority to correct the case. The Supreme Court rules on the lower court case, and if it has not done its job properly, the remedy only lies in trying the case again.

Trumbull v. Campbell
orig. ed. 8 Ill.502

(Ill. Rep.: Trumbull v. Campbell 8 Ill.502)
December Term 1846

Lynman Trumbull was appointed secretary of state on February 27, 1841, and continued to hold office until March 4, 1843, when he was superseded by the appointment of Thompson Campbell. The legislature, on March 3, 1843, appropriated "to the secretary of state, for making the index to the journals of the senate and house of representatives and laws, for copying laws, and making marginal notes and indeed to laws, the sum of six hundred dollars." The next day, which was Trumbull's last day in office, Trumbull estimated he had done two-thirds of the work, asked for, and was paid $400. Campbell subsequently performed the rest of the services, and alleging Trumbull had been overpaid, brings this action of assumpsit in the Sangamon circuit court (Judge not identified in the opinion) to recover the alleged overpayment to Trumbull. The court awarded $200 to Campbell. Lincoln represented Trumbull on the appeal.

The Supreme Court, with Justice Treat writing the opinion, reversed the judgment of the lower court, saying: "The only point in this case is, whether the action as between the parties can be maintained. The question was discussed at the bar with much ability, and some embarrassment has been felt in determining it." Treat went on to say no action could be brought by Campbell. If Trumbull was overpaid, the state could sue to recover it. If Campbell did some of this work, he should be paid by the state, even if Trumbull had been paid for the same work.

Lincoln cited six common law cases, and treatises as authorities, and prevailed. Apparently the embarrassment mentioned by Treat was because of the political nature of the trial. We assume he wasn't the judge in the Sangamon circuit court case, although he tried many cases there.

Cooper v. Crosby & Robbins
orig. ed. 8 Ill.506

(Ill. Rep.: Cooper v. Crosby et al. 8 Ill.506)
December Term 1846

Crosby executed a mortgage to Cooper upon several lots in Springfield, and conveyed his equity of redemption (the right of a mortgagor to redeem the property after it has been forfeited by law, upon paying the amount of the mortgage, accumulated interest and costs. The right to redeem is limited by a certain number of years, by statute.), to Robbins. Cooper foreclosed the mortgage, making Robbins a party to the suit. There was $608 due on the mortgage at the time. Cooper bought the property at the sale for $269.50. Two days later, Cooper served notice he would move to set aside the sale at the next term of the circuit court, which he did, stating he misunderstood the advice from his attorneys as to how he should bid, that Crosby was insolvent, and that Robbins could exercise his right of redemption by paying $269.50, plus ten percent interest and costs, and thus Cooper would not recover his entire $608. His motion was denied.

The Supreme Court, in an opinion written by Justice Purple, affirmed the decree. The bidding at the sale of mortgaged property in default would be opened, on motion, if it were shown that there had been any injurious mistake, misrepresentation, or fraud, and if so, the property will be resold. Such was not the case here.

Lincoln represented Cooper on the appeal, and presumably was not the one who gave Cooper the misunderstood advice.

Schaffer et al. v. Weed et al.
orig. ed. 8 Ill.511
(Ill. Rep.: Shaeffer et al. v. Weed et al. 8 Ill.511)
December Term 1846

Schaffer et al. furnished materials and did work on a house for William Weed, and upon his death the job was left unfinished. About seven month's after Weed's death, this petition for a mechanic's lien is filed, under a statute saying mechanic's liens have to be filed within six months after the money is due. The court ruled for the Weeds. Lincoln represented Schaffer et al. on the appeal.

The Supreme Court, in an opinion written by Justice Caton, with a concurring opinion by Justice Purple, reversed and remanded the decree. Firstly, a mechanic's lien cannot be impaired except by his consent. Secondly, although Schaffer et al. cannot effect a mechanic's lien, they still have a claim against the estate for the materials and work done. This case should be remanded for further proceedings consistent with this opinion.

Anderson v. Ryan
orig. ed. 8 Ill.583
(Ill. Rep.: Anderson v. Ryan 8 Ill.584)
December Term 1846

This is an appeal from a judgment against Anderson in an action of trespass for assault, debauchery, and carnal knowledge of daughter of Ryan, rendered in the Coles circuit court before Judge Wilson. Lincoln, representing Anderson in the appeal, contended there had been no loss of services proved by Ryan, as father of the girl. This had been a necessary element under common law in an action of this sort. It was proven the daughter had lived with her family, and was four months advanced in pregnancy by Anderson, when the action was brought.

The Supreme Court, with Justice Lockwood writing the opinion, affirmed the circuit court, saying that loss of services to the father was no longer a necessary element. Justice Lockwood cited Heart v. Prince 21 Wend. 81 (which strongly supported Ryan's side, but was not included in the large list of authorities cited by his attorneys in the appeal) as follows: "As this question was never been discussed in this court, previous to the case at the bar, we feel authorized in extracting from that opinion, because it furnishes reasons fully justifying the doctrine, in action of seduction brought by the parent, that loss of service need no longer be proved to sustain the action." One reason given for this was "If it were otherwise, says Littledate, Justice, in Maunder v. Venn, no action could be sustained for this injury in the higher ranks of life, where no actual services by the daughter are usual." Also: "the views presented by Chief Justice Nelson (Heart v. Prince) place the ground of this action upon the elevated consideration of protecting the moral purity of female character. Such an object must meet a cordial response in every noncorrupted heart. This opinion also satisfactorily vindicates the modern doctrine, as more in accordance with the original design of the action for seduction. It has long been considered as a standing reproach to the common law, that it furnished no means to punish the seducer of female innocence and virtue, except through the fiction of supposing the daughter was a servant of her parent, and that in consequence of her seduction, the parent has lost some of her services as a menial. It is high time this reproach be wiped out." Later: "This action ought, then, no longer to be considered as a means of recovering damages for the loss of menial services, but as an instrument to punish the perpetrator of flagitious outrage upon the peace and happiness of the family circle."

Justice Koerner wrote a concurring opinion stating loss of service was still an essential element, however: "I consider that the loss of service in a case of seduction is still the just and only legal foundations of the actions, and that it is the rule of evidence merely which has undergone a change in the course of time, by the decisions of the courts according to a more just and refined feeling of society on this subject, at once so delicate and so painful." The law, from the seduction itself, will presume the loss of services resulted.

Lincoln was on the losing side in this, and had to insist on the only argument which could have won the case for his client, despite it being an outmoded doctrine just ripe for being overthrown in the Illinois Supreme Court. Koerner showing his reverence for the common law, said loss of services is still an essential element, but is presumed to exist, and cannot be disproved by the defendant. A rather strained compromise of tradition and the practicality of agreeing that carnal knowledge, resulting in pregnancy, should be punished.

Lincoln also argued that loss of services was not an essential component of a case like this in Grable v. Margrave (4 Ill.372), and was successful.

Enos et al. v. Hunter
orig. ed. 9 Ill.211

(Ill. Rep.: Enos et al. v. Hunter 9 Ill.212)
December Term 1847

Hunter brings an action in equity in Sangamon County to compel the conveyance of certain land to him based on the following facts: In 1820 Hunter was indebted to one Schuller for a large sum of money, and conveyed the premises in question in Madison County to one Hempstead to secure the debt. Hunter paid off the debt, and Hempstead was willing to reconvey the property. However, Hunter wished the property to be held in trust for him by someone else, and he had enough confidence in Enos to have the property conveyed to him. Enos agreed to convey the property to Hunter upon his request. However, he moved to Sangamon County, and died before Hunter requested him to do this. This action was commenced in 1838 against Enos' heirs to require the conveyance, and it was so decreed.

The supreme court, in an opinion written by Justice Caton, reversed the decree and remanded the cause, to be reconsidered. Caton agreed jurisdiction had been acquired by the court under common law rules that a court of equity had the power to compel a person located in its jurisdiction to convey property in another county out of it's jurisdiction. However there was some question as to what the widow could testify to, because of the confidentiality of husband/wife communications, and the allowance of oral evidence to prove a constructive trust on real estate. The lapse of time also should be entitled to very great consideration, and "admonishes us that we should be careful and not disturb this legal title without the most satisfactory truth. Here the conveyance was made to Enos in 1821, and we hear of no pretense of claim by the complainant or anyone else, until seventeen years after, and two years after the death of the grantee, who, from aught that appears up to the time of his death, enjoyed the undisputed possession of the premises as his own, and paid the taxes upon the land. If this be not a stale claim, it is not probable that we shall meet with one soon."

Bruen et al. v. Graves
orig. ed. 9 Ill.283

(Ill. Rep.: Bruen et al. v. Graves 9 Ill.283)
December Term 1847

The Bruens brought an action of ejectment against Graves. They claimed title under a deed executed by the auditor of the state who sold the property because the taxes had not been paid. The sale had been made in 1833, but the deed was not executed until 1840. Graves contended the deed was invalid because even though the auditor had the power to sell the property for taxes in 1833, by 1840 this power had been repealed. The court sustained Grave's contention, and gave him the judgment.

The supreme court, in an opinion written by Justice Wilson, reversed the judgment, and remanded the cause for further proceedings. The matter had already been settled in a previous case in the same term of the supreme court (Bruce v. Schuyler 9 Ill.221). The authority of the auditor to make deeds after the passage of the act of 1833, of land sold by him prior to that time, was not abrogated by the act of 1833, but still existed in full force.

Taylor et al. v. Taylor et al.
orig. ed. 9 Ill.303

(Ill. Rep.: Taylor et al. v. Taylor et al. 9 Ill.303)
December Term 1847

This was a bill in chancery filed to sort out the rights of the various ancestors of James Taylor by the children of James by his second marriage. In 1820 James bought certain land and had it conveyed in the names of two of his minor children of his first marriage, Isaac and William. He died in 1841 without having made any provision for this land. The decree was rendered for the petitioners, the children of the second marriage.

The Supreme Court, in an opinion written by Justice Caton, affirmed the decree. The presumption of law is, when a father purchases land in name of his children, unaccompanied by any extraordinary or explanatory circumstances, that it was intended as an advance or gift to them. This presumption however, may be rebutted by circumstances, as was done here. On this, Justice Caton said "But after all, the most that can be said on this subject is, that no fixed and definite rule can be found to guide us but the intention of the father, at the time the purchase was made, which must be gathered from all the lights which the attending circumstances afford. Now, in this case, I confess that we have so much light that I have a great difficulty in seeing my way clear. Indeed, it rarely occurs where the evidence is so equally balanced, when all taken together, as to leave the mind so nearly upon an equipoise." The most convincing evidence was that Isaac and William had bought some of the land at various times from their father, and sold it back to him. Thus they obviously believed the father owned the land, and had not intended to give it to them.

Moore et al. v. Capps
orig. ed. 9 Ill.315

(Ill. Rep.: Moore et al. v. Capps 9 Ill.315)
December Term 1847

In September of 1836, Capps obtained a decree against Moore et al. for the specific performance of a contract. In September 1847, a writ of error was presented for appeal to the supreme court on the grounds that some of the defendants in the 1836 case were minors, and thus the five year restriction on time to file an appeal did not bar some of the co-defendants from appealing. All of the parties asking for this appeal had been of adult age in 1836. The petition for appeal, which was demurred to because of the statute of limitations, was granted.

The supreme court, in an opinion written by Justice Treat, ruled that the demurrer should have been sustained, and dismissed the writ of error. The statute of limitations will not run against a minor until he comes of age. However, the parties bringing this appeal were of full age when the judgment was rendered in 1836, and those who were of full age cannot avail themselves of the non-age of some of their coparties to accomplish indirectly what they should not be allowed to directly.

Further proceedings in this matter are Enos et al. v. Capps (12 Ill.255), and Enos v. Capps (15 Ill.277).

Chauncey v. Jackson
orig. ed. 9 Ill.435

(Ill. Rep.: Chauncey v. Jackson 9 Ill.436)
December Term 1847

This was an action of attachment against the schooner General Thornton under an act entitled "an act authorizing the seizure of boats and other vessels by attachment in certain cases." Jackson was the master of the General Thornton, and served for two months, rendering services worth $50 a month. He received $180 for transporting cargo during that period. He was not paid by the owner, and the court rendered a judgment in his favor for $100. Chauncey, the owner of the schooner, pleaded the master was not allowed to attach a vessel under common law, and asked for an accounting of the $180.

The supreme court, in an opinion written by Justice Treat, reversed the judgment and remanded the cause. The master is covered under the Illinois statute, which gives a lien against a vessel to anyone "employed in any capacity" in the running and management of the vessel. Maritime law did not give a master this right, but that is changed by this statute. However, Jackson did not account for the $180, and that is the reason the cause is remanded.

Orr v. Thompson, for use of Curtis
orig. ed. 9 Ill.451

(Ill. Rep.: Orr v. Thompson, for use of Curtis 9 Ill.451)
December Term 1847

Shelby and Orr executed a note to Thompson, jointly and severally, for $14.50 to be paid in twelve months. The note was unpaid and Thompson sues both before a justice of the peace. Shelby appeared and confessed judgment in the amount of $19.50. About six months later, the same justice of peace issued process against Orr, reciting the previous proceedings and requiring Orr to show cause why a judgment should not be entered against him. Orr pleaded Thompson had died, and the proceedings were irregular. The justice of peace rendered judgment against him for $20.25. The circuit court affirmed this judgment. Herndon represented Orr on the appeal at least.

The Supreme Court, in an opinion written by Justice Treat, reversed the judgment and remanded the cause. The action against Orr was improper. It could not have been regarded as a continuation of the first suit when judgment was rendered against Shelby. It must be treated as a new and independent action against Orr. A new suit can be brought, with the heirs of Thompson as the complainants. The previous proceedings constituted no bar to a subsequent suit to enforce the liability of Orr, as one of the makers of a joint and several promissory note.

Edwards et ux. v. Patterson
orig. ed. 10 Ill.126

(Ill. Rep.: Edwards et ux. v. Patterson 10 Ill.126)
December Term 1848

Edwards et ux. (wife) had obtained a judgment and execution against Patterson. Patterson made a motion in the Mason circuit court to quash the execution and to set aside a sale made under it, because the record was not adequate. Edwards and wife moved to amend the record, which was refused; and the execution was quashed, and the sale vacated.

The supreme court, in an opinion written by Justice Treat, affirmed the judgment. Treat said: "The evidence on which the court acted is not in the record. We can not, therefore, inquire into the propriety of its decision. The clerk has copied an affidavit and some other papers, but they are not thereby made a part of the record. A bill of exceptions should have been taken embodying the evidence."

Seeley v. Peters
orig ed. 10 Ill.130

(Ill. Rep.: Seeley v. Peters 10 Ill.130)
December Term 1848

Peters brought an action of trespass against Seeley, when Seeley's hogs entered Peters' land and damaged his crops. Evidence was offered that Peters' fence was in poor condition. Peters asked for and received an instruction to the jury that it was not the duty of the landowner to have an adequate fence to keep out straying animals, but the duty of the owner of the animals to keep them from straying. Judgment for Peters. Seeley objected to Judge Caton's ruling, and appealed on the grounds the instructions were improper. Herndon represented Peters on the appeal at least.

The supreme court, in an opinion written by Justice Trumbull, reversed the judgment, and remanded the cause for further proceedings. The English common law required the owners of live stock to keep them fenced up. The Illinois legislature passed a law in 1819 that the English common law would be the common law of Illinois if they were applicable and of a general nature. However, Justice Trumbull said: "However well adapted the rule of common law may be to a densely populated country like England, it is but ill adapted to a new country like ours . . . Perhaps there is no principle of the common law so inapplicable to the condition of our country and people as the one which is sought to be enforced now for the first time since the settlement of the State." Thus Judge Caton's ruling was improper, and the judgment is reversed.

Justice Caton dissented in a twenty page opinion. The legislature is the proper body to define what parts of the English common law are "applicable" to Illinois, rather than the courts. He said: "By the construction given to the word applicable, we (the supreme court) assume the right to disregard any other provision of the common law, which in our judgment would be inconvenient, and no one can safely advise his client relying upon the common law." He concluded, "Although this case by itself may be insignificant, yet the principles involved are important, and I have felt that I could not say less than I have, in assigning the reasons which led me to the conclusion at which I have arrived."

Sargeant, for use of Huntington v. Kellogg & Kellogg
orig. ed. 10 Ill.273

(Ill. Rep.: Sargeant v. Kellogg et al. 10 Ill.273)
December Term 1848

John Sargeant sold land to the Kelloggs, and as part of the consideration they gave a note to John. John assigned it to Alexander Sargeant, after its maturity, who brings an action of debt on the note against the Kelloggs in the Kendall circuit court. The Kelloggs plead John did not have the title he promised to have in the land, and thus the consideration failed. Judgment for the Kelloggs.

The Supreme Court, with Justice Treat writing the opinion, affirmed the judgment. Where a note is assigned after maturity, the makers (Kellogs) are entitled to interpose the same defense against the assigner, as they could if the action were brought by the payee. Also unliquidated damages arising out of contracts may be set off in actions on contracts.

There was some confusion as to whether the land had been properly described. The statute law said that to constitute a valid claim to unsurveyed public lands, the claim must, "be so plainly marked and designated as to be distinguished from adjacent lands." The description here, along with other details said "situate on the east side of Fox River, nearly opposite of Gorton's flouring-mill, beginning at a small burr oak tree and running on William Wilson's old line, supposed to be an east course, to a forked hickory tree adjoining Daniel Pierce's, thence a south course to a white oak stump and a red oak stump on the bank of Fox River, opposite Gorton's mill, etc." The jury was instructed natural objects may be used when they fully answer the purpose of the statute. And in this case found the description adequate.

Trustees of Illinois & Michigan Canal v. Haven & Haven
orig. ed. 10 Ill.548

(Ill. Rep.: The Board of trustees of the Illinois and Michigan Canal v. Haven & Haven 10 Ill.548)
June Term 1849

This was a case submitted on agreed facts to the Will county circuit court wherein Philo and Orlando Haven sought damages from the canal trustees for damages incurred by their milling operation, because of diversion of water in the Des Plaines River by the construction of the canal. It was agreed water had been diverted and damages sustained. The canal trustees contend that the land had been granted by the United States to Illinois to build a canal from Lake Michigan to the Illinois River; land and water within ninety feet of the canal were included in that grant, which precluded Havens' claims. The court held for the Havens.

The Supreme Court, in an opinion written by Justice Trumbull, affirmed the lower court judgment. The act of congress in 1822 did vest in the state land for the canal, including ninety feet on each side of the canal, but it did not apply to the sixteenth sections. Havens' land and mill were in the sixteenth section which were not public lands in 1822, because they had been granted to the state by congressional ordinance in 1818 for the use of schools. The Havens owned land on both sides of the river, and by common law, thus owned the rights to the water in the river along their property lines. The interference by the canal trustees was unlawful, and the Havens were entitled to damages.

McConnell v. Holobush et al.
orig. ed. 11 Ill.61

(Ill. Rep.: McConnell v. Holobush et al. 11 Ill.61)
December Term 1842

Delahay purchased certain property from Manchester and gave him a mortgage in 1839. Delahay sold the property to McConnell, with the mortgage still owing. McKee is owed money by Manchester, and he sues him, recovering a judgment which can be enforced against any interests in land Manchester might have. McKee assigned his rights, and Manchester and others occupied the property, at least since 1843, and made improvements and additions. McConnell brings this action to disencumber the property by the payment of the amount due on the mortgages, to McKee and Manchester as the court should direct; and asks that certain rents and profits received by the assignees of McKee, be applied in extinguishment of the amount due them. Judge Minshall, in the Pike circuit court, dismissed the bill, perhaps because of the confusions in the facts.

The Supreme Court, in an opinion written by Justice Caton, restated the facts simply, reversed the decree, and sent the matter back to the circuit court for rehearing; with an order for the court to apply certain well established rules: a mortgagee in possession (Manchester) must account for rents and profits actually received. A mortgagee in possession is authorized, and even bound, to keep the property in necessary repairs, and to preserve it. He is not authorized to make new improvements; and if he does so, he may not tack these costs onto the mortgage, or pay it out of rents and profits.

Wright v. McNeely
orig. ed. 11 Ill.241

(Ill. Rep.: Wright v. McNeely 11 Ill.241)
December Term 1849

Wright's lands are sold by the sheriff to Samuel Hill for $353.27, which was the amount of principal, interest, and costs due on a judgment in favor of Hill against Wright. McNeely and Johnson were owed money by Wright, and obtained a judgment against him for $294.41. McNeely and Johnson redeemed the land from Hill, and it was proven they promised to allow Wright to redeem the land whenever he could pay off the amount of both judgments. This was done in October 1846 and this bill was filed in February 1848. It was proven the land was worth $1800. Wright brings this action of specific performance to redeem the land, and McNeely, who had bought out Johnson, refuses. The bill is dismissed, leaving McNeely owner of the land.

The Supreme Court, in an opinion written by Justice Caton, modifies the decree specifically to declare McNeely's judgment against Wright satisfied. For Wright to have succeeded in redeeming the land, he would have had to prove he tendered the money. Justice Caton said: "We are satisfied that an agreement is proved, substantially as charged in the bill, but there is an insuperable objection to a decree for its specific performance. The complainant (Wright) has totally failed in his attempt to prove a tender of the money; nor has he brought it into court as he should have done, even if he had proved a tender. This was indispensable, as we consider this simply as an agreement for the conveyance of land."

Also McNeely's judgment is deemed satisfied, since he keeps the land, and it is worth substantially more than the amount he paid to redeem the land from Hill, and his own judgment against Wright.

Lincoln, Herndon, and Logan represented Wright on the appeal at least. Somebody before the original case was brought for specific performance should have advised Wright to make an effective tender of payment of the proper amount to McNeely, when he asked to buy the land back as McNeely had promised to do.

Webster & Huntington v. French et al.
orig. ed. 11 Ill.254

(Ill. Rep.: Webster & Huntington v. French et al. 11 Ill.254)
December Term 1848

An act of the legislature authorized the sale of Quincy House, in Quincy, Adams County, owned by the state, and established procedures for an auction of sealed bids. The bids ranged from $15,250 by Jacob Bunn to a bid by Webster and Huntington for $21,100. In addition there was a bid promising to pay $500 more than any other bid, and another by Ash and Diller to pay $601 over the highest bid. The governor sold the property to Ash and Diller for $22,201, which was the aggregate of $21,000 plus $500 plus $601. This action was a bill filed in Sangamon Circuit Court before Judge Davis to enforce the conveyance of the property to Webster and Huntington who had the highest specific bid. It was agreed by both parties to dismiss the bill so it could be appealed. There were four lawyers on each side of the appeal, and were five pages of serious briefs submitted. Lincoln and Herndon, Logan and Brayman represented Webster and Huntington, and Stuart, Edwards, Browning and Bushnell represented the governor's side. Of special interest: Stuart and Edwards included a classic U.S. constitutional case in their brief, Madison v. Marbury, 1 W.S. Cond. Rep. 278, holding the acts of the governor were executive, and thus could not be restrained or directed by the U.S. Supreme Court. Lincoln's side argued the bid of Ash and Diller was not a specific bid, and a total subversion of the manifest intention of the legislature.

Judge Caton, writing for the court, agreed with Lincoln, and revised the decree and remanded the case. When the terms of a sealed bid auction give one party an unfair advantage over another, it prevents fair competition. Allowing practices as in this case would preclude all possibility of a specific bidder getting the property, and would discourage any prudent bidder from participating in future sealed bid auctions.

This case was reheard, and appeal taken reported at 12 Ill.302. Lincoln won here, but received a surprising set-back in the second appeal.

Adams et al. v. County of Logan
orig. ed. 11 Ill.336

(Ill. Rep.: Adams et al. v. The County of Logan 11 Ill.337)
December Term 1848

The Illinois legislature authorized the establishment of the counties of Menard, Logan, and Dane in 1839. Several people, the plaintiffs in this action, proposed that if the county seat of Logan county was established in Postville, they would give land and erect a building for the county seat. In 1841 the legislature authorized Postville as the county seat of Logan County, and the parties donated the land and erected the building. Later on the legislature authorized the move of the county seat to Mount Pulaski. The county owned building and land in Postville were sold, and Adams et al. brought an action in the Logan Circuit Court before Judge Davis to recover the proceeds of the sale. Judgment rendered for the county of Logan. Adams et al. appealed, represented by S.T Logan and Stuart and Edwards, and Lincoln and Herndon represented the County of Logan. All of the other four attorneys had strong connections with Lincoln, and this is one of the few appellate case in which all five participated. The five had participated in Webster v. French, 11 Ill.254, but there were also other attorneys involved in that case.

The Supreme Court, with Justice Caton writing the opinion, affirmed the judgment of the lower court. The grants by Adams et al. were unconditional, as there were neither conditions in the deeds nor any separate written instruments to establish any conditions on the gifts. A conveyance of land to a county, in consideration of the location of the county seat at a particular place, does not deprive the legislature of the right to remove the same, whenever the public good shall require a change. Nor does such conveyance, if unconditional, give the donors of property a right of action for damages sustained in consequence of such removal.

Pearl & Holland v. Wellman & Wellman
orig. ed. 11 Ill.352
(Ill. Rep.: Perl & Holland v. Wellman & Wellman
et al. 11 Ill.352)
December Term 1849

The Wellmans recovered a judgment against Pearl, who appealed. The appeal bond was entered into by Pearl with Holland as his surety in April 1846. At the December Term, 1846, the judgment was reversed. At the ensuing term of the Supreme Court, a rehearing was granted, and the judgment of the lower court was affirmed. This suit is brought against Pearl and Holland for nonpayment of the appeal bond, which would have satisfied the judgment. Pearl and Holland, represented by Lincoln and Herndon, pleaded the judgment had not been affirmed because the evidence produced was inadequate. Holland pleaded separately there had been sufficient delay to excuse him. Decision was rendered for the Wellmans, and judgment awarded to them of $909.41, plus interest and costs.

The Supreme Court, in an opinion written by Justice Trumbull, affirmed the judgment. The evidence was adequate to prove the judgment had been affirmed, despite minor discrepancies in proof. The surety, Holland, is not excused because of mere passiveness, or delay, in the Wellmans' proceeding against the principal (Pearl). The fact the cause was originally reversed, did not excuse his liability.

Lewis v. Moffett
orig. ed. 11 Ill.392
(Ill. Rep.: Lewis v. Moffett 11 Ill.392)
December Term 1849

Lewis, Johnson and Moffett entered into a partnership in Springfield named Lewis, Johnson & Co. in February of 1848. Johnson and Moffett agree to perform services, and Lewis to furnish a foundry and machine shop, plus to purchase stock for the firm. The firm was dissolved by mutual consent in August 1848. The partnership owned a patent on an "atmospheric churn," which it tried to sell. Lewis, when in St. Louis on personal business, sold the churn for $5,047. In the distribution of the assets of the partnership, he claimed a commission for making this sale, while his partners refused him saying it was a general obligation of each partner to do what he could to promote the common good. The circuit judge, Davis, entered a decree allowing Lewis a commission of $1,000 and directing the remaining assets to be divided equally. Logan, Stewart and Edwards represented Lewis, and Lincoln and Herndon, and Conkling represented Moffett on the appeal.

The Supreme Court, in an opinion written by Justice Caton, reduced a portion of the decree which if followed would have allowed Lewis more than the $1000 he was awarded, and affirmed the rest. Justice Caton recognized Lewis must have done a superb job of salesmanship when "testimony shows, and all now seem to admit, that the invention is really valueless." Under the partnership agreement, he did not agree to provide services. So any he rendered should be compensated for. $1,000 is a proper amount for this valuable service. Lewis had claimed $12,000 originally, so Lincoln et al. did a good job in proving the value of Lewis' miraculous services to be much less.

Austin, adm. of Austin v. People ex rel. Burr et al.
orig. ed. 11 Ill.452

(Ill. Rep.: Austin, adm. of Austin v. People,
for use of Burr et al. 11 Ill.453)
December Term 1849

This was an action of debt brought by the People of the State of Illinois against Seth Austin, administrator of Elijah Austin on a guardian's bond. The penalty of the bond was $600. Judgment for the People for $600, although the declaration filed by the People was for $500.

Justice Treat, in his opinion for the Supreme Court, reversed the judgment, and remanded it for further proceedings. It was the duty of the jury to find the amount of the debt as well as the damages. This was not done.

Lincoln and Herndon represented the People, on appeal at least. The facts are so minimal it is impossible to understand the inconsistency between the amount of the debt and the total penalty in the bond and whether or not the case was mishandled.

People ex rel. Davenport v. Brown et al.
orig. ed. 11 Ill.478

(Ill. Rep.: The People ex rel. Davenport v.
Brown et al. 11 Ill.479)
June Term 1850

The Illinois constitution provided that a county could adopt township organization if a majority of the citizens of a county voted affirmatively for it. Woodford county had such an election; and 153 voted for it, and 107 voted against it, out of a total of more than six hundred legal voters in the county. County Judge Brown, and his associate judges, refused to organize the townships. The people ex rel. Davenport bring this petition for a mandamus to compel the judges to act. The court dismissed the petition. Lincoln represented the People in the Woodford circuit court, and on the appeal the only indication in the supreme court opinion, is that Peters represented the People.

The supreme court, in an opinion written by Justice Treat, affirmed the judgment. The county courts were created and their jurisdiction conferred by the constitution. None of its powers could be taken away except in the mode prescribed in the constitution. The power of the county court over the business of the county continues until the township organization is adopted by an affirmative vote of a majority of all the legal voters of the county. The language of the constitution to establish townships is clear and explicit. It does not mean a majority of those casting votes, but a majority of the legal voters in the county. This did not happen here, so the county judges acted properly in denying the petition for a mandamus.

Morris et al. v. The City of Chicago
orig. ed. 11 Ill.650

(Ill. Rep.: Morris et al. v. The City of Chicago 11 Ill.650)
June Term 1850

The City of Chicago wanted to widen Madison street, between Wells and State streets. It followed the procedure mandated for condemnation of the necessary land to accomplish this, and the commissioners estimated the damage to the owners of the land to be appropriated to be $8,740.17; to which they added $96 as compensation to the city for its expenses. The aggregate sum of $8,836.17 was then apportioned against the lots deemed to be benefitted by the widening of the street. These beneficiaries appeal.

The Supreme Court, with Justice Treat writing the opinion, reversed the judgment and remanded it for a new hearing. Chicago maintained no appeal could be made, because the act under which condemnation was made was silent as to conferring any right to appeal. The court said the right of appeal here was granted by the general provision regulating appeals. The statute provides, that appeals "shall be allowed in all cases, where the judgment or decree appealed from be final, and shall amount, exclusively of costs, to the sum of twenty dollars, or relate to a franchise or freehold." This judgment clearly relates to a freehold, since the city was to acquire ownership of the land condemned. However, the fatal objection to the proceeding of the commissioners was the addition of the $96 in the award. The city must bear its own expenses, and not pass them through to the property owners that are beneficiaries.

Godfrey v. The City of Alton
orig. ed. 12 Ill.29

(Ill. Rep.: Godfrey v. The City of Alton 12 Ill.29)
November Term 1850

Godfrey and Gilman owned land along the Mississippi River, and it was added to the City of Alton in 1832. A survey was made and the land along the river was designated as a public highway and landing. Lots were sold, and buildings were erected. Godfrey brings this action in 1850 against the city, seeking damages for trespass **quare clausum fregit**. This is an old English common law action translated as "trespass whereas he broke the close (meaning boundaries of the land)." The court rejected his claim, and found for the city.

The Supreme Court, with the opinion written by Justice Caton, affirmed the judgment. The survey with sales and land use being made in reliance on it, constituted sufficient evidence of intent by Godfrey to dedicate the road along the river for public use including a landing. Dedication of property for these uses requires no particular form or written documentation. The statute of frauds (which requires transfer of real property to be made in writing with specific formalities) does not apply. It is purely a question of intention, and the intention of Godfrey was very clear here. He cannot change his mind.

City of Alton v. Illinois Transportation Company
orig. ed. 12 Ill.38

(Ill. Rep.: City of Alton v.
Illinois Transportation Company 12 Ill.37)
November Term 1850

The City of Alton brought an action of ejectment in the Madison circuit court to recover possession of an easement on property along the Mississippi River which had been dedicated for public use. In 1818,

Easton, claiming to be the owner of the land, laid out a plan for Alton, and reserved two blocks along the river for public use. Subsequently, Whiteside and Reynolds set up a claim for some land, including a portion of what Easton had reserved. These parties settled their controversy in 1821, by executing and interchanging deeds, upon the construction of which rests the decision in this case. A plot had been recorded. There were some inconsistencies between the deeds, and both with the recorded plot. In the thirty years between this settlement and the lawsuit, the area was developed and the Illinois Transportation Company became involved. The facts of the case don't include its involvement but it seems logical its transportation system in some way impeded what the city deemed was dedicated for public use. The court rejected Alton's case, and it appealed.

The Supreme Court, with an opinion written by Judge Caton, reversed the lower court and remanded the cases. The case had been submitted on agreed facts, and there are many pages stating the agreement, and the lengthy briefs of the attorneys. Justice Caton relied on several long standing common law principles in his interpretation of the intent of the parties as indicated by the deeds: 1) a construction which requires that an entire clause of a deed should be rejected, will not be adopted, except upon unavoidable necessity (which was not true here); 2) when a deed refers to a plot, which has upon its face that to which the expressions of the deed can apply, the court will connect the two, rather than reject the words of the deed; 3) if a deed will admit of two constructions, it should be construed against the grantor.

Atwood v. Caldwell et al.
orig. ed. 12 Ill.96

(Ill. Rep.: Atwood v. Caldwell et al. 12 Ill.95)

November Term 1850

Atwood brought an action in the Madison circuit court to prevent the assignees of the Bank of Illinois selling certain lands, and to enforce a conveyance of title of the same lands to Atwood. The lands had belonged to the bank, which was in liquidation. The statute of the act putting the bank in liquidation specified: "The real estate of said bank shall be appraised by three householders, or a majority of them, on oath, to be appointed by the judge of the circuit court in the county, where the real estate may be situated" and when so appraised shall be sold. Atwood had these certain lands appraised, and tendered $500 (which was more than the appraisal) for the lands. The assignees refused to sell him the lands, and had the court appoint appraisers, who valued the lands at $2,122.50. The court dismissed the request of Atwood.

The supreme court, in an opinion written by Justice Treat, affirmed the dismissal decree. An appraisal made by anyone of these subject lands, other than appraisers appointed under the terms of the applicable statute, is not binding on the assignees of the bank. The assignees of the bank had a proper appraisal made, and ordered a public sale. Atwood had an opportunity to buy the property at that sale, and has no just cause to complain of the assignees actions.

Williams et al., exec. of Trotter v. Blankenship et al., adm. of Trailor
orig. ed. 12 Ill.122

(Ill. Rep.: Williams et al., exec. of Trotter v.
Blankenship et al., adm of Trailor 12 Ill.121)
December Term 1850

Blankenship, administrator of Archibald Trailer, deceased, brought an action against Williams, the executor of George Trotter, deceased, in a justice of the peace court. After a hearing, the justice of the peace awarded $43.18 to Blankenship. Williams contended the justice had no authority to render the judgment, when Blankenship tried to enforce the judgment in county court. The county court affirmed the justice's judgment, and Williams appealed to the circuit court, who affirmed the decision of the county court.

Williams, represented by Lincoln and Herndon, appealed to the Supreme Court, which reversed the lower courts, in an opinion written by Justice Treat. The statute conferring powers to the justice of peace courts gives authority to handle cases when the claims do not exceed $100 when an executor is the plaintiff, but only up to $20 when an executor is the defendant. Also consent cannot confer jurisdiction, so the fact the parties appeared before the justice of the peace, and contested the merits of the case, can have no bearing on the proper decision.

Warren v. Chambers et al.
orig. ed. 12 Ill.124

(Ill. Rep.: Warren v. Chambers et al. 12 Ill.124)
December Term 1850

Warren brought an action in assumpsit against Chambers et al. as partners. They made a general denial. The record on appeal indicated the money had been paid to one of the defendants, and the point in controversy was whether the other defendants were partners, and thus jointly liable. Judgment was rendered for the defendants.

The supreme court, in an opinion written by Justice Trumbull, reversed the judgment and remanded the cause. According to the pertinent statute, the issue of partnership status among the defendants could only be proven by them under a plea in abatement. Since they made a general denial instead, their evidence of no partnership was improperly received.

Justice Treat dissented stating the proper interpretation of the statute is the issue could be raised by either a plea in abatement or a general denial.

See Chambers et al. v. Warren 13 Ill.318, for further action in this case.

Smith & Dunlap, Assignees of State Bank v. Dunlap orig. ed. 12 Ill.184

(Ill. Rep.: Smith et al. v. Dunlap 12 Ill.183)
December Term 1850

James Dunlap made a note to the Bank of Illinois for $131,480.52, to be paid in State of Illinois indebtedness. The note became due, and was unpaid. The Bank of Illinois went into liquidation, and assigned this note to John J. Hardin and Samuel Dunlap, who died. David Smith et al. are his successors. They bring this action to collect $131,480.52. The Sangamon circuit court, Judge Davis presiding, awarded them $38,361.93. The assignees appeal, and are represented by Lincoln and Herndon, Browning and Bushnell, and Williams and Lawrence, who appear for the creditors of the Bank of Illinois. S.T. Logan stands alone, defending for James Dunlap. At the maturity of the note, state of Illinois indebtedness had values of its obligations ranging $.20 to $.42 on the dollar.

The Supreme Court, in an opinion written by Justice Treat, affirmed the circuit court. Where a promisor undertakes to pay a certain number of dollars in specific articles, like grain, cattle or other commodities, he must deliver the articles on the day named, or he will be bound to pay the sum stated in money. However, when he promises to pay in bank notes, or other evidences of indebtedness, which purport on their face to represent dollars, and can be counted as such, the sum is expressed to indicate the number of dollars of the notes or evidences to be paid, and not the amount of the debt. If the debtor fails to deliver them according to the terms of the contract, he is responsible only for their real, not their nominal value. Their cash value is the true amount of the debt to be discharged. Such was the case here.

See Dunlap v. Smith et al., assignees of State Banks (12 Ill.399) for further proceedings in this matter.

Eames, adm. of Eames v. Blackhart
orig. ed. 12 Ill.195

(Ill. Rep.: Eames v. Blackhart 12 Ill.195)
December Term 1850

The facts are well summarized in the opinion: "Joseph Eames, a resident of Oquawka, on his return home from St. Louis, died suddenly of cholera on board a steamboat upon the Mississippi River. Just before his death he delivered up to the defendant (Blackhart) his money, and requested him to keep and deliver it to his family . . . After his return, the defendant paid over to the plaintiff (Thaddeus Eames), who is administrator of said Joseph Eames deceased, two hundred and fifteen dollars in gold, and twelve dollars in paper money. This suit (assumpsit) was brought upon the ground that the defendant did not pay over all the money he had received from the deceased. A variety of facts were proven upon the trial, mostly of a circumstantial character, tending to show that the deceased had more money with him, and that the defendant received a larger sum than we had accounted for."

At the request of Blackhart the jury was instructed: "That it is not incumbent on the defendant to account for what Joseph Eames did with his money, and unless they believe from the evidence, that the said defendant received more money from Joseph Eames than he delivered to the plaintiff, they will find for the defendant." Judgment for Blackhart, and Eames had objected to the instruction, and this is the error he presents to the supreme court to obtain a reversal.

The supreme court, in an opinion written by Justice Trumbell, reversed the judgment and remanded the cause. There is a general proposition that one man is not bound to show what another has done with his money, but such a state of circumstances may exist as to make it incumbent on a person, who would discharge himself from liability, to show what another has done with his money. Here the instruction was wrong. It was up to the jury to decide whether or not Eames had in his possession at the time of his decease a larger sum of money than Blackhart accounted for, "It is not the province of the court to draw inferences from the evidence, or determine what it does and does not prove, and if it do so in a manner calculated to mislead the jury, the judgment will be set aside and a new trial granted."

McHenry v. Watkins
orig. ed. 12 Ill.233

(Ill. Rep.: McHenry v. Watkins 12 Ill.232)
December Term 1850

Watkins recovered a judgment against McHenry and Perkapile for $462.64. By virtue of an execution of this judgment the sheriff sold to Watkins several tracts of land as the property of McHenry for $350 (this reduced the amount of the judgment by that amount--no money changed hand). Perkapile paid $270.25 on the judgment. Later Watkins entered a motion to set aside the sale of two of the tracts of land, which were bid at $75 each, because McHenry had no title to them. The court sustained this motion, ordering execution against McHenry for the amount for which the lands were sold. Execution was entered to collect $150. McHenry enters motion to quash this execution, and the court overrules it. Lincoln and Herndon represent McHenry on the appeal.

The Supreme Court, in an opinion written by Justice Treat, reversed the lower court, remanding the case to that court to quash the execution. The judgment had already been satisfied, in fact had been overpaid. The $350 in effect paid by McHenry on the purchase of the land, reduced by $150 for the lots to which he had no title, plus $270.25 paid by Perkapile, exceeded the judgment awarded Watkins of $462.64. Perhaps the size of the numbers confused the officials of Cass county where the trial and execution of the judgment took place.

Whitecraft et al. v. Vanderver
orig. ed. 12 Ill.235

(Ill. Rep.: Whitecraft et al. v. Vanderver 12 Ill.234)
December Term 1850

Vanderver brought an action in debt to recover the penalty for cutting trees, as specified in a statute which stipulated a penalty of eight dollars per tree for certain specific types, and three dollars per tree for the others; if the trees were cut without the permission of the owner. Vanderver was awarded $476 after the mathematics of how many trees of each value were cut. Whitecraft et al., who apparently had cut down the trees, appealed. Vanderver is represented by Lincoln and Herndon on the appeal.

The Supreme Court, in an opinion written by Justice Trumball, reversed the judgment, and remanded the cause, with permission for Vanderver to amend his declaration. He started the opinion as follows: "All the facts stated in the declaration may be true, and yet the defendants below have committed no act that would subject them to this action. It is not alleged that they felled the trees without having first obtained permission so to do from the owner of the land etc." The want of permission from the owner is a necessary ingredient to constitute the offense, and "he who would make a party liable under the statute, must allege all the facts upon which the statute creates the penalty."

The circuit court case was tried in Christian county, and we have no indication whether Lincoln and Herndon handled the trial there. We assume not, because of the fundamental, fatal error of inadequate pleading.

Enos et al. v. Capps
orig. ed. 12 Ill.255

(Ill. Rep.: Enos et al. v. Capps 12 Ill.255)
December Term 1850

Capps brought an action in chancery to prove an equitable interest in certain land against several people, including two minors. In 1836 a bill was confessed against all the defendants, and a decree entered requiring the land be conveyed to Capps. In 1847 a decree was sworn out in the name of all former defendants against Capps to reverse the decree. Capps said that since more than five years had elapsed, it was too late. The court dismissed the decree. Lincoln and Herndon represent all the former defendants.

The Supreme Court, in an opinion written by Judge Treat, reversed the decree against the two minors, but upheld it against all the other former defendants. Neither a default nor a confessed judgment can be taken against a minor. A guardian ad litem should have been appointed to protect their interests, but none was in this case. Why one was not appointed is not clear; perhaps Lincoln and Herndon did not represent these defendants when Capps originally brought his action in equity against them. It was brought in their home court (Sangamon County), however.

Also in chancery, as at law, a decree jointly binding on several defendants, so that each is liable for the whole; if reversed at all must be reversed as to all; but where a decree in form is joint, but is several in its effect, it may be reversed as to a part of the defendants. Here Capps becomes a tenant in common with the two minors.

The original action in this matter was Moore et al. v. Capps (9 Ill.315). Also see subsequent action in Enos v. Capps (15 Ill.277).

Ward v. Owens et al.
orig. ed. 12 Ill.283

(Ill. Rep.: Ward v. Owens et al. 12 Ill.282)

December Term 1850

This was a bill in chancery brought by Owens et al. against Ward to set aside a conveyance. A decree was entered for Owens et al., and Ward appeals saying the evidence presented was not adequate to support the decree. Lincoln and Herndon represented Owens et al. in the appeal. No record of who represented them at the hearings.

The Supreme Court, in an opinion written by Justice Treat, agreed with Ward, and reversed the decree, remanding the cause for further proceedings. The opinion, which contains no other facts about the issue or the hearing, says "The record fails to show that any evidence was given to sustain the averments in the bill. The statute authorizing testimony to be introduced orally at the hearing, was only designed to change the mode of taking proof in chancery cases, and does not dispense with the necessity of incorporating it into the record. The evidence, or the facts proved by it, ought to be stated in the record. The court will not presume that any other proof was made than that what appears in the record."

This case was originally heard in Cumberland county. Here is another case in which Lincoln and Herndon represented clients in the Supreme Court, with Justice Treat writing the opinion, where seemingly inadequate work was done by the attorneys for the same client in the circuit courts. Two others are Whitecraft v. Vandeveer, 12 Ill.234 (Christian county) and Enos et al. v. Capps (Sangamon county), all in the December Term 1850.

Linton, Adm. of Nott v. Anglin
orig. ed. 12 Ill.284

(Ill. Rep.: Linton, adm. of Nott v. Anglin 12 Ill.283)

December Term 1850

Linton, as administrator of Nott, deceased, sued Anglin in the Clark circuit court, for $535.18 in an action of debt. The declaration says the plaintiff resided in Clark County, and the process was issued to Coles county, where Anglin could be found, and served there. Linton pleaded the court had no jurisdiction over him because he was not a resident of Coles county and judgment was rendered for Anglin on this ground. Lincoln and Herndon represented Anglin in defending the appeal.

The Supreme Court, in an opinion written by Justice Caton, reversed the judgment and remanded the cause. The pertinent statute provides "it shall not be lawful for any plaintiff to sue a defendant out of the county where the latter resides, or may be found, except in" certain specified cases, "when process may issue against the defendant, to the county where he resides." Caton said, "We have no doubt that the legislature intended to use the word 'resides' in such a sense as to include the place where the defendant, for the time being, might be, whether that was his permanent place of residence, or not. Were a different construction to prevail, transient persons would be placed on a better footing than permanent residents, which, taking the whole law together, we think was not the intention of the legislature. The court, having acquired the jurisdiction to issue its process beyond its territorial jurisdiction, the object was to reach the defendants and if he could only be reached at the place of his permanent residence, the object of the law in conferring the jurisdiction would be defeated."

Whoever represented Anglin at the trial in the Clark circuit court presented an ingenious idea. Judge Wilson bought it there, but the Supreme Court decided otherwise.

Penny v. Graves, assignee of White
orig. ed. 12 Ill.287

(Ill. Rep.: Penny v. Graves, assignee of White 12 Ill.286)
December Term 1850

Penny gave a note to Wilson and Beard for $52.13 stating: "This being for twelve per cent interest on account of hogs bought." Wilson and Beard assigned the note to White, who assigned it to Graves. The note becomes due, and Graves brings an action to collect the amount due from Penny. Penny sought to introduce evidence from two witnesses that it was agreed orally between himself and Wilson and Beard that interest would not be paid, if interest were not asked of Penny by the people who sold him the hogs. No interest was demanded by those sellers, so Penny believes he doesn't owe the money specified in his note. Judgment for Graves, when the evidence of the oral agreement was disallowed. Lincoln and Herndon represented Graves, and Stuart and Edwards, Penny on the appeal at least.

The Supreme Court, in an opinion written by Justice Trumbull, affirmed the judgment. The court said the law was clear: "Parol evidence is inadmissable to vary, contradict, or explain, the terms of a written agreement, and yet it is allowable to show by parol, that the consideration of a promissory note has wholly or in part failed, or that it was given without consideration." It is sometimes difficult to apply this rule, but it seems clear here. The effect of the parol evidence here was to show the note, although absolute in terms, was in fact conditional. If Penny had intended the note to be conditional, he should have expressed it on the terms of the note. He now wants to change the written terms of his promise, to the detriment of innocent transferrees of the note, by parol or oral evidence, and the law does not permit this.

Compher et al. v. People
orig. ed. 12 Ill.290

(Ill. Rep.: Compher et al. v. The People 12 Ill.289)
December Term 1850

This was an action brought on a bond executed by Compher, as collector of Peoria county. The other defendants were his sureties. The sureties argued they should be discharged from their liabilities because the legislature changed the revenue laws after they agreed to be sureties for a collector. The Tazewell circuit court, with Judge Davis presiding, held for the People and did not discharge the sureties. Lincoln and Herndon, among others, represented the People on the appeal, and submitted a brief which contained the cogent argument the Supreme Court used in it opinion.

The Supreme Court, in an opinion written by Justice Trumbull, affirmed the judgment stating that the changes did not prejudice the sureties: "The power to control the revenue is one of the highest attributes of sovereignty. Without this power, no government could exist, and it cannot be supposed that the general assembly intended to part with this important prerogative, or to contract that no change should be made in the manner of collecting the revenue, during the continuance in office of any of its collectors. Parties who go security upon bonds of this character, do so with the full knowledge and expectation that the revenue laws will be changed, and the duties of the collectors altered as the public interests may require, and they have no right to complain of any duties of this principal, especially when such alterations are in nowise prejudicial to their interest. Such are the changes of the law under consideration."

Major v. Hawkes et al.
orig. ed. 12 Ill.298
(Ill. Rep.: Major v. Hawkes et al. 12 Ill.297)
December Term 1850

Hawkes et al. were partners with Major. The partnership was dissolved, and Major paid Hawkes some of the partnership money. The facts indicated Hawkes was indebted personally to Major at that time, and that Hawkes was insolvent. It was suggested by counsel that the money had been returned by Hawkes to Major, but not proven. The remaining parties sued Major for improper stewardship of partnership accounts, and the verdict was against Major. Lincoln and Herndon represented Hawkes et al. on the appeal.

The Supreme Court, in an opinion written by Justice Trumbull, reversed the lower court, and remanded the cause. Upon the voluntary dissolution of a partnership, each of the partners, in the absence of any agreement to the contrary, retains the right to collect debts due the firm, and give discharges therefor. Hawkes had, therefore, just as much right to receive the money from Major as either of the other partners. To deprive Major of the benefit of the payment made to Hawkes, it was incumbent upon the other partners to show the payment had not been made in good faith. This was not done, so judgment is reversed, but remanded for a new trial if the other partners believe they can prove bad faith.

Webster et al. v. French et al.
orig. ed. 12 Ill.302
(Ill. Rep.: Webster et al. v. French et al. 12 Ill.301)
December Term 1850

In the case of Webster and Huntington v. French et al. (11 Ill.254), Lincoln represented Webster and Huntington, and succeeded in reversing a judgment in a lower court which had awarded a bid to certain property owned by the State of Illinois to another bidder. The cause was remanded for a new hearing, and Webster et al. brought this case to have their bid accepted as the highest bid. The legislative enactment authorizing the bidding for this specific state property, provided that the governor shall received written, sealed bids "until the first day of July, A.D., 1949." It was proven conclusively the bid of Webster et al. was received on July 2. Therefore Webster's bill was dismissed, and his attempt to buy the property rejected. Lincoln and Herndon, and others, represented Webster et al. on the appeal.

The Supreme Court, in an opinion written by Justice Caton, affirmed the decree. The word "until" was used as a word of limitation, and was peremptory. The act had to be done within the time specified. It was argued that since the sealed bids had not been opened when Webster's bid was received, no one was harmed. Probably so, but a peremptory condition must be complied with.

In the prior case, also written by Justice Caton, it was simply stated that Webster's bid had been received on June 30. It The earlier case seemed a remarkable triumph for Webster, and Lincoln, as two bids higher than Webster's were rejected. It had to be a serious disappointment to win a tough case like that, only to find, through some inadvertence, the "winning" bid was submitted a little late. July 1 was a Sunday, which is interesting, but of no importance here.

The People ex rel. Stephenson v. Marshall orig. ed. 12 Ill.391

(Ill. Rep.: The People ex rel. Stephenson v. Marshall 12 Ill.391)
June Term 1851

The People, represented by Lincoln and Wingate, bring this application for a mandamus (to require an official to act) to the Supreme Court, to require Judge Marshall to hold court at Raleigh, Illinois.

In 1847 the legislature divided Gallatin county, and Saline county was organized, with Raleigh established as the county seat. Afterwards courts were held in Raleigh at regular times. In 1851 the legislature passed an act combining Gallatin and Saline counties, with a new county seat at Equality. There was no vote of the people authorizing this. Judge Marshall held court in the new county seat pursuant to the act, and would not hold court at Raleigh. Hence this petition for mandamus to order him to do so. The facts are not disputed. The major issue relates to the authority of the legislature to make the changes in the counties and the county seats without the affirmative vote of the people.

The Supreme Court, in an opinion written by Justice Caton, granted the mandamus. An affirmative vote of the people is required under the constitution to do any of the things the legislature did here. Justice Caton stated: "If the constitution is still to be regarded as an instrument of that social character which has hitherto always been attributed to all American constitutions,--if it is still to be considered as a law to the law makers, as well as to the citizens, a law which cannot be compassed or provisions are not frittered away, by establishing a rule which will, in every instance, allow its provisions to be disregarded, which will permit the legislature to do the precise and identical thing which the constitution in most express and unequivocal terms, has declared shall not be done, without the vote of the people interested."

Dunlap v. Smith et al., assignees of State Bank
orig. ed. 12 Ill.399

(Ill. Rep.: Dunlap v.
Smith et al., assignees of State Bank 12 Ill.399)
June Term 1851

This is a continuation of the situation presented in Smith v. Dunlap, 12 Ill.184, wherein Dunlap won the right to pay off a $131,480.52 note he made to the Bank of Illinois, to be paid in State of Illinois indebtedness. When the note became due, State of Illinois indebtedness was not worth face value, so the Supreme Court affirmed a judgment against Dunlap for $38,361.93 to discharge his total indebtedness. Lincoln and others represented Smith et al. Presumably in this continuation he and others still represented them, but this short opinion does not acknowledge who counsel for either side was, and it does not state who wrote the opinion.

In this action, Dunlap entered a motion in the Sangamon circuit court to pay all, or part, of the judgment in notes and certificates of the Bank of Illinois with face value of $28,127.35. Five days after Dunlap gave the note to the Bank of Illinois, and before it became due, the legislature passed an act putting the Bank of Illinois into liquidation; which provided, among other things, for paying out the liquid assets of the bank, pro rata, and issuing certificates for the balance due; which certificates should be received for any debt due the bank. Judge Davis rejected this offer of Dunlap, and overruled the notion.

The Supreme Court reversed this judgment, and remanded the cause. Dunlap had the right to discharge the judgment in the notes and certificates of the bank. The anonymous Justice impliedly rebuked the attorneys for Smith et al., stating "It is to be regretted that, in so important a case as this, the parties have not thought proper to bring before the court the whole transaction out of which Dunlap's indebtedness arose. Had this been done, it is possible that the court might be called upon to pronounce a different judgment; but as the case is presented in the record, by which alone the court must be governed, Dunlap's right to discharge the judgment in notes and certificates of the bank is clear."

In the first case Dunlap won the right to discharge his debt of $131,480.52 by paying a lesser amount, measured by the value of State of Illinois indebtedness at the time the note became due. This case gives him additional benefit in that he can discharge the obligation by paying the adjudicated amount of money with indebtedness of the bankrupt bank at its face value, which probably could be brought by Dunlap at a discount. Logan represented Dunlap in the first appeal, and presumably here, against an impressive array of attorneys, including Lincoln. In the first case he succeeded in establishing Dunlap could pay off $133.480.52 with $38,361.93 in real money, and with this decision, it is reduced further. The facts of the case do not indicate the degree of the additional savings.

Ballance v. Rankin
orig. ed. 12 Ill.420

(Ill. Rep.: Ballance v. Rankin 12 Ill.419)
June Term 1851

Rankin brought an action of ejectment against Ballance for the recovery of a lot in Peoria. Ballance asked the judge to charge the jury that since Rankin had asked for compete title to the lot, he could not recover an undivided interest in the same lot. The judge refused, and Rankin obtained a judgment for one undivided part of the premises claimed. Ballance appealed.

The Supreme Court, with Justice Treat writing the opinion, reversed the judgment. The Revised Statutes of Illinois covering the action of ejectment provides that "if such plaintiff claims any undivided share or interest in any premises, he shall state the same particularly in such declaration." Judge Treat says this is imperative, and not directory. The declaration in ejectment is intended to apprise the defendant of the precise character of the estate sought to be recovered against him. Thus if he wishes he can let the matter pass by default, and if he chooses to defend he knows precisely what issue to prepare himself for his defense.

In an action the plaintiff cannot recover a different estate than the one he claims.

See Rankin v. Ballance (13 Ill.706) for further proceedings in this matter.

Lewis v. Lyons & Frances
orig. ed. 13 Ill.117
(Ill. Rep.: Lewis v. Lyons et al. 13 Ill.116)
December Term 1851

Lyons died in 1842. Prior to that time he and Irwin had sold some property, and had taken a mortgage; which was in default and foreclosed upon. This was still pending when Lyons died, and remained so during a five year service of one Saunders as administrator, who resigned in 1848. In 1851 the decree of foreclosure was revived, and the Lyon's share was awarded to his widow. Lewis, appointed as administrator of the estate, seeks to have the mortgage money paid to him in his official capacity. There seemed to be no other debts or assets in the estate. Decree denied.

The supreme court, in an opinion written by Justice Caton, affirmed the judgment. When the debts are paid, the residue of an estate belongs to the heirs, and an administrator is no longer needed. Caton said: "It would be a mockery of justice for a court of chancery to require the heir to pay over the money to the administrator, when he has no debts to pay and no legitimate use for it, merely for the purpose of allowing him to retain and use it for perhaps two years, and then to pay it back to the heir, retaining his costs and commissions - costs uselessly made and commissions earned by no beneficial services, but in a business which he seeks, through an expensive suit in chancery, and which can benefit himself alone."

Dorman et ux. v. Yost
orig. ed. 13 Ill.127
(Ill. Rep.: Dorman et ux. v. Yost 13 Ill.128)
December Term 1851

Robinson died intestate in 1819, leaving considerable real and personal estate. In 1826, his administrators settled with the probate court showing a debt against the estate of $1,008.87, consisting chiefly of a debt due the

Bank of Illinois. In January 1827, the legislature passed a special act, authorizing John Lane to sell enough of the real estate to discharge this debt. During the same month, Lane sold several tracts of land for $1,057, and applied the proceeds to the payment of the debt to the bank. The heirs of Robinson (the Dormans) subsequently recovered their lands by ejectment, which was sustained by the Supreme Court on the ground that the act of the legislature, and the proceedings under it, were unauthorized and void (Lane v. Dorman, 4 Ill.238). In 1841, Lane was appointed administrator do bonus non (of the goods not administrated), and he applied to the White circuit court and obtained an order for the sale of enough land to satisfy the sum of $1,008.87. The order was reversed, and cause remanded (Dorman v. Lane, 6 Ill.143). Yost, who succeeded Lane who was deceased, brought this petition in 1849 to sell the land, and an order was entered authorizing him to do so. Lincoln represented the Dormans on the appeal.

The Supreme Court, in an opinion written by Justice Treat, reversed this judgment. The opinion was very short. The debt to be paid off by this sale had already been discharged. Lincoln prevailed. There is very little detail to indicate why Lane had brought this second petition to sell land to pay off the same debt. Whatever it was, Lincoln defeated it, with Justice Treat concluding: "The petition does not disclose the least necessity for the application."

Petition of Smith
orig. ed. 13 Ill.138

(Ill. Rep.: Petition of Smith for habeas corpus 13 Ill.139)
December Term 1851

Smith petitioned the supreme court to recover custody of two infants, the children of Alexander, who died in December, 1851, leaving a daughter aged thirteen, and a son aged eight. In his last sickness he requested Shoup to take charge and educate his daughter, and made a like request to Hansby respecting his son. In January, 1852, Smith was appointed guardian of the children, and claimed the right to control them, which was denied by Shoup and Hansby. Smith then bought his petition for habeas corpus to obtain custody of the children. Evidence was offered that the mother was deceased; that the children preferred to stay with Shoup and Hansby; and that Smith was not a suitable person to have custody of the children.

In a per curiam opinion, the supreme court denied the petition. It is the duty of the court to consider the best interests of the children, and that would not be done by putting them under the control of Smith.

McKinley v. Watkins
orig. ed. 13 Ill.140
(Ill. Rep.: McKinley v. Watkins 13 Ill.140)
December Term 1851

Watkins and McKinley had traded horses in 1845; afterwards they had some dispute about the trade, and Watkins threatened to sue unless McKinley would give him a horse or the worth of the horse which McKinley had got from Watkins; the horse which Watkins had received in exchange having died. McKinley promised that, if Watkins would not sue, he would give him $50, or a horse worth that sum. Upon this promise Watkins brought his action against McKinley. Judgment for Watkins, who was represented by Herndon on the appeal at least.

The supreme court, in an opinion written by Justice Trumbull, reversed the judgment and remanded the cause. There was no evidence that Watkins had assented to McKinley's statement. The promise of McKinley to pay $50 if Watkins would not sue was incomplete until accepted by Watkins. He then quoted Story on Contracts: "A mere offer, not assented to, constitutes no contract; for there must be not only a proposal, but an acceptance thereof."

Newsom v. Luster et al.
orig. ed. 13 Ill.175
(Ill. Rep.: Newsom v. Luster et al. 13 Ill.176)
December Term 1851

This is an action of **quare clausum fregit** brought by Luster et al. against Newsom. Luster et al. attempted to prove title by presenting two deeds in the chain of title executed commencing thirty years ago. The question in the case is whether these deeds can be adequately proven to be valid. The deeds were accepted by the Sangamon circuit court before Judge Davis, and judgment rendered for Luster et al. The Supreme Court, in an opinion written by Justice Trumbull affirmed the judgment.

The first deed had been executed and recorded. The deed could not be produced for the trial, but under statutes on "conveyances," if a deed cannot be produced, and it is proven that it is "lost, or not in the power of the party wishing to use it, a transcript of the record, certified by the recorder may be used." It was proven the deed was lost, and not in the power of Luster et al., so the certified copy was properly accepted as valid.

The second deed had not been acknowledged or recorded. The deed was presented, and proven by the handwriting of the grantor. None of the parties to the deed, including the witnesses could be found. After citing the authorities from many states in similar cases, many of whom said the proof of handwriting of a witness is the only acceptable proof, Justice Trumbull said, "In this state the question has now arisen for the first time; and in determining it I have no hesitation in holding that proof of the handwriting of the grantor to a deed furnishes altogether more satisfactory evidence of its execution than would proof of the handwriting of subscribing witness."

Penny v. McHenry
orig. ed. 13 Ill.227

(Ill. Rep.: Perry v. McHenry 13 Ill.227)
December Term 1851

McHenry purchased a tract of land, and paid his own money for it. Penny had been a tenant on the land, and influenced McHenry to buy it. He maintains they had an oral agreement that McHenry would convey half the land to him, and brought this action in chancery to compel the conveyance on the one-half he claims. The decree was dismissed, and Penny, represented by Logan and Stuart and Edwards, appeals. McHenry is represented by Lincoln and Herndon.

The Supreme Court, in an opinion written by Justice Trumbull, affirmed the decree. There is no record of the briefs, or cases submitted by the respective attorney's, to support their sides. However, Justice Trumbull referenced at least 18 cases, apparently cited by Penny's attorneys, which were dismissed as not applicable. One must assume Lincoln, in his oral argument addressed each case, and distinguished it from the present situation.

A parol agreement, relating to the sale of lands, or an interest therein for a longer period than one year, is within the statute of frauds (which requires such to be in writing), and is not valid. Even if Penny's testimony is believed, the agreement falls within this rule.

Penny claimed a resultant trust (a trust implied by law from the intentions of the parties to a given transaction). However, such a trust can only arise in favor of a person who claims to have furnished some, or all, of the consideration money. Such was not the case here.

McAtee v. Enyart
orig. ed. 13 Ill.242
(Ill. Rep.: McArtee v. Engart 13 Ill.242)
December Term 1851

Enyart conveyed certain property to McAtee for a consideration of $350, when the land was worth $1000. Enyart had a serious drinking problem, and had been indicted for larceny for stealing a pair of shoes. McAtee befriended him, and Enyart contends that McAtee took fraudulent advantage of him. There was much evidence surrounding the particular transaction, and Enyart's history of drinking and problems with the law. Judge Davis, in the Sangamon circuit court, heard the case and decreed the conveyance annulled, and required the land to be reconveyed to Enyart. Logan and Stuart and Edwards represented McAtee on the appeal, and Lincoln, Ferguson, and Herndon represented Enyart.

The Supreme Court, in an opinion written by Justice Treat, affirmed the decree. Inadequacy of consideration in the conveyance of land as between the vendor and the vendee would not justify the interposition of a court of equity to set aside a sale, unless the inequality was so gross and palpable as to shock the conscience and convince the judgment; but where fraudulent practices are used under such peculiar circumstances as to make the vendor a prey of the vendee, the aid of the court may be obtained. Such was the case here.

Tuller v. Voght
orig. ed. 13 Ill.277
(Ill. Rep.: Tuller v. Voght 13 Ill.278)
December Term 1851

Tuller owned a carriage drawn by four horses, Voght bought an action in trespass to recover for injuries he sustained when he was riding a horse, and was hit by Tuller's carriage, which its driver (not Tuller) was driving in an alleged careless and dangerous fashion. The court awarded $1000 to Voght.

The supreme court, in an opinion written by Justice Caton, reversed the judgment and remanded the cause, with leave for the plaintiff to amend his declaration. Tuller had no liability under the common law which had a well settled rule that the master is not liable for the willful trespasses of the servant, which were not committed in furtherance of the business of the master. However, the statutes of the state specify that the owners of any carriage running upon a public highway, for the conveyance of passengers, shall be liable for any injuries caused by its driver, in the same manner as such driver would be liable. Thus if the driver were negligent, the owner would be liable. However, the pleadings in this case were inadequate. The declaration did not show the carriage was "for the conveyance of passengers." Caton concluded: "For aught that appears, it may have been only for the transportation of goods or for the private use of the owner, without reference to the accommodation of the traveling public. For this reason, the declaration is defective under the statute."

State Bank by Manly et al. v. Gibson
orig. ed. 13 Ill.308

(Ill. Rep.: Manly et al. v. Gibson 13 Ill.308)
December Term 1851

This is an action of ejectment brought by the trustees of the State Bank of Illinois against Gibson to recover possession of certain real property in Petersburg. The petitioners offered in evidence a certificate of the county surveyor, his oral testimony that the property in dispute was on that certificate, and that the property had been conveyed to several parties in succession, with the State Bank of Illinois having title at the time of this action. Gibson objected, and the evidence was rejected, because the petitioners did not introduce the original town plat of the addition. Verdict for Gibson. Lincoln and Herndon represented Manly et al. on the appeal.

The Supreme Court, in an opinion written by Judge Treat, reversed the judgment, and remanded the cause. Lincoln argued the plat of the town is no part or parcel of a man's title. It is not the best evidence of which the nature of the case admits. An actual survey is the best. Treat said the question of whether the premises in question are owned by either party is one of fact. And any evidence to solve the question is properly admissible. The certified copy of a survey made by the county surveyor is competent. He may be called as a witness.

This case was reheard on appeal at 14 Ill.136.

Chambers et al. v. Warren
orig. ed. 13 Ill.318

(Ill. Rep.: Chambers et al. v. Warren 13 Ill.319)
December Term 1851

This is the trial of a cause that had been remanded (Warren v. Chambers et al. 12 Ill.124). Chambers et al. had filed a bill of discovery against Warren, who filed an answer in response to it. Chambers et al. made two objections during the case, and since Judge Woodson ruled against them in both, and judgment was rendered for Warren, based their appeal on what they contended were erroneous rulings. First they objected to Warren's answer as being more than responsive to the bill of discovery, and they wanted the excess to be stricken. Secondly, the judge instructed the jury that they had made Warren their witness by seeking answers to the bill of discovery, and now were bound by his statements, and they could not be permitted to discredit it. Herndon represented Warren on the appeal at least.

The supreme court, in an opinion written by Justice Trumbull, reversed the cause and remanded it. The first ruling was proper, however; Chambers did have the right to ask the court to exclude from the jury any parts of the answer that were not responsive or in any manner not connected with or explanatory of it. However, if the entire answer here is not responsive to the bill of discovery, it is explanatory of it, and could go to the jury. However, the second ruling was erroneous. It is true Chambers is not at liberty to discredit Warren's answer by impeaching his general reputation for truth, but he may controvert the correctness of the statements made by his own witness by the introduction of other evidence, and in that way discredit his testimony.

Moody v. Peake
orig. ed. 13 Ill.343

(Ill. Rep.: Moody v. Peake 13 Ill.344)
December Term 1851

The opinion of the court was simply signed "per curiam" (on behalf of the court). This was an agreed case in the Sangamon circuit court, intended to raise the question of right of unnationalized persons to vote at a charter election in the city of Springfield. However, the record failed to show that the court took any action in the case. There was therefore, no judgment to be reviewed. It is obvious the supreme court can not review a judgment not yet rendered, so the writ of error was dismissed.

Gardner et al. v. Watson et al.
orig. ed. 13 Ill.347

(Ill. Rep.: Gardner et al. v. Watson et al. 13 Ill.347)
December Term 1851

Corneau executed a note to Gardner, and Watson et al. were the sureties. The note was in default. Gardner obtained a judgment, and told Corneau he would not execute the judgment as long as Corneau would pay interest on the judgment, and costs. There was no time limit set. The judgment was rendered in 1842, and in 1850 Watson et al. bring this action for an injunction to restrain Gardner from collecting the judgment and a perpetual injunction is granted. W.B. Herndon, and Stuart represented Watson et al. on the appeal at least.

The supreme court, in an opinion written by Justice Trumbull, reversed the decree and dismissed the bill. The agreement was entirely too indefinite to be enforced in a court of equity. An agreement to be binding must be mutual, and if Gardner could not compel Corneau to pay the interest for any particular length of time, neither could Corneau compel Gardner to suspend execution for any definite period. The statement made by Gardner was nothing more than a mere indulgence, determinable at the will of the party by whom it was made. An agreement, without consideration, to enlarge the time of payment, will not discharge the surety.

Harris v. Shaw et al.
orig. ed. 13 Ill.456

(Ill. Rep.: Harris v. Shaw et al. 13 Ill.457)
December Term 1851

Harris brings an action of ejectment to recover twenty acres of land in Tremont, Illinois he had given to the county of Tazewell, in accordance with the conditions of an act of the Illinois legislature stipulating that if anyone gave the county twenty acres of land it would build the county courthouse on the property. Later the county moved the county seat to Pekin; under the authority of a legislative act, which also specified the courthouse in Tremont would be used for education. Harris had sold land in Tremont in the sixty acres remaining from a large parcel that contained the twenty acres donated. Harris now wants the land and building returned to him, since it is no longer used for the county seat. The court disagreed, and judgment rendered for Shaw et al. Lincoln, Logan, and Stuart and Edwards represented Harris on the appeal, where, despite this amalgamation of the leading attorneys in the circuit, they lost.

The Supreme Court, in an opinion written by Justice Trumball, affirmed the judgment. Harris gave the land unconditionally; but "Had the land been granted upon condition that it should be used for a particular purpose, it would unquestionably have reverted to the donor when it ceased to be thus used. But it was competent for the legislature to make it a condition precedent to the location of the county seat upon the land of any individual, that he should convey twenty acres of the tract in fee-simple absolute to the county. The owner was not obliged to accept such a proposition, but having done so, and made his deed accordingly, he can not complain when the legislature, to promote the public good, and in the exercise of an undoubted right, subsequently provide for a change of the county seat.

Barret v. Alton and Sangamon Railroad Company
orig. ed. 13 Ill.504

(Ill. Rep.: Banet v. The Alton and Sangamon Railroad Company 13 Ill.504)
December Term 1851

The railroad was created under authority of an act of the legislature to complete a railroad from Alton to Springfield. It provided for stock to be issued for $100 per share, with a subscriber to pay 5% down, and the balance at stated intervals to be specifically called for by the board of directors. Barret subscribed for 30 shares. He also had substantial real estate interests in New Berlin, through which the planned railroad would traverse. Before the completion of Barret's payments, the legislature authorized the company to change the location of the road, but without changing the termini. The railroad found it would be more efficient to shorten the line, which then would not run through New Berlin. Barret saw economic detriment to himself by this move, and refused to pay any more installments on his stock. The railroad brings this action in assumpsit in the Sangamon circuit court, and Judge Davis awards it $1,351. Lincoln represents the railroad, and Logan and E.B. Herndon represent Barret.

The Supreme Court, in an opinion written by Justice Treat, affirmed the judgment. Firstly, the alteration of the company charter did not excuse Barret from paying his subscription. The special reasons which may have influenced Barret to become a subscriber cannot be taken into consideration. There was no fraud, and the subscription was not conditional. Whereas it is possible for an alteration in the charter to work a dissolution of the contract of subscription, this alteration was not material enough to do so. The general features of the project remain unchanged. Secondly, the power to make calls for additional payments was vested in the board of directors, who properly made the calls.

Klein v. The Alton and Sangamon Railroad Company orig. ed. 13 Ill.514

(Ill. Rep.: Klein v. The Alton and Sangamon Railroad Company 13 Ill.514)
December Term 1851

This case has substantially the same facts as Barret v. The Alton and Sangamon Railroad Company (13 Ill.504), with two additional questions which did not arise in that case. Logan and E.B. Herndon again represented the defendant (Klein) on appeal, and Lincoln represented the railroad. This also was an action brought by the railroad to force a subscriber to pay the agreed amount for stock in the railroad. The Sangamon circuit court, Judge Davis presiding, gave judgment again for the railroad.

The Supreme Court, with Justice Treat writing the opinion, again affirmed the lower court judgment. Klein had pleaded he gave a note for the 5% down payment, which was paid after the stock was subscribed. The contract was complete when he gave the note and agreed to pay for the stock. Failing on this, he pleaded the company could keep his 5% per share, and he rescinded his obligation to pay the balance. However, the right of forfeiture belongs exclusively to the corporations. He could not forfeit his down payment, and abandon his obligation.

Ryder v. Alton and Sangamon RR Co.
orig. ed. 13 Ill.516

(Ill. Rep.: Ryder v. The Alton & Sangamon Railroad Company 13 Ill.516)
December Term 1851

This was an action of assumpsit brought by the railroad against Ryder to recover the assessments made on fifty shares of stock he was alleged to have subscribed in a new corporation. Ryder was president of the commissioners in the offering, whose duty was to collect the stock assessments. He signed up for twenty shares at one time and thirty at another. He changed his mind, and set up several reasons for this. He lost the case in the Madison circuit court before Judge Underwood. The judgment against him was affirmed by the Supreme Court, with Justice Treat writing the opinion.

The first plea argued by him was his knowledge of the subscription of 1000 shares by the City of Alton, and 2000 by certain persons residing in the City of New York, wherein Alton gave a proxy to those investors, and guaranteed them a six percent return. Ryder believed this defrauded him from getting equal treatment. Justice Treat said all stockholders had to be treated equally, and were in this case. The obligation Alton made to the investors did not affect the other stockholders, since it did not obligate the corporation to pay anything.

Secondly, he refused to take the thirty shares, and another person, Godfrey, agreed to take the shares himself. However, the intended arrangement was left incomplete and unconcluded. Thus Ryder was still primarily liable to pay for these shares.

Thirdly, he didn't pay the down payment of five percent of the cost, and by the provisions of the charter, one could not become a stockholder unless he paid that. However, as a commissioner, it was his duty to collect the down payment, and it is assumed he paid even if he didn't write himself a check for the amount. Treat said, "Besides, it was his official duty to require payment from subscribers, and he ought not be allowed to set up his violation of that duty to defeat the action."

Finally, he contended the corporate books could not be offered in evidence. Wrong again. Such books are competent evidence to show prima facie that the prerequisites of a statute have been complied with so as to give the corporation an existence.

Rankin v. Ballance
orig. ed. 13 Ill.706
(Ill. Rep.: Rankin v. Ballance 13 Ill.707)
June Term 1852

Rankin recovered a judgment against Ballance in the Peoria circuit court. Balance appealed to the Supreme Court, who reversed the judgment and remanded the cause. This case, Ballance v. Rankin, was reported as 12 Ill.420. Rankin then sued out a writ of error to the circuit court on the original judgment. Ballance brings this motion to the Supreme Court to dismiss this writ of error.

The Supreme Court, in a Per Curiam (author unknown), granted the motion, and dismissed the writ of error. Where a judgment has been reversed on appeal and stands for hearing **de novo** in the circuit court, a writ of error will not lie to hear exceptions to the same judgment.

Metzker v. The People
orig. ed. 14 Ill.101
(Ill. Rep.: Metzker v. The People 14 Ill.101)
December Term 1852

Metzker was convicted under an indictment charging him with the sale of spirituous liquor in less quantities than a quart, which was forbidden under an act of 1851. The court ordered that Metzker should stand committed until the fine ($25) and costs adjudged against him should be paid. Prior to February, 1851, licenses to sell spirituous liquors in quantities less than one quart, could be granted for a period of one year. The act of 1851 exempted from the prohibition, sale of liquors by physicians or druggists in good faith. Metzker objected to the indictment since it did not aver that he did not have an unexpired license effective prior to February 1851, nor did it show he was not a physician or druggist.

The Supreme Court, in an opinion written by Justice Caton, affirmed the judgment. The two exceptions did not have to be averred in the indictment. If either of them applied to the defendant, he should plead in defence. Metzker also objected to the imprisonment until he paid the fine and costs. Justice Caton held it was proper to do so under the statutes. The criminal code gave the judge this power for any conviction of a violation stated in the code. This was enacted before 1851, but there was a provision regulating the sale of spirituous liquors then, and this modification does not abrogate the power of the judge to imprison the defendant pending his payment of the fine and costs.

Casey v. Casey
orig. ed. 14 Ill.112

(Ill. Rep.: Casey v. Casey 14 Ill.112)
December Term 1852

This is an action to set aside the sale of an inheritance, made by the complainant to the defendant, on the ground of fraud.

Sarah Piggot died in New York City, leaving an estate subsequently valued at $13,000. The first knowledge the complainant had of this, or that he was an heir entitled to one-eighth of the estate, was brought to him by the defendant, who learned of the existence of the estate from a friend in New York. He went to New York, and although he wasn't an heir himself, represented himself as acting for the heirs. He then visited the complainant in Tennessee, and depreciated the value of the estate, reciting potential problems and valuing the estate as worth about $3,000. Complainant sold his one-eighth interest to the complainant for $75. Defendant then bought the other shares as well (no facts are given as to how much he paid for them or what he said to induce the sales), and was paid $13,000 from the estate. Complainant believes he has been ill served, and the Jefferson circuit court agrees, awarding a decree to the complainant for one-eighth of the total estate. Lincoln, Logan, and Walter B. Scates, represented the defendant on appeal, and were unsuccessful.

The supreme court, with Justice Caton writing the opinion, affirmed the decree. A party who voluntarily interferes with and manages an estate in behalf of heirs, as their representative, and as such acquires information to which a stranger would not have access, assumes the obligation to his principals which properly appertain to the character of the agent, and entreating with them for the estate, he is bound to disclose how he has acted, and every matter which it was important for them to know, unless such disclosures were distinctly dispensed with. Where confidence is reasonably reposed, that confidence must not be abused. The party relied upon must see that he meets fully and fairly the responsibility of his position, and does not take any advantage, either to the injury of another or for his own gain.

State Bank, by Manly et al. v. Gibson
orig. ed. 14 Ill.136

(Ill. Rep. Manly et al. v. Gibson 14 Ill.136)
December Term 1852

This was an action of ejectment brought by the trustees of the State Bank of Illinois against Gibson to recover the possession of two lots in the town of Petersburg. The bank acquired legal title to the lots in February, 1843, but the 1842 taxes had not been paid. The circuit court issued judgment against these lots for unpaid taxes, and they were ordered to be sold. Gibson brought the lots from the purchaser at that sale. The bank contended the sale was improper because the collector did not file a proper report, and the bank was not liable to pay real estate taxes because of its special tax status. Judgment was rendered for Gibson.

The Supreme Court, in an opinion written by Justice Treat, affirmed the judgment. Even though the bank paid an annual tax based upon its paid-in capital, it still had to pay real estate taxes on land it owned. Thus the taxes were a proper lien to justify the tax sale. The tax sale judgment contained all the necessary information, and the failure of the collector to file his report did not violate it. A party claiming title under a sale for taxes, makes out a **prima facie** case, by the production of the sheriff's deed founded upon a valid judgment. If one wants to contest this, the burden of proof is thrown on the party contesting the tax title.

This case was earlier appealed at 13 Ill.308, when a judgment for Gibson was reversed on appeal and the cause remanded.

Gutzweller v. The People
orig. ed. 14 Ill.142

(Ill. Rep.: Gutzweller v. The People 14 Ill.141)
December Term 1852

The city of Alton provided in its charter in 1837 the power to grant licenses for the sale of spirituous liquors in quantities less than one quart, with the receipts from such licenses to be appropriated for the support of paupers within the city. In 1851 the state enacted legislation forbidding the sale of spirituous liquors in amounts less than one quart. Alton issued a license to Gutzweller to sell liquor in the lesser quantities after this legislation was passed. Gutzweller did so, and was found guilty. Herndon represented the people on the appeal at least.

The supreme court, in an opinion written by Justice Caton, affirmed the judgment. The state had the power to prevent the sale of liquor in less than specified amounts everywhere in the state. Therefore, the license set up as a defense in this case, was issued without authority of law, and can afford no protection to Gutzweller for the commission of an act which was in express violation of the law.

Pierce v. Short
orig. ed. 14 Ill.144
(Ill. Rep.: Pierce v. Short 14 Ill.144)
December Term 1852

Hungerford executed a note to Thornton, who assigned it to Pierce, who assigned it to Short. The note is in default, and evidence is presented that Hungerford has no means of paying the note. Short sues Pierce, in reliance on his obligation as an assignor. Judgment rendered for Short.

The Supreme Court, in an opinion written by Justice Treat, affirmed the judgment. The pertinent statute makes the assignor (Pierce) liable to the assignee (Short), where the latter, by the exercise of due diligence, prosecutes the matter to insolvency; where a suit against the maker would be unavailing; and where the maker had absconded or left the state when the note fell due, or, if assigned after maturity, when the assignment was made on the happening of any one of these contingencies, the assignee may at once resort to the assignor. The assignee must show he used due diligence to collect the note from the maker. In this situation, Short showed, **prima facie,** that a suit against the maker would have been unavailing, and consequently that he had a good cause of action against Pierce; who could not rebut the evidence, was liable as an assignor to Short.

Shillinger v. Shillinger
orig. ed. 14 Ill.147
(Ill. Rep.: Shillinger v. Shillinger 14 Ill.146)
December Term 1852

George Jacob Shillinger came to Illinois from Philadelphia in 1848, leaving his wife, Elizabeth, who promised to join him when he asked her to. She failed to do so, and George brought this action for a divorce under a statute providing if a wife refuses to live with her husband for at least two years, a divorce will be granted. The parties stayed in touch, and George sent her money. George's brother left Philadelphia in 1851 to come to Illinois, and at George's request, asked Elizabeth to accompany him. She refused. Since the suit was filed by publication, and Elizabeth was never served, the court appointed a master, as specified in the statute, to hear evidence. He reported he believed a divorce should be granted, and the court decreed a divorce at the March term, 1852. Herndon represented George.

The supreme court, in an opinion written by Justice Trumbull, reversed the decree. A court has no authority to decree a divorce when the other party does not appear, without proof to sustain its allegations. The general statement of the master is not enough. There was not enough evidence in the decree to grant the divorce. The master's report, so far as showing a refusal by Elizabeth to join George for a space of two years, fails to show any such refusal until 1851, and a few months before this bill was filed.

Ross v. Irving & Pryor v. Irving
orig. ed. 14 Ill.171

(Ill. Rep.: Ross v. Irving & Pryor v. Irving 14 Ill.170)
December Term 1852

These two cases were argued conjointly, since they each contained the same issue on appeal. Irving sued Ross and Pryor for ejectment from land he proved he owned, and was awarded a judgment. However, Ross and Pryor had made improvements on the land, and were entitled to be paid for them. The applicable statute of Illinois, commonly called the "occupying claimants' law," provides that when an adverse possessor of land, complying with all conditions of same, makes improvements on the land, he is entitled to be compensated for those made prior to receive notice he is an adverse possessor. The mode of assessment of the value of such improvements was to present the facts to seven appointed commissioners. In this case this was done, and the seven commissioners reported their assessment to the circuit court. Irving moved to quash that report on the ground the law under which it was made is unconstitutional. The court agreed, and that is the sole issue to be decided on this appeal. Lincoln, Williams, and Thomas represented Ross and Pryor on the appeal.

The Supreme Court, in an opinion written by Justice Trumbull, held the law was constitutional, as Lincoln contended, and reversed the judgment and remanded the case for further proceedings. The contention the law was unconstitutional because it infringed upon the right of trial by jury was rejected. Trial by jury is only required on issues of fact, in civil and criminal cases, and cannot be extended so as to embrace the case of a mere assessment of damages or valuation of property.

The Alton & Sangamon Railroad Company v. Carpenter orig. ed. 14 Ill.190

(Ill. Rep.: The Alton & Sangamon Railroad Company v. Carpenter 14 Ill.189)
December Term 1852

This was a proceeding in the Sangamon circuit court before Judge Dickey to condemn the railroad company's right of way over Carpenter's land; and the only question on appeal is the proper measure of damages in the case. Carpenter was awarded $326.96. Lincoln and Herndon represented the railroad, and requested the following instruction to the jury (which was refused): "That, in estimating the damage done to the land by the construction of the railroad, they are to deduct the advantage which they believe the land will derive from its construction; and in estimating such advantages, they are not to be confined to the advantages peculiar to this tract of land, but they are to consider as such advantage, whatever increased value they may believe the land bears in common with other land beyond what they may believe it would bear if the road was not constructed, nor to be constructed at all; and that if in their opinion, such increased value is equal to, or greater than the damage done, they are to give no damage at all."

The Supreme Court, in an opinion written by Judge Trumbull, reversed the judgment and remanded the cause. It is obvious from reading the pertinent statutes that the legislature never contemplated the payment of damages to the owner of a tract of land for the privilege of constructing the railroad through it, when the additional value to be given to the land by its construction was fully equal to the injury which it would occasion.

After these proceedings were instituted, the legislature passed a statute amending the law condemning right of way for purpose of internal improvement, as follows: "it is expressly declared that no benefits or advantages shall be estimated which may accrue to land affected in common with adjoining lands on which the public work does not pass." Whether this was allowed as a limitation on the requested instruction to the jury at the rehearing is not known, and there is nothing in the Supreme Court records subsequent to this case to give the answer.

Petersburg, president & trustees v. Mappin et al.
orig. ed. 14 Ill.193
(Ill. Rep.: Town of Petersburg v. Mappin et al. 14 Ill.193)
December Term 1852

Mappin and Estel obtained a license from the town of Petersburg to keep a grocery; and they, with Atchinson and Lanning as sureties executed a bond to the corporation, in the penalty of five hundred dollars, conditioned that they would keep an orderly house, and would not keep the same open on Sunday nor permit gaming or riotous conduct therein. One or more of these conditions was apparently breached, because the town recovered a judgment against all the obligers for the amount of the bond and costs. When the obligers were perfecting an appeal, the trustees of the town suggested a compromise in that the citizens of the town would vote to advise what the trustees should do. 114 of the 130 voters petitioned the board to release the judgment upon the payment of costs of $38 by the obligers. The obligers were then released. However, eighteen months later, the board changed its mind, and filed this bill in equity against the obligers, alleging there had been no valid consideration for the release, and praying it be set aside, and execution be issued for the collection of the judgment. The court dismissed the bill.

The Supreme Court, in an opinion written by Justice Treat, affirmed the decree. The trustees of the town possess only such powers as are specifically conferred by the act of incorporation, or are necessary to carry into effect the powers expressly granted. They have no power to give away the funds of the town. They may sue and be sued, and the power to prosecute suits on behalf of the corporation, includes the right to compromise doubtful controversies. This was done here, and was within the power of the trustees. Whether the arrangement was judicious or not is not the question. A mere error of judgment would not vitiate the settlement.

Jones v. The People
orig. ed. 14 Ill.196
(Ill. Rep.: Jones v. The People 14 Ill.196)
December Term 1852

Jones was indicted for selling spirituous liquor in quantities less than one quart, under the statute prohibiting retailing intoxicating drinks, approved

February 1, 1851. He contended the act was unconstitutional. Verdict and judgment for the People, and Jones is fined $25.

The supreme court, in an opinion written by Justice Trumbull, affirmed the judgment. The statute is constitutional. Trumbull said: "The powers of the several States to regulate or even prohibit the retail of spirituous liquors within their limits, is expressly sanctioned by the Supreme Court of the United States, in the license cases. 5 Howard, 504, and there is nothing in the constitution of Illinois to prevent the exercise of this power. By virtue of its police power, every State must have the right to enact such laws as may be necessary for the restraint and punishment of crime, and for the preservation of the public peace, health and morals of its citizens. It is upon this principle that the sale of lottery tickets, and of cards, and other instruments of gaming is prohibited; and who ever questioned the constitutionality or validity of such laws? A government that did not possess the power to protect itself against such and similar evils, would scarcely be worth preserving."

Alton and Sangamon RR Co. v. Baugh
orig. ed. 14 Ill.211

(Ill. Rep.: The Alton and Sangamon Railroad Company v. Baugh 14 Ill.210)
December Term 1852

The railroad was assessed damages of $480 for the company's right of way over Baugh's land. Lincoln and Herndon represent the railroad, and Logan represents Baugh. The appeal is based on the railroad's contention that the following instructions given the jury were improperly given, and consequently a new trial should be awarded. The challenged instruction was "that after the assessment and payment of damages in the case, the railroad company will not be bound to make fences for Baugh, on either side of the road to make cattle guards for him across the road; nor will Baugh have the right without consent of the company, to make cattle guards across or under said road."

The Supreme Court, in an opinion written by Justice Trumbull, affirmed the judgment. The first part of the instruction does not seem to prejudice the railway in any fashion. We assume it does not want the obligation to build fences or cattle guard. Perhaps it was included in the appeal because it was not deemed severable from the instruction dealing with potential problems to the railroad giving the right to the land owner to build fences and cattle guards which might obstruct the right of way.

Perhaps the objection and appeal was to get another chance to try the action, with the expectations of lowering the amount of damages the second time around. Since the appeal was not allowed, the $450 stands, and Baugh cannot build fences or cattle guards on the right of way.

Dunlap v. President and Trustees of Mount Sterling
orig. ed. 14 Ill.251

(Ill. Rep.: Dunlap v. President and Trustees of Mount Sterling 14 Ill.250)
December Term 1852

The town of Mount Sterling, following procedures authorized by its charter, decided to open a street across land owned by Dunlap. As prescribed in the charter as a means of measuring damages suffered by a landowner in such an event, six disinterested freeholders in the city were summoned to determine the damages. They decided Dunlap was not damaged, and Dunlap appealed to the circuit court. His appeal was denied from which judgment he brings this appeal to the supreme court. Herndon represented Mount Sterling on the appeal at least.

The supreme court, in an opinion written by Justice Treat reversed the judgment and remanded the cause. The town of Mount Sterling has the power to open roads, and has a proper procedure to do so outlined in its charter. The decision to do so is made by the trustees, with damages measured by six disinterested freeholders. The court cannot inquire into the expediency of opening the street, but it can review the amount of damages awarded the landholder. Thus the circuit court should have accepted the appeal from the trustees' decision, and decided whether Dunlap was treated fairly by the six disinterested freeholders.

Reed v. Johnson
orig. ed. 14 Ill.257

(Ill. Rep.: Reed v. Johnson 14 Ill.257)
December Term 1852

Reed sued Johnson for trespass for injury done by Johnson's cattle to Reed's growing corn, before a Justice of the Peace. The circuit court in Menard county dismissed the action stating that corn was real estate, and the Justice of the Peace only had jurisdiction over personal property.

The Supreme Court, in an opinion written by Justice Trumbull, reversed the judgment, and remanded the cause. The court traced some of the history of the evolution of the definitions of what constituted personal property, and concluded: "There is no fixed rule by which to determine in every case, when they [growing crops] are to be deemed personal, and when real estate; and the present case may, as we conceive, be decided either way without any violation of principle, and upon respectable authorities." The court continued the pragmatic view of this case as follows: "It will certainly be more convenient to allow justices of the peace to entertain jurisdiction of such cases. It often happens that the owner of a field of corn has no other interest in the land where it grows than to raise the crop from it; and if compelled to resort to an action of trespass **quare clausum fregit** in the circuit court, for every injury to the corn while maturing, the expense and delay of the proceeding will often deter him from an attempt to assert his rights. In this very case, for aught that appears, the owner of the corn may have been a mere tenant, and had no interest in the land except to raise the crop of corn. The bill of exceptions shows that the corn was protected by a good and sufficient fence; that the cattle of the defendant came over the fence and committed the injury to the corn, for which alone damages were claimed; and we see nothing either in the law, or the subject-matter of the suit, which should prevent a justice of the peace from entertaining jurisdiction of the case."

Webster v. People
orig. ed. 14 Ill.365

(Ill. Rep.: Webster v. The People 14 Ill.365)
June Term 1853

Webster was sued in a justice of the peace court by Tisdel in the name of the State of Illinois for hawking and peddling goods without a license. Under an Illinois statute, persons doing such hawking and peddling needed a license, and if one didn't have one, a person could bring an action of debt against him, with a $100 penalty, half going to the state, and half to the person who entered the complaint. The justice of the peace dismissed the complaint for informality. Tisdel appealed in the Carrol circuit court, since such an appeal right was stipulated in the statute. Webster said the act was criminal in nature, and in a criminal action if the defendant is released on the pleadings, the state's right to appeal is limited. He also asked the court to charge the jury that if there was any reasonable doubt of his guilt, he should be acquitted; again saying it was a criminal case, and criminal practice rules applied. Judge Wilkinson refused to so charge the jury, and judgment was rendered against Webster.

The Supreme Court, with Justice Caton writing the opinion, affirmed the judgment. The statutory offense is not criminal, since a civil remedy is specified in the statute. The right of the appeal in the statute applies to both parties. Also since it is civil, rather than criminal, "proof convincing the judgment, although a doubt might still remain, in our opinion, was all that was required to authorize the jury to render the verdict which they did."

Bryan v. Bates
orig. ed. 15 Ill.87
(Ill. Rep.: Bryan v. Bates 15 Ill.87)
December Term 1853

Bryan was arrested by Marshall Bates for being drunk in public. Justice Scates states the facts in his supreme court opinion as follows: "Defendant was marshall of the city of Springfield, and as such it was his duty to preserve the peace and arrest etc., all offenders for violations of the city ordinances; and that plaintiff was drunk, in violation of a city ordinance; that the plaintiff disturbed the peace by violent, tumultuous and offensive language, calculated to provoke a breach of the peace, and in like violation of the ordinances of the city; all of which were committed in his view. Wherefore he gently laid his hands upon him and imprisoned him until he could take him before the mayor of the city, according to law . . ." Judgment was rendered for Bates. Herndon represented Bryan on the appeal at least.

The supreme court, in an opinion written by Justice Scates, affirmed the judgment. The power of the cities and their ministerial authorities was not changed by the new constitution. The applicable ordinance clearly set out the authority of the marshall to make such an arrest.

Johnson v. Donnell et al.
orig. ed. 15 Ill.97
(Ill. Rep.: Johnson v. Donnell et al. 15 Ill.98)
December Term 1853

Donnell et al., being mortgagees of a mortgage executed by Johnson, brought an action to foreclose the mortgage because Johnson was delinquent in his payments. The bill asked for a strict foreclosure (a foreclosure in which the mortgagor has no right to redeem, or buy back, the property at some future time). The bill asserted the property was of less value than the amount due on the mortgage, and Johnson had no means of paying any balance after the mortgage premises were sold. Johnson did not contest these allegations, and a decree of strict foreclosure was entered.

The supreme court, in an opinion written by Justice Caton, affirmed the judgement. Johnson maintained since an Illinois statute provided the right of a mortgagor to redeem the property in the certain time limits, the court could not order a strict foreclosure. Caton said the statute did not forbid strict foreclosures, so this right of the courts to order one could not be taken away by implication. It was no argument against a strict foreclosure that such a right would be abused by the court. Caton said:

"This record then, justifies the conclusion that it was for the interests of both parties, at the time the decree was rendered, that a strict foreclosure should be decreed. And so long as such cases might frequently arise, we may well presume that it was not mere inadvertence on the part of the legislature that the power to enter such decrees was not taken away. This power may be abused by the courts. If this were a valid argument against the exercise of the power, in order to satisfy it would be necessary to deprive the courts of all power to do justice as well as injustice, for these are very few powers which are held, either by courts or others, which may not be abused or perverted. Also since Johnson did not contest the evidence we cannot do so now. He was discharged from an obligation greater than the value of the property, and the mortgagees received the property with absolute title. This was the best result either one of them could attain by the judgement of the court.

People ex rel. Stevenson et al. v. Higgins
orig. ed. 15 Ill.110

(Ill. Rep.: The People ex rel. Stevenson v. Higgins 15 Ill.110)
December Term 1853

The act creating the "Illinois State Hospital for the Insane" provided for naming of trustees who were charged with general responsibility to run the hospital; also including a medical superintendent, who should be a skillful physician, should be appointed for ten years, and who could be removed before that term only for infidelity to the trust reposed in him, or on account of incompetency. Higgins was appointed medical superintendent, and the trustees wanted to remove him; resolving at a board meeting that he "does not possess the kind of qualifications which are necessary to the discharge of the duties of said office, etc." The People on behalf of the trustees, brought this action to remove Higgins, and he demurs; which was sustained, and the matter ended. the People appeal.

The supreme court, in an opinion written by Justice Caton, reversed the judgment and remanded the cause. The statute was silent as to who had the authority to remove the medical superintendent. However, Caton said "It was the design of the legislature to confer upon the board of trustees the management of this institution and to confer upon them all necessary powers for that management and control, as the most probable way of accomplishing, in the highest degree, the great and benevolent purpose of its creation, "This included the power of removal, but only for the two stated causes so that "No change of political parties or other inferior consideration could ever disturb him in his high and responsible position." Also the reasons stated by the board complied with the statute: "The substance is the same, though, perhaps, expressed in more delicate or less offensive terms."

Gibson v. State Bank by Manly et al.
orig. ed. 15 Ill.140

(Ill. Rep.: Gibson v. Manly et al. 15 Ill.141)
December Term 1853

The statutory law on ejectment specified that within one year after a judgment for ejectment, the party against which the judgment was rendered could have the judgment vacated, and a new trial on the matter ordered. And if he lost again, he could petition the court to consider the matter again, if it were done within the same year. In this case, Gibson brought an action of ejectment against Manly et al., and they were ejected from the subject property. They asked for a second trial within a year, which resulted in a judgment against them. This judgment was brought to the supreme court, and affirmed, after year had expired. Manly et al. then made a motion to the court to vacate the judgment and grant a new trial, which motion the court granted. Manly et al. were represented by Herndon.

The supreme court, in an opinion written by Justice Caton, reversed the judgment. Manly et al. had one year to have the ejectment vacated, if they could prove it was the proper thing to do. They brought the proper action within one year, and failed. They appealed the case, and relied on the supreme court to reverse the judgment. The court did not reverse the judgment, and since it was then too late to bring a second suit to reverse the judgment, the judgment becomes conclusive, and they have no remedy. Apparently, if Manly et al. really had good cause to have the ejectment vacated, they should have moved for a new trial before the supreme court had acted on their first attempt.

Stewartson v. Stewartson
orig. ed. 15 Ill.145

(Ill. Rep.: Stewartson v. Stewartson 15 Ill.146)
December Term 1853

Mary Jane Stewartson married William Stewartson in 1848, and had, at her marriage, "$320 and upwards, which afterwards came to the use of the appellee [William], and was appropriated by him." Shortly after the marriage, $40 of Mary Jane's money was used to buy land, which was purchased in her name. In 1850, William abandoned Mary Jane, and left her in possession of the dwelling-house, and a few articles of personal property, some of which she sold. She then bought, in her own name, another forty acre tract of land, unimproved, but contiguous to appellee's (William's) farm. In 1852 Mary Jane filed for divorce, and obtained a decree of divorce, and $50 a year alimony. This action is brought by William to change the terms of the financial settlement. The court heard the facts, and decreed that Mary Jane convey to William title in the last tract of land she bought, and the alimony was reduced to $30 per annum. Lincoln and Moulton represented Mary Jane on the appeal.

The Supreme Court, in an opinion written by Justice Caton, affirmed the decree. Caton said, "Before we should feel justified in disturbing a decree of this kind, we ought to be able to say that manifest injustice has been done." Then, "We are not disposed to disturb the decision of the circuit court. There can be no question as to the propriety of that portion of the decree which directs the complainant to convey to the defendant the forty acres which she entered with the proceeds of the property which she had sold, belonging to him. It was bought with his money, and there can be no doubt he had the right to claim it as his own. While there is undoubted propriety in allowing her to retain the forty acres which he had entered in her name, with money she had brought to him at the marriage, it is worthy upon consideration upon the question of alimony, that that forty acre tract had all been improved by him and constituted a part of his farm and by those improvements its value must have been much enhanced, and rendered immediately available and productive for her support."

O'Bryne v. Stout
orig. ed. 15 Ill.180
(Ill. Rep.: Byrne v. Stout 15 Ill.181)
December Term 1853

Stout sued O'Bryne in an action of trover and conversion, and recovered a judgment for $3. Lincoln represented Stout on the appeal.

The evidence was somewhat conflicting, but it clearly involved a hog Stout said he owned, which wandered from home frequently and mixed with O'Bryne's hogs. Stout came over to O'Bryne's to get the hog, but the hog was not there at the time. O'Bryne said he could have him; and Stout said when the hog returned, O'Bryne should bring him to Stout's place. Stout said, in effect: "that he had a hold upon plaintiff (O'Bryne); that he intended to chastise him; and that he would send plaintiff to the penitentiary, and would make him pay for the hog."

The Supreme Court, in a short opinion written by Justice Caton and containing mostly a recitation of abbreviated facts, reversed the judgment. Stout failed to show either an unlawful taking, or an actual conversion. "Castrating a scrub male hog running around one's stock is not such a proof of change of property as to be evidence of a conversion or appropriation to plaintiff's use." "Every element of a conversion is wanting." Then, for good measure: "Besides, there are very strong reasons, from the whole evidence, to doubt the defendant's (Stout) title to the hog." The judgment was reversed, and cause remanded for a new trial.

W. M. Cowgill & Co. v. Long
orig. ed. 15 Ill.202
(Ill. Rep.: Cowgill et al. v. Long 15 Ill.203)
December Term 1853

Legislative authority was given to school districts to assess a school tax, and specific details were prescribed as to how this should be done; including a requirement that a school tax could not be assessed for a given year unless it was reported to the county clerk by July 1. On July 20, 1850, the inhabitants of a school district in Menard county voted a tax of $500 for the purpose of erecting a school house in the district. Cowgill and Frackelton were charged $28.26 to be paid by May 14, 1851, and filed this bill against the collector to enjoin him on the grounds the assessment was improper. However, while this suit was pending, and on January 21, 1853, the legislature passed an act identifying this specific tax, and remedying the defects. The court dismissed the bill.

The Supreme Court, in an opinion written by Justice Treat, affirmed the decree. It is essential for the validity of a school tax that the provisions in the law be exactly followed. This was not done here, and if that was all there was to it, Cowgill and Frackelton would not owe this tax. However, the legislature had the power to correct this, and did so. When the act was passed, Cowgill and Frackelton had not paid the tax, and still had time to do so before their property was seized and sold to taxes. "If the property has since been sacrificed to pay the tax, it is the result of their own neglect."

Pate v. People
orig. ed. 15 Ill.221

(Ill. Rep.: Pate v. People 15 Ill.221)
December Term 1853

This was an action of debt, brought by the People against J.W. Pate and C.L. Pate upon a recognizance bond made by J.W. and C.L. in which they jointly and severally pledged $150 to guarantee the appearance of J.W. at a trial charging larceny. J.W. did not appear as agreed. Judgment was rendered against C.L. for the entire amount of penalty. Lincoln represented C.L. on the appeal.

The Supreme Court, in an opinion written by Justice Treat, affirmed the judgment. It is well settled an action of debt will lie upon a recognizance. The statute that authorizes a surety to surrender his principle in discharge of his obligation does not exclude the common law remedy of action on the debt. In this action the whole amount of the recognizance is recoverable. It matters not what may be the form of remedy. The sum named in the recognizance is forfeited by a failure to perform a condition. It is not like the case of an ordinary bond, where the penalty is designed to enforce pecuniary liability; and where the amount really due, and not the penalty is recoverable.

Sullivan v. People
orig. ed. 15 Ill.233

(Ill. Rep.: Sullivan v. People 15 Ill.233)
December Term 1853

Sullivan was indicted for selling spirituous liquor in less quantities than a quart in May, 1853 without having a license to keep a grocery. He was found guilty and fined $10. He was represented by Lincoln on the appeal.

The Supreme court, in an opinion written by Judge Treat, affirmed the judgment. Lincoln contended the statute of 1845 under which Sullivan was convicted was not in force. In 1851, another statute on the same subject provided a fine of $25. This act of 1851 was expressly repealed by an act passed in February 1853. Because of another statute specifying no act repealed by the legislature is revived by the subsequent act being repealed, the 1845 statute was not revived. However, on February 12, 1853, the legislature had passed an act stating that all laws in force on the subject of spirituous liquors which were in force on February 1, 1851 are hereby in full force and effect as if never repealed. If Sullivan had been indicted between February 7 and February 12, 1853, Lincoln's contention there was no law forbidding such sale would have prevailed. Sullivan probably was selling spirituous liquor in less quantities than one quart then, but was unlucky enough not to be caught.

Warren v. Jacksonville, president & trustees
orig. ed. 15 Ill.236

(Ill. Rep.: Warren v. The President and Trustees of
the Town of Jacksonville 15 Ill.236)
December Term 1853

Warren acquired title to certain land in Jacksonville through parties who had allowed a public street to run through the property, but who had not formalized a grant to the city for public use of the street. Warren brings an action of ejectment against the city, and judgment is rendered against him, Herndon represented Warren on the appeal at least.

The supreme court, in an opinion written by Justice Scates, reversed the judgment and remanded the cause for a new trial. The public is an ever-existing grantee, capable of taking dedications for public uses, and its interests are sufficient consideration to support them. The mode of making dedications is immaterial. They are not within the statute of frauds and are good by parol. The intention of the party, manifested by express consent, or acquiescence in the user, will govern in determining whether it is a dedication. Scates then said, in reversing the judgment because the evidence was not sufficient to warrant the judgment: "The use and occupation of this portion is only about seven years without any proof of assent or dissent. It was over lands lying uninclosed and in common. While so much land lying in common in this country remains free to public uses and travel until circumstances induce owners to inclose, we can deduce no strength of inference or conclusion from mere travel across it by the public without objection from the owner. It is neither the temper, disposition, fashion or habit of the people, or custom of the country, to object to community enjoying such privilege until owners wish to inclose."

Humphreys v. Spear & Spear
orig. ed. 15 Ill.275

(Ill. Rep.: Humphreys v. Spear et al. 15 Ill.275)
December Term 1853

This was an action of assumpsit, brought by D. and T.P. Spear in the Sangamon circuit court before Judge Davis against Humphreys. The Spears stated Humphreys owed them $135.71 for goods he had bought. Humphreys objected to the Spears proving their case by submitting the entrees in their books to the jury. This was allowed, and verdict and judgment entered for the Spears.

The Supreme Court, in an opinion written by Justice Treat, affirmed the judgment. Treat reviewed the evidence, with the Spears recalling how entries were made in the book. "They then proved by their clerk that he and the plaintiffs [Spears] were the only attendants in the store; that they served their customers promiscuously, each entering upon a slate the credit sales made by him during the day, and they all assembled at night, and the clerk transcribed the entries from the slate into the book, called the blotter or day-book." He then said, "It is well settled in this country, that entries made by a clerk, in the regular and usual course of business are admissible in evidence after his death, on proof of his handwriting; and during his life, if authenticated by him."

Enos v. Capps
orig. ed. 15 Ill.277

(Ill. Rep.: Enos v. Capps 15 Ill.277)
December Term 1853

Capps filed a bill in chancery against the heirs at law of P.P. Enos, alleging their ancestor had acquired land in trust for Capps, and praying that they be compelled to convey the land to him. A decree was entered in 1836 requiring the heirs to convey the land to Capps. The heirs were all then minors. In 1853 Z.A. Enos, one of the heirs, sued out a writ of error to reverse the decree. Capps pleaded the writ of error has not been sued out in five years after entering the decree, and thus void. Herndon represented Enos, and Logan represented Capps, in this action concerning the writ of error.

The supreme court, in an opinion written by Justice Treat, dismissed the writ of error. Under the common law an infant, who was sued in respect of land derived from ancestor, might stay the action until he arrived at full age. This was changed by statute, allowing the decree against the minor heirs to be in force when it was rendered. However, the heirs had a right to sue out a writ of error for its reversal, at any time within five years after arriving at full age. If Enos had attained his majority within five years before this writ of error was requested, he should have replied that fact in his plea. Since he did not plead this, he loses. However erroneous the decree may be, it is now conclusive upon the parties.

Prior cases in this proceeding are Moore et al. v. Capps (9 Ill.315) and Enos et al. v. Capps (12 Ill.255).

Nichols, adm. of Prentice et al. v. Thorton
orig. ed. 16 Ill.113

(Ill. Rep.: Nichols, adm. of Prentice et al. v. Thorton 16 Ill.112)
December Term 1854

Thorton filed a bill for the conveyance of three lots, which he alleged were purchased by Prentice, since deceased, with Thorton's money. Prentice had intended to convey the property to Thorton, but was prevented by protracted sickness and death. Decree entered for Prentice, on the appeal at least.

The supreme court, in an opinion written by Justice Scates, affirmed the decree. When one person purchases property in his name with the funds of another, a resultant trust is created, and the property should be conveyed to the one who furnished the funds. The ownership of the funds may be proven by parol (oral) evidence.

People v. Blackford et al.
orig. ed. 16 Ill.166
(Ill. Rep.: The People v. Blackford et al. 16 Ill.165)
December Term 1854

Blackford was tax collector of White county for 1846 and 1847, and gave a bond with Williams and Mitchell as sureties. In 1850, the state recovered a judgment against the obligors for $2,302.70, the arrearage of revenue due the state for the years 1846 and 1847. In 1851 the General Assembly passed an act giving Blackford authority to collect delinquent taxes (he was no longer collector), giving him power to enforce payment by distraining personal property, obtaining judgment against real estate, authorizing him to keep the 10% interest rather than paying it to the state, and extending the time of settlement until April 1852. Blackford and his sureties then filed this action in equity for an injunction against any further proceedings under the judgment. It alleged he had credits coming of $753.16, and the sureties were discharged from liability because the act of the legislature extended the date of settlement with the county court. The court granted the credit of $753.16, and ruled sureties were discharged. Lincoln represented Blackford et al. on the appeal.

The Supreme Court, in an opinion written by Justice Treat, reversed that portion of the decree, which released the sureties, and affirmed the rest. The provisions of the legislative act did not prejudice the sureties, since it diminished their potential liability because of the special powers it gave Blackford to collect delinquent taxes. The extension of time for the settlement with the county court also did not prejudice them.

Edmunds v. Myers & Myers
orig. ed. 16 Ill.207
(Ill. Rep.: Edmunds v. Myers et al. 16 Ill.207)
December Term 1854

Myers et al. filed a bill in equity in Logan circuit court for a recision of a contract he made with Edmunds, whereby Edmunds assigned certain interests in a "horological cradle" for $2,000, paid for by transferring title to a certain tract of land, plus $500. Myers et al. contend there was misrepresentation, as they thought he had a patent for the machinery that sustained motion of the cradle, when his patent merely covered the design. Judge Davis decreed the contract should be rescinded, and the land reconveyed and the money returned. Lincoln represented Myers et al. in the appeal.

The Supreme Court, in an opinion written by Justice Scates, reversed the decree and dismissed the bill. Firstly, Myers and others had made some sales of the cradle, and did not offer to account for those. A basic principle in chancery is that he who seeks equity must do equity. Here the contract was executed by the performance of Myers and others, and to restore the status quo, a party seeking equity must account for the fruits of his execution. Secondly, they did not prove fraud. Scates said, "But the defendants [Myers et al.] wholly failed in their evidence. No witness testifies to any representation whatever being made to them."

This case should be read with Edmunds v. Hildreth et al. (16 Ill.214), and Myers and Myers v. Turner (17 Ill.179). The Hildreth case states the Myers did not contract with Edmunds, but acquired their interest from Turner, who had acquired it from Edmunds. The outcome of all three is based on the absence of proven fraud, and in the Turner case, Turner recovers on the $500 promissory note given him by the Myers. See also Hildreth v. Turner (17 Ill.184) wherein Turner recovers on a note given him by Hildreth, as part of the transaction.

Edmunds v. Hildreth et al.
orig. ed. 16 Ill.214

(Ill. Rep.: Edmunds v. Hildreth et al. 16 Ill.214)
December Term 1854

This case is in all respects like Edmunds v. Myers et al. (16 Ill.207), except that Edmunds sold to Hildreth and one William Turner, the said patent for several states, for ten thousand dollars, and that Turner sold his interest to the two Myers for five thousand dollars. They were not parties to the agreement between Edmunds and Hildreth and Turner. Judge Davis in the Logan circuit court rescinded the contract and ordered Edmunds to return the consideration. Lincoln represented Hildreth et al. on the appeal.

The Supreme Court, in an opinion written by Justice Scates, reversed the lower court. Justice Scates said, "We are unable to find any ground to sustain this decree." Then, "I have already, in the other case, given my views of the supposed equities, upon the supposition that the fraud was established, and they apply equally to this case . . . Suppose there was fraud, the party defrauded and those injured by the fraud, could alone take advantage of it to annul the contract." The Myers had no contract with Edmunds.

Justice Scates is referring to Edmunds v. Myers and Myers (16 Ill.207).

Gilman et al. v. Hamilton et al.
orig. ed. 16 Ill.225

(Ill. Rep.: Gilman et al. v. Hamilton et al. 16 Ill.225)

December Term 1854

In 1835, Gideon Blackburn raised money from many benevolent grantees to purchase land from the government to establish a seminary. He conveyed the land to trustees of the school directing them, among other things, to erect a building on a certain portion of the land. The trustees sold some of the land at various times to pay taxes and decided since there was not enough money to build, they would use the trust property to establish a Blackburn Theological Professorship. Most of the land was sold to Coffin, and the professorship was endowed under a decree of the Sangamon circuit court, which was reversed by the Supreme Court (12 Ill.360) and the cause remanded. Hence this action was brought, which decreed the land could not be conveyed, and directed the trustees to carry out the wishes of Blackburn. Lincoln and Smith represented the appellants, Gilman et al., on the appeal.

The Supreme Court, in an opinion written by Justice Scates, affirmed the decree. A charity must be accepted upon the terms proposed. It cannot be altered by any agreement between the heirs of the grantor and the trustees. The intention of the donor will control, unless it is impractical; and in that event it may be altered cy-pres (as near as may be). Granted the land itself was not valuable enough to provide funds to build, but the trustees should have sought other funds to carry out the wishes of the grantor. Secondly, the decree of the court transferring land is not a judicial sale, and anyone purchasing the land is charged with notice of the facts of the trust. Such a case as here does not allow Coffin to fall under the rule of an innocent purchaser. A trust is stamped upon the property itself, and it will follow it into the hands of those who acquire it by purchase or otherwise.

Crosby v. Gipps
orig. ed. 16 Ill.352
(Ill. Rep.: Crosby v. Gipps 16 Ill.352)
June Term 1855

Gipps brought an action, under an act of 1852, entitled "Roads", for the supposed obstruction of a road leading from Washington to Tremont, Illinois before a justice of the peace. The statute provided a penalty against any offender under that act, which could be prosecuted by anyone. The justice of the peace held for Gipps, and Crosby appealed the decision to the circuit court. Crosby had contended at the trial that one Goodchild had previously prosecuted him for the same act, before the same justice of the peace, who had ruled for him. Crosby asked the judge to charge the jury that if it believed the current case covered the same cause as the Goodchild case, it should hold for him. This instruction was refused, and judgment was rendered for Gipps.

The supreme court, in an opinion written by Justice Caton, reversed the judgment and remanded the cause. Goodchild had as much right to prosecute Crosby as Gipps did. Judgment in the Goodchild case, if it were the same cause or offense, whether rendered for the plaintiff or defendant, was a bar to a subsequent prosecution brought by anyone against Crosby for violation of the statute.

Buckner et al. v. Hamilton
orig. ed. 16 Ill.487
(Ill. Rep.: Buckner et al. v. Hamilton 16 Ill.487)
June Term 1855

Hassen agreed in writing to convey certain real estate to Hamilton, who in turn executed an agreement to transfer his interest - one half to Buckner, trustee, and one half to Joseph and Jabish Eddy, and he covenanted not to impair their interests. Despite this promise, he then released Hassen from his obligation, and this action was brought by all three grantees on the covenant not to impair their interests. Hamilton demurred, stating that separate actions should have been brought for each half interest - one by Buckner and one by the Eddys. The demurrer was sustained, and Hamilton won.

The court of appeals reversed the judgment, and remanded the cause. The action had been properly brought by the three parties. The covenant not to impair the interests of Buckner and the Eddys was joint, and if a covenant is joint, suit must be brought buy all those having legal interests.

Chicago, Burlington & Quincy RR Co. v. Wilson
orig. ed. 17 Ill.123

(Ill. Rep.: The Chicago, Burlington & Quincy Railroad Company v. Wilson 17 Ill.122)

December Term 1855

An application for a mandamus was filed with Judge Wilson asking for the appointment of commissioners to fix compensation to be made for appropriating certain lands for use of the railroad, as provided in the legislative act establishing the railroad. Judge Wilson denied the petition, so the application for mandamus is now brought to the Supreme Court. Lincoln represented Wilson, who owned some of the land to be acquired, and objected.

The court, in an opinion written by Justice Caton, granted the mandamus. The charter of the railroad was authorized to construct a railroad on the prescribed route "with such appendages as may be deemed necessary for the convenient use of the same," and to acquire the right of way or title to land necessary therefor. The railroad sought this land to build work shops, and such are necessary appendages. Also this power is not exhausted by an apparent completion of the road, if an increase of business shall demand other appendages, or more room for tracks.

It was also contended that Judge Wilson acted in his judicial capacity, and the Supreme Court does not have the power to force him to reverse his decision. Caton said, "We cannot by mandamus control the judicial action of any inferior tribunal. We can, in such a case, only set it in motion, and require it to act one way or the other, but without determining how it shall act." However, here the judge was acting as a ministerial officer rather than judicial. He is compelled to act, if such a case is made as the statute directs. Such was the case here.

Justice Skinner wrote a concurring opinion. He wanted it made clear that property sought to be condemned is a decision to be made by the courts, as it is not the sole province of the corporation to determine what property its exigencies require.

Browning v. City of Springfield
orig. ed. 17 Ill.143

(Ill. Rep.: Browning v. The City of Springfield 17 Ill.142)
December Term 1855

Browning brought an action for damages against the City of Springfield, alleging that it was the duty of the city to keep its streets in repair, which duty had been neglected, in consequence of which thereof he had fallen, and broken his leg. The city demurred to this, which was sustained by Judge Davis in the Sangamon Circuit Court. Browning, represented by Lincoln and Herndon, appealed, and was successful. The judgment was reversed and cause remanded.

Justice Scates in his opinion for the court pointed out the difference here from ordinary negligent acts. This was negligence in not doing something, as opposed to an affirmative action. English common law had no remedy against a city for failure to act, even though by specific statue it was required to do things, like repairing the streets. Scates citing many authorities summarized erosion of this common law precedent, stating there should be liability if all the following applied: First, the city is under a legal obligation to repair the place in question; Second, the obligation is a matter of so general and public concern a criminal action would lie against the city for non repair; and thirdly, the place is out of repair; and lastly, the plaintiff sustained damages. He pointed out the city had the means to make the repairs. It had taxing powers and also, "all public property of the city is vested in the corporation, with power to cause all male inhabitants of twenty-one years to work three days on the streets." In affirming the city had potential liability in this case, Scates concluded: "With such lights for our guide, and such authorities for our sanction, we not only feel authorized but required to afford the protection sought, and more especially as we think the decisions based upon sound sense in accordance with strict morality, and keeping pace with the progress of improvements of the age."

Turley et al. v. County of Logan
orig. ed. 17 Ill.151

(Ill. Rep.: Turley et al. v. The County of Logan 17 Ill.150)
December Term 1855

In 1853 the General Assembly passed an act for the removal of the seat of justice for Logan County, by the vote of the people. Later the vote was taken, and resulted in favor of removal. Turley et al. filed a bill to restrain the county officers from erecting buildings at the new location on the ground that, as appeared by the journal, the act had not been read in the House of Representatives the full number of times required by the constitution; and so was not law. The injunction was allowed. In 1854 the same legislature met, and on the recollection of the members, and by manuscript minutes of the clerk, amended the journal, so that it showed the bill had been read the requisite number of times. Logan County submitted this to the court, the bill was dismissed and the injunction was dissolved. Lincoln represented Logan County on the appeal.

The Supreme Court, in an opinion written by Justice Scates, affirmed the decree. The same legislature may correct its journals. It had also been argued that there was a law that a county seat shall not be changed unless upon a petition of a majority of the voters. However, this act is merely advisory, and does not deprive the legislature of the right to do so without petition.

Justice Skinner wrote a concurring opinion stating, "I do not deem it necessary upon this record to decide upon the effect upon acts of the General Assembly, duly authenticated by the signatures of the presiding officers of the respective Houses and the approval of the Governor, of the absence of evidence in the journals of their regular passage; and upon this point I reserve my opinion."

Armstrong v. Mock
orig. ed. 17 Ill.166

(Ill. Rep.: Armstrong v. Mock 17 Ill.165)

December Term 1855

Mock brought an action of replevin against Armstrong for 141 head of cattle. Armstrong filed four pleas, and there was no formal joinder in the pleadings on the fourth plea. Armstrong asked for certain instructions to the jury, which were refused, but no exception was taken to the judge's ruling. Judgment for Mock. Lincoln and Herndon represented Armstrong on the appeal at least.

The Supreme Court, in an opinion written by Justice Scates, affirmed the judgment. Proceeding to trial without a formal issue, is, after verdict, treated as a waiver of either issue or plea. Thus Armstrong has no issue on appeal here to reverse the lower court judgment. Also, "The court has repeatedly held, that the exception must be taken on the trial, and that fact must appear on the face of the record." So Armstrong loses another issue on the appeal, and the appeal itself. Six earlier Illinois cases were cited to support the court's opinion in this case.

The opinion is short, but contains enough information to indicate Armstrong received less than adequate representation at the trial.

Booth et al. v. Rives
orig. ed. 17 Ill.175
(Ill. Rep.: Booth et al. v. Rives 17 Ill.174)
December Term 1855

This was an action of assumpsit brought by Rives against Martin and Booth. The jury was waived, and the issue was tried in the Edgar circuit court before Judge Harlan. Lincoln represented Rives, and Logan represented Booth et al. on the appeal at least. The evidence was conflicting, and the judge awarded judgment for Rives for $380.

The Supreme Court, in an opinion written by Justice Caton, affirmed the judgment. He said, "The controversy in this case is purely one of fact, and we think the finding of the court is sustained by the evidence. After reciting the facts on each side, he said, "It is at any rate not that clear a case of finding against the evidence as the rule of law requires to justify this court in reversing the judgment."

Myers & Myers v. Turner
orig. ed. 17 Ill.179
(Ill. Rep.: Myers et al. v. Turner 17 Ill.179)
December Term 1855

These are two action upon promissory notes brought by Turner against John and George Myers. The Myers had given the notes to Turner when they acquired certain rights in the "Horological cradle" from him and which he had acquired from Edmunds. Since the notes are due and unpaid, Turner brings these actions against the assignees. They plead failure of consideration. Judgment for Turner. Stuart, Edwards, Lincoln and Herndon represented Myers et al. on the appeal.

The Supreme Court, in an opinion written by Justice Caton, affirmed the judgment. The language in the assignment of the rights was very clear. There was sufficient consideration, even if the invention may have little value. Caveat Emptor. The Myers also pleaded fraud. Caton said, "There is not near as much suspicion of fraud in this case as there was in Edmunds v. Myers, 16 Ill.207, and yet in that case we reversed the decree and dismissed the bill because the charge of fraud was not sustained. That suit grew out of this same transaction."

Hildreth v. Turner
orig. ed. 17 Ill.184
(Ill. Rep.: Hildreth v. Turner 17 Ill.184)
December Term 1855

This is an action on a promissory note brought by Turner, which had been given to purchase certain rights in a "Horological cradle." Hildreth pleads lack of consideration. Judgment for Turner. Stuart, Edwards, Lincoln, and Herndon represented Hildreth on the appeal.

The Supreme Court, in an opinion written by Justice Caton, affirmed the judgment. Caton said, "The first question in this case is precisely like that decided in Myers v. Turner, ante, and is determined in the same way for the reasons there assigned. This record presents the additional question: whether the assignment or transfer of a patent right is operative, until it is recorded as required by the patent laws of the United States . . . This act has been repeatedly held by the federal courts to be merely directory as between the parties . . . It is sufficient that the question has been settled by the federal courts, whose particular province it is to construe the acts of Congress. We follow these decisions, not only because they are authority, but also because we are satisfied they are sustained by sound legal reasoning."

Moore & Munn v. Vail for use of Melick
orig. ed. 17 Ill.185
(Ill. Rep.: Moore & Munn v. Vail for use of Melick 17 Ill.184)
and
Moore & Munn v. Dodd
orig. ed. 17 Ill.185
(Ill. Rep.: Moore & Munn v. Dodd 17 Ill.185)
December Term 1855

These are two cases brought against Moore et al. on the same covenant in a deed for breach of a covenant in 1855. There were some evidentiary questions as the facts were reported in this case. The basic facts are:

Lynch was the true owner of subject land in 1835, when certain judgments were obtained against him, and became liens upon the land. In January, 1836, the land was sold on execution, to satisfy these judgments. In April, 1836, the right of redemption not having expired, Lynch, remaining in possession, conveyed to Charles Collins. In June 1836, Collins conveyed an undivided interest to Munn, and another third to Moore. In September, 1836, Collins, Munn, and Moore made the deeds now sued on, which were full covenant deeds. Lynch remained in actual possession until the Spring of 1837. In 1839, the land, not having been redeemed from the execution sale, was conveyed by the sherrif to the purchaser. In 1842, Lynch, under the execution title, took possession, and thus was the supposed eviction, on which the plaintiffs sued Moore et al. as a breach in the warrantee promising absolute title. Moore et al. plead the constructive eviction occurred in 1836, and thus the plaintiffs cannot bring an action because the sixteen year statute of limitations has expired. Judgment for the plaintiffs. Lincoln represented Moore et al. on the appeal least.

The Supreme Court, in an opinion written by Justice Caton, affirmed the judgment. The law is clear that if, at the time this conveyance was executed (September 1836), the premises were actually in possession of a third party claiming under a paramount title, that, of itself, amounted to an eviction. However, Lynch had possession then, in subordination to the title which he had conveyed to Collins, and he could have been evicted by an action of ejectment. Lynch did not hold possession under a paramount title. Thus, no constructive eviction in 1836; and thus the statute of limitations did not start to run until 1842, when Lynch did have possession under a claim of paramount title.

Davis v. Scarritt
orig. ed. 17 Ill.202

(Ill. Rep.: Davis v. Scaritt 17 Ill.202)
December Term 1855

Scarritt brought an action in assumpsit against Davis and William Pankey on two notes to him signed by "Pankey & Davis," who Scarritt said were partners. Pankey pleaded non-assumpsit (did not make a promise to pay the money) and payment. Davis pleaded non-assumpsit, and filed an affidavit stating he was not a partner of Pankey at the time these notes were given. A witness testified the notes were in the handwriting of Pankey. The Morgan circuit court refused to hear Davis' evidence, and entered a judgment against Davis; Pankey having been dropped as defendant.

The supreme court, in an opinion written by Justice Caton, reversed the judgment and remanded the cause. Davis should have been allowed to present his evidence. Caton cited two Illinois precedents on this subject, stating "It was there held that the affidavit of one of the defendants denying the existence of the partnership or the execution of the instrument sued on, was sufficient to entitle the party making the affidavit to make the defense."

Loomis & Taylor v. Francis for use of Pierce
orig. ed. 17 Ill.206

(Ill. Rep.: Loomis & Taylor v. Francis for use of Pierce 17 Ill.205)
December Term 1855

This action was an application to the Sangamon circuit court to make Taylor a party to a judgment, in the case of Francis, sheriff of Sangamon county, for the use of Pierce, against Loomis and Taylor. Pierce submitted an affidavit saying that his attorney in his suit against Loomis and Taylor, had released Taylor from his liability, and taken judgment against Loomis alone, without Pierce's consent or knowledge. The execution of the judgment against Loomis was returned "no property found." Also the attorney who released Taylor was "unmarried, was without means, and absent from the State, and that recourse against him would be worthless." Judge Davis granted the application, and added Taylor to the judgment, **nunc pro tunc** (literally, now as then--a thing done now shall have the same legal force as if it had been done then). Lincoln and Herndon represented Loomis and Taylor, and Stuart and Edwards represented Pierce, on the appeal at least.

The Supreme Court, in an opinion written by Justice Caton, reversed the judgment, and remanded the cause. When Taylor was brought into court in this proceeding, he should have been allowed to plead. Also the judgment should not have been **nunc pro tunc**, since that would have imposed a lien on Taylor's property as of the date of the original judgment, which would have been unjust to purchasers and encumbrancers of Taylor's property from that date.

This seems to be another case where someone wished malpractice insurance had been invented.

Manning et al. v. Warren et al.
orig. ed. 17 Ill.267

(Ill. Rep.: Manning et al. v. Warren et al. 17 Ill.267)
December Term 1855

Stone gave Manning a conditional mortgage on certain land in exchange for him guaranteeing a note of Stone's. The note was in default. Manning paid it, and the mortgage because absolute on Manning. It was recorded in May, 1837, and in 1842 was conveyed to the co-complainants with Manning in this action in equity to foreclose the mortgage. Stone in March 1837 had conveyed a portion of the land to Kirkland, which deed was recorded in July 1838. The defendants here claim title through Kirkland, and had held possession for more than seven years before this action was brought and paid taxes. Defendants pleaded the statute of limitations had expired, and judgment was rendered for the defendants.

The supreme court, in an opinion written by Justice Skinner, affirmed the decree. Manning et al. could have brought an action in law of ejectment anytime during those seven years. Since the mortgage had been recorded before the deed; and thus the buyer Jim Kirkland had actual notice of a prior lien on the land. They did not do so, and are barred in a court of law from doing so now, because of the statute of limitations. The concurrent remedy in a court of equity here is foreclosure of the mortgage, which would attain the same results as an action of ejectment. Skinner cited many cases from various common law jurisdictions that although the statute of limitations may not in terms apply to a court of equity, the equity court will refuse relief when the bar is complete at law. Where courts of equity have concurrent jurisdiction with courts of law and the party proceeds in equity, if barred at law he will also be barred in equity.

Weightman et al. v. Hutch
orig. ed. 17 Ill.281

(Ill. Rep.: Weightman et al. v. Hutch 17 Ill.281)
December Term 1855

This was a creditors' bill filed by Hutch against Weightman and Preston. Hutch had obtained a decree in chancery against Preston for $3,069.50. Execution was attempted, and no property belonging to Preston could be found. It was proven that Preston had conveyed his land to Weightman after the suit was commenced, and for inadequate consideration. Because of this fraud, the circuit court of Tazewell county, by order of Judge Davis, set aside the conveyance from Preston to Weightman.

The supreme court, in an opinion written by Justice Caton, affirmed the judgment. The only question was whether Hutch had the power to obtain this relief without having pursued other remedies in a court of law, Caton said: "A party has a right to the same remedies to enforce the collection of a decree in chancery for a specific sum of money, which he has to enforce a judgment at law. Our statute gives him an execution upon such a decree, the same as a judgment at law, and he must have the same right to remove out of his way fraudulent conveyances."

Batterton et al. v. Yoakum
orig. ed. 17 Ill.288

(Ill. Rep.: Batterton et al. v. Yoakum 17 Ill.288)

December Term 1855

David Batterton owned several tracts of land and died leaving all his estate, by his will, to his wife to own as long as she should remain his widow (and not remarry), except so much of a described piece of his land as might be necessary to sell to pay all his just debts. The widow, who was the executrix of his will, applied to the court to sell a portion of the land to pay certain indebtedness of David Batterton, and land was sold under this procedure to Yoakum, who was also the crier at the auction. The plaintiffs are heirs of David Batterman and seek in this action to eject Yoakum, and to recover the premises for themselves. The court holds for Yoakum. Herndon represents the Batterton heirs, on the appeal at least.

The supreme court affirmed the judgment. The widow, remaining alive and unmarried, still had a life interest in the estate. To recover in ejectment, the plaintiffs must have such an estate in the land as entitles them to present possession, and where there is an outstanding life estate, as here, the heirs cannot maintain such an action. Even if the procedure of the sale was irregular, the heirs can't reverse the sale. Perhaps if they could have included their mother (the widow) in the action, they could have prevailed. The court did not rule on the propriety of the claim the sale was void, since the heirs did not have an adequate claim to title.

Illinois Central RR Co. v. County of McLean et al.
orig. ed. 17 Ill.291

(Ill. Rep.: Illinois Central RR Co. v.
County of McLean & Parke 17 Ill.290)
December Term 1855

This action in chancery is brought in the McLean circuit court by the Illinois Central railroad to enjoin the collection of a tax assessed by the County of McLean upon the property of the railroad company in that county. The McLean circuit court held for the County of McLean. Lincoln, Brayman and Joy represented the railroad, and Logan, and Stuart and Edwards, represented McLean county.

The supreme court, in an opinion written by Justice Scates, reversed the decree, and made the injunction against the collection of the tax perpetual. The legislature had enacted a special state tax for railroads, exempting its property from taxation, upon the payment of a certain proportion of its earnings (to the state). McLean county contended this was unconstitutional, since the general rule of the constitution intended to apportion the burden upon the actual appraised value of all property, in a manner which would, as far as possible, make it operation "uniform in respect to persons and property within the jurisdiction of the body imposing the same." Justice Scates said "And had the rule stopped here, there could be little room left for construction. But there are exceptions to it (in the constitution), which show that an inflexible, universal rule was not intended. And it becomes a question how far the legislature may depart from it--in what instances--and whether the present is warranted as one falling within the exceptions." He stated this was a proper exception, and it was for the legislature and not the court to make the exceptions. The only duty of the court was to make certain the legislature did not make an exception "in palpable violation of the constitutional rights of the tax-payer."

Justice Skinner wrote a separate, concurring opinion, agreeing with the reversal but questioning some of the reasoning.

This is the case in which Lincoln had to sue the Illinois Central Railroad company to recover his $5,000 legal fee.

Johnson v. Richardson & Hopkins
orig. ed. 17 Ill.302

(Ill. Rep.: Johnson v. Richardson et al. 17 Ill.302)
December Term 1855

Brush and Thompson rented a room in Johnson's hotel. Thompson was carrying $3,000 belonging to other parties, which he deposited in the hotel safe. He had $300 of his own money, and Brush had $434 of partnership money (Richardson and Hopkins were his partners); and each of them elected to keep those sums in their room. In the morning, Brush's $434 had been stolen. Richardson and Hopkins bring this action on the case to recover the partnership money, and the jury awarded them $286 (two-thirds of $434). Johnson appealed, and the only two questions considered on the appeal were the judge's refusal to give two requested instructions to the jury: 1) Plaintiffs could not maintain their action because Brush was not joined, and he was a joint owner with them of the stolen partnership money. 2) Since Brush knew there was a hotel safe, and chose to keep the money, the innkeeper was not liable for the loss. Lincoln represented Johnson, and Logan represented Richardson and Hopkins, on the appeal at least.

The Supreme Court, in an opinion written by Justice Skinner, affirmed the Sangamon circuit court opinion. As to 1.), the proper plaintiffs for injuries to property are all the joint owners of the property, but where the remedy is to seek the recovery of damages, and not a specific thing, the non-joinder of one or more of the joint owners can only be defeated by a plea of abatement. If this is not done, as here, the plaintiffs may recover as to their proportionate interests, as here, in the damages. Brush can still bring an action against Johnson to recover his one-third interest. As to 2.), innkeepers are bound to protect the property of their guests, and in case of loss, can only absolve themselves from liability by showing they were not at fault. The burden of proof is on the innkeeper. "We do not intimate an opinion that innkeepers are responsible in all cases of loss of their guests property. The guest may unnecessarily expose his money to danger, or unnecessarily carry with him large sums, which no prudent man would do in a country where exchange can readily be obtained." Neither was the case here.

Sinklear v. Emert
orig. ed. 18 Ill.63

(Ill. Rep.: Sinklear v. Emert 18 Ill.63)

December Term 1856

Walter Sinklear, an infant, was left with Emert, when Walter's father went to California, and who promised to pay Emert $50 a year for Walter's board for two years, plus extra for clothing, doctor's bills, and medicine. Walter's father never sent any money, and didn't return. Emert brings this action against Walter's guardian to recover the amount of the debt owed by Walter's father. Judgment for Emert. Herndon represented the guardian on the appeal at least.

The supreme court, in an opinion written by Justice Caton, reversed the judgment. This was a special agreement, made by the father of an infant, to pay for his board. There can be no pretense for charging the infant or his estate with the amount. It is not like the case of necessaries furnished an infant on his credit.

Lake v. Campbell
orig. ed. 18 Ill.106

(Ill. Rep.: Lake v. Campbell 18 Ill.106)
December Term 1856

This is an appeal from an action of ejectment brought by Campbell against Lake in the DeWitt circuit court. Lake, through his agent (Blackford), leased a certain house in Mount Pleasant to Campbell for four years, at a yearly rent of $100, effective July 1, 1856. Lake then had trouble finding a suitable place for himself to live, and told Campbell he couldn't have the house in July because he wanted it for himself. Campbell brings this action of ejectment to force Lake to vacate the premises and give him possession, and is successful. Lake maintains that since he never gave Blackford written authority to lease the house, the lease was invalid because it violated the statute of frauds (general term given in English and U.S. common law to require documents in writing, usually under seal, in all contracts and deeds pertaining to real estate).

Justice Scates, writing for the Supreme Court, affirmed the judgment. His opinion cites the history of the English statute of frauds, and compares its pertinent terms with the Illinois statute of frauds. Blackford did have oral authority to make the lease, and that was adequate. He was "Lawfully authorized" which is all the Illinois statute requires. As between the parties, the lease was valid. The statute of frauds requiring written documents and registration of deeds is primarily designed to protect third parties, who acquire interests in the land and who are protected when doing so if they have neither actual or constructive notice of prior interests in the land.

Phelps v. McGee
orig. ed. 18 Ill.155
(Ill. Rep.: Phelps v. McGee 18 Ill.155)
December Term 1856

Phelps entered into a contract with McGee in June 1854, agreeing to deliver to him 5000 bushels of corn on or before August 15, 1854, at Port Isabel on the Illinois River. The corn was not delivered by that time, because McGee did not call for it. McGee demanded the corn on May 31, 1855, and Phelps failed to deliver it. McGee brings an action of assumpsit in the Cass circuit court, and judgment is entered in his favor for $1,131. Lincoln represented Phelps and Logan represented McGee, on the appeal.

The Supreme Court, in an opinion written by Justice Caton, reversed the judgment, and remanded the cause. First, Phelps claimed the court had no jurisdiction over him, since he did not reside in Cass county, and process in this action was served in Fulton country. The pertinent statute is: "It shall not be lawful for any plaintiff to sue a defendant out of the county where the latter resides or may be found, except in cases where the debt, contract or cause of action occurred in the county of the plaintiff, or where the contract may have been specifically payable." Here the contract "occurred" in Cass county, and Phelps was properly brought into this action. However, the lower court erred in measuring the damages as if the breach had occurred in May 31, 1855, rather than August 15, 1854. Phelps was guilty of breach of contract, if at all, at that time. This cause is remanded for a new trial.

Neteler et al. v. Culies et al.
orig. ed. 18 Ill.188
(Ill. Rep.: Neteler, interpleaded with Hurd et al. v. Culies et al. 18 Ill.188)
December Term 1856

Culies, et al. sued Israel A. Hurd, William C. Hurd, and John H. Neteler in assumpsit as joint makers of a promissory note, payable to Williams, and assigned by him to Culies et al. The note, in the amount of $120.69 was signed by "Hurds & Neteler." Judgment was rendered for Culies et al., who were represented on the appeal by Herndon at least.

The supreme court, in an opinion written by Justice Skinner, reversed the judgment, and remanded the cause with leave to the plaintiffs below to amend their declaration. The lack of pleading that the signature on the note was that of the defendants was a fatal error, and thus the case could not be proven against them. It would seem the representation of Culies et al. at the trial was inadequate.

Christian County v. Overholt & Squier
orig. ed. 18 Ill.223

(Ill. Rep.: County of Christian v. Overholt et al. 18 Ill.223)
December Term 1856

The parties agreed that Overholt et al. would build a courthouse for the County of Christian, according to certain plans and specifications, to be paid for in installments at certain levels of completion of the project. One payment was due when the foundations were completed. When this was done, Overholt demanded payment of the contractual amount due. The county did not agree the specifications had been met, and refused to pay. Overholt et al. stopped the work, and never did any more on the project. This action is in assumpsit to recover what was already owed, plus the anticipated profits which would have occurred to Overholt if he had finished the contract. The jury found for Overholt. Lincoln and Logan represented the county, and Stuart and Edwards, represented Overholt et al. on the appeal.

The Supreme Court, in an opinion written by Justice Caton, reversed the judgment, and remanded the cause. Caton cited a previous Illinois Supreme Court case as precedent for this opinion: "This is substantially the same question as that decided in Palm and Robertson v. Ohio and Mississippi Railroad Company (**ante,** p. 217), and if there be any difference, it is in favor of that case. The plaintiffs could only recover for prospective profits where they have been prevented from going on, either by some affirmative act of the defendant, as by being ordered to desist from further work, or by the omission to perform some condition precedent to the further prosecution, as to furnish or do something necessary to its further progress." In this case the payments for work when the foundation was completed was independent of the agreement to build and complete the court house. The issue of whether the money is due for finishing the foundation should be litigated (and thus the case is remanded), but prospective profits are not recoverable.

McConnel v. Delaware Mutual Safety Fire Insurance Co. et al. orig. ed. 18 Ill.229

(Ill. Rep.: McConnel v. The Delaware Mutual Safety Insurance Company et al. 18 Ill.229)
December Term 1856

Roney, a merchant, had an insurance policy covering fire damage to his property, including goods for sale. His premises burned, including all his inventory. The insurance company paid him, and he bought more goods. Arson was then suggested, and Roney transferred all his inventory to the insurance company. Gordheart and Acherland were owed money by Roney for goods he had purchased. They recover a judgment against Roney. This is an action in equity to sort out who is entitled to what, and the decree is entered in favor of the insurance company (which is represented by Lincoln on the appeal at least).

The Supreme Court, in an opinion written by Justice Caton, affirms the decree. Caton said the law was clear: if Roney defrauded the insurance company, he may be compelled to refund what is paid him. The degree of proof to establish fraud must be the same as that required in a criminal case. Every legal presumption is in favor of his innocence, and the guilt must be established by evidence excluding or overcoming every fair and reasonable hypothesis of his innocence. Caton was clearly convinced Roney was guilty of arson and agreed with the judge and jury in the circuit court.

Caton said it was impossible to go through in detail the immense mass of evidence in the record, without extending the opinion to unreasonable and unjustifiable length, but "this is the less important, as such a minute discussion of facts could be of little or no value as a precedent, which is the great purpose of reported cases."

Roney had one artificial leg. One telling bit of evidence against him was in the pressing emergency of the fire, he was seen at the scene of the fire dressed completely, "with his watch in his pocket and with a cane in his hand." Caton went on to say: "Now we would naturally suppose that a man with his affirmity alone in the house, awakened out of a sound sleep by the smoke of the fire, of the extent and location of which he was ignorant, and so suffocated as to endanger his life before he could get the door open, would take but little time in making his toilet, but would rather be content to secure the artificial member as a means of locomotion, and then rush to the door out of the suffocation, and give the alarm."

People v. Watkins & Watkins
orig ed. 19 Ill.117

(Ill. Rep.: The People v. Samuel Watkins et al. 19 Ill.117)
December Term 1857

Joseph, Samuel and Lewis Watkins gave a recognizance filed in court in the amount of $3,000, conditioned upon the appearance of Joseph for trial of a charge of murder of one David Watkins against him. Joseph was indicted, and failed to appear and answer to the charge. The court declared the recognizance forfeited, and served a writ on Samuel and Lewis; Joseph was not found. The two Watkins (represented by Lincoln & Herndon on the appeal at least) brought this motion to quash the writ, which the court denied. They then demurred, which was overruled, and the pleaded fifteen pleas to the action about which Justice Breese in writing for the supreme court, said: "very few of which were properly pleadable in such a case." The opinion, in reciting the facts of the case, is very vague. We do know the Watkins won in the lower court, despite the denial of the motion and overruling of the demurrer, because the people filed the appeal.

The supreme court reversed the lower court, and remanded the cause for a new trial. Justice Breese shredded the fifteen pleas, one by one, and then said in summary: "So that among all the pleas, but two are considered as appropriate, the eleventh and twelfth, and the twelfth defective in not averring the time of death of Joseph Watkins. It is surprising the Circuit Court should have treated seriously these pleas, and required replications to them, and demurrers to the replications, encumbering the record with matters foreign to and obscuring the real points in controversy." The eleventh plea of the record was inadequate. This was quickly disposed of by saying the record of the action on the recognizance in the court was a proper record, which imports absolute verity.

The supreme court, Justice Breese at least, obviously thought the trial Judge, Woodson, in the Menard circuit court did a poor job. Presumably Lincoln & Herndon represented the Watkins in that court, and influenced a miraculous judgment; only to be found out and indirectly chastised for encouraging obfuscation. The Watkins should have recognized that a valiant effort had been made on their behalf.

Partlow, assignee of Clapp v. Williams et al.
orig. ed. 19 Ill.132

(Ill. Rep.: Partlow, assignee of Capps v.
Williams et al. 19 Ill.132)
December Term 1857

Williams et al. executed a note to Clapp (who assigned his interest to Partlow) to pay $6,500 in forty days, "in sight exchange, on New York city, or its equivalent, and if not paid at maturity, to forfeit and pay three percent per month thereafter, as liquidated, agreed and assessed damages." The note was in default and Partlow's attorney (Lincoln and Herndon on the appeal at least) moved the court to direct the clerk to assess the damages at three percent per month. The court (Judge Davis in Vermilion county) overruled this motion, and directed interest of ten percent per annum.

The Supreme Court, in an opinion written by Justice Caton, overruled the circuit court and remanded the cause. Caton said: "This case is precisely within the rule laid down by this court, in the case of Stevenson v. Unkefer, 14 Ill.R. 103. The note was not payable in money, nor in anything of a fixed an determined value like money. It was payable in sight exchange on New York city, which is ever fluctuating in value." Because it is payable in an article or commodity of fluctuating value, the parties may stipulate any consideration they choose as penalty for default. The usury laws have no application. And in any event, if the Williams had wanted to plead usury, it would have had to have been done by a special plea before judgment was rendered. This was not done.

Illinois Central RR Co. v. Morrison & Crabtree
orig. ed. 19 Ill.136

(Ill. Rep.: Illinois Central Railroad Company v.
Morrison & Crabtree 19 Ill.135)
December Term 1857

Morrison and Crabtree contracted with the railroad to ship 400 head of cattle from Urbana to Chicago, at a rate less than the first class rate, because they signed a release to the railroad of its liability for any claims resulting from any damage on injury to the stock. During the shipment a few cattle died, and many suffered greater than expected weight reduction because of delays, etc. on the trip. Judgment was rendered for $1,200 for Morrison and Crabtree. Lincoln represented the railroad.

The supreme court, in an opinion written by Justice Breese, reversed the lower court, and remanded the cause. The plaintiffs contended the railroads, as common carriers, were bound by common law rules as such; and had absolute liability for any damages caused by the shipment, despite the fact they had signed releases in consideration of lower rates. Justice Breese said: "Until the establishment and use of railroads for the conveyance of property, it was not generally considered that common carriers could, by special contract, limit their liability, or take themselves out of the severe rules which governed such business. At this time railroads have acquired much of the carrying trade of the country, and reversing the former order of things, now carry the very animals which propelled the old machines used for that purpose." Then: "Transportation of live stock in railroad cars, in their rapid motion, is attended with great hazard, against which if the companies owning them had no power of protection, irretrievable ruin to them might be the necessary consequence."

Accordingly the courts of England and in most of the older states of our country, had declared railroad companies could protect themselves from their absolute liabilities as common carriers, by special contracts. However, they cannot restrict their liability from their own gross negligence or willful misfeasance. Neither of these two situations were charged here, but probably would have been if the case were retried.

Justice Breese closed by saying: "As the Circuit Court seemed to have entertained views of the law different from those here expressed, the judgment is reversed, and the cause remanded for further proceedings not inconsistent with this opinion."

Illinois Central RR Co. v. Brock, Hays & Co.
orig. ed. 19 Ill.166

(Ill. Rep.: The Illinois Central Railroad Company v.
Hays et al. 19 Ill.166)
December Term 1857

Hays agreed with the railroad to ship live fat hogs from Okaw, Illinois, to Chicago. Evidence was taken that indicated the trip should take about one full day, but it took three days in this situation. The weather was excessively cold, many hogs died; and the others lost about twenty-five pounds, when the normal expectation would have been about one and one-half pounds. The jury found for Hays et al., and awarded $860.25.

Lincoln represented the railroad, on the appeal at least, and contended the damages were excessive.

The Supreme Court, in an opinion written by Justice Skinner, affirmed the judgment. The only question in the case was whether the evidence justified a verdict for the amount for which the judgment was rendered. It did.

People v. Witt et al.
orig. ed. 19 Ill.169

(Ill. Rep.: People v. Witt et al. 19 Ill.169)
December Term 1857

Farnham, who was accused of forgery, and Moore executed a recognizance to the State promising the payment of $500, if Farnham did not appear at the proper time for further legal procedures. He was not present for such proceedings, and the People bring this action of debt, offering as evidence of the recognizance the record of the Schuyer circuit court, and the proceeding before the same court reciting the default of the cognizors, which adjudged the recognizance forfeited. The defendants (represented by Lincoln and Herndon) argued **nul tiel** record (not proper record), insisting a formal judgment of the recovery of a sum certain is essential to the forfeiture of a recognizance. Judgment entered for the defendants.

The Supreme Court, in an opinion written by Justice Skinner, reversed the judgment and remanded the cause, citing for Illinois cases as precedent, a formal judgment of recovery of a sum certain is not essential to the forfeiture of a recognizance (Pinckard v. The People, 187). Three other cases held the recognizance of record, and judgment of forfeiture are sufficient evidence to authorized judgment of execution, and in an action of debt to authorized judgment for the amount of the recognizance.

Lincoln and Herndon convinced Judge Walker in the Schuyler circuit court; but were defeated in the Supreme Court, four cases to none.

Sprague v. Illinois River RR Co. et al.
orig. ed. 19 Ill.174

(Ill. Rep.: Sprague v.
The Illinois River Railroad Company et al. 19 Ill.173)
December Term 1857

Sprague, represented by Lincoln & Herndon, on the appeal at least, brought an action in the Cass circuit court, as an owner of land in Cass county, to enjoin the county against purchasing $50,000 worth of stock in

The Illinois River Railroad Company. The railroad had been incorporated by authority of legislature, to construct a line from Jacksonville to La Salle, which would pass through Cass county; and the Cass county residents had approved a subscription of $50,000 to invest in the project. Subsequent action of the legislature amended the railroads authority to allow it to consolidate with any other intersecting railroad line; and the railroad then decided to locate its line from Virginia, in Cass county,to Pekin, and to cross the river at Pekin to connect with the Peoria and Hannibal line. Sprague believed this diminished Cass county's, or his interests, and seeks to have the purchase of stock by the county enjoined. The court decreed the county was liable to pay for the stock

The supreme court, in an opinion written by Justice Caton, affirmed the decree. The attention here was not of such a nature as to excuse any stockholder from paying his subscription. The effect of any amendment of a charter must be measured by how it effects the value of the stock, rather than by any adverse effect on any particular property owner who might suffer personal loss if a line is located other than where it was originally planned. Caton cited Barret v. The Alton and Sangamon Railroad Company, 13 Ill.504, as the most satisfactory exposition of the general principles of law, governing the respective rights of corporations and individual stockholders therein; and on those principles the county must complete its stock subscription. The common benefit to all the stockholders, rather than the benefit of one or a few of them, should control the action of those managing the enterprise. Justice Caton wrote an eloquent opinion and concluded: "This whole proceeding seems to have been prosecuted upon the supposition that it was proper for the court to consider some ulterior interest or object which the shareholders had in view when they subscribed, rather than suppose that they could or ought to have no other object but the real value of the stock and to promote its interest." Lincoln represented the railroad in the Barret case, which established the principle which defeated him in this one.

McDaniel et al. v. Correll et al.
orig. ed. 19 Ill.226

(Ill. Rep.: McDaniel et al. v. Correll et al. 19 Ill.226)
December Term 1857

This is a bill in chancery to set aside the will of William McDaniel, deceased. The jury found that "the paper produced was not the will of said William McDaniel." Some of the devisees under the will were non-resident children. No process was ever issued for them, and the publication of notices of the proceedings on the will were inadequate by the standards at that time, but would have been adequate under a legislative act of February 12, 1857. Lincoln and Herndon, and Conkling represented Correll et al. on the appeal, and Logan and Stuart and Edwards represented McDaniel et al.

The Supreme Court, in an opinion written by Justice Caton, reversed the decree and remanded the suit, as requested by Logan et al. Summons was necessary to bring non-residents into court. A subsequent act of the legislature could not correct the flaws in this case. Caton said: "They can no more impart a binding efficacy to a void proceeding than they can take one man's property from him and give it to another."

Also other infants, who may have been mentioned in the summons issued, were not protected by the appointment of a guardian ad litem.

Another objection overcome on the appeal involved a party bringing the appeal being properly served by summons, and still complaining about the process. Caton said: "Nor is the objection a valid one that these appellants, as to whom all the proceedings may have been regular, cannot take advantage of defects and irregularities as to parties who are not here complaining, and who, if they were consulted, might prefer that the decree should stand. Any one who is a party to the decree may take advantage of these objections as well as the infants or non-residents themselves. These appellants have a right to see and insist that all the other defendants shall be bound by the decree as well as themselves." The parties not properly served, or represented in the case of the infants, could have reopened the proceedings at a later date. The successful parties wanted to avoid that possibility, so pursued this appeal.

People ex rel. Billings v. Bissell
orig. ed. 19 Ill.229

(Ill. Rep.: People ex rel. Billings v. Bissell 19 Ill.229)
December Term 1857

The People on behalf of Billings bring this application of mandamus to require Governor Bissell to perform certain acts. Billings owned two $1,000 bonds of the state, and there Billings wants the governor to issue him new bonds for the arreage and believes the governor is required to do this under a legislative act entitled "An act to fund the arrears of interest accrued and unpaid on the public debt of the State of Illinois," approved February 18, 1857. The governor does not agree. Billings is represented by Stuart and Edwards, and Lincoln and Herndon. Logan represents the governor.

The Supreme Court, in an opinion written by Justice Caton, denies the application. The court does not have the constitutional authority to order the governor to perform any public duty. Caton answered a basic argument of Lincoln et al. as follows: "It is urged upon us, that in a government of laws there must be an adequate remedy for every wrong, and that where a clear right exists, there must be some mode of enforcing that right. While human society is governed by so imperfect a being as man, this can be true only in theory. If we were to compel the governor or the legislature to right every wrong which may arise from the omission of duty, then surely they must, in order to make this utopian system perfect, have the power to compel us to do right in every case." Then, "In the formation of the government, equal confidence was rightfully reposed in each department, to which appropriate and independent duties were assigned. If we unintentionally err, and do a party never so great a wrong, there is, and from the nature of our institutions, can be no remedy. If we perversely or corruptly do an intentional wrong, the constitution has provided the only remedy, which is by impeachment; and so of the executive. When acting within the limits assigned to each, neither can control or dictate to the other."

Prettyman et al. v. Wilkey et al.
orig. ed. 19 Ill.235

19 Ill.234

December Term 1857

S.P. and James Bailey conveyed certain real property (two adjacent lots in Pekin) to D.M. Bailey in 1831, for the payment of certain debts they owed D.M. and others. D.M., in the same year, executed to Stanford a power of attorney to carry out the trust duties arising from the deed. Stanford, under that power, with the knowledge of the Baileys, sold the property to Menard and Doolittle, in his own name. D.M. knew of the sale, and received the purchase money. Menard and Doolittle, and those claiming under them were in actual possession of the property since 1831, claiming fee simple title. In 1850, D.M. Bailey conveyed the same property to Reeves, who conveyed to Prettyman. Also S.P. and James Bailey conveyed the same property to Prettyman. All had notice that Menard and Doolittle had adverse possession of the property. Reeves brought an action in ejectment against the current people in possession of the land,

and the action was decided in their favor. This action is brought in the Tazewell circuit court to enjoin the recovery under that action of ejectment, and to obtain a conveyance of the legal title to the sixteen complainants, all Menard and Doolittle heirs. Decree for the Menards and Doolittles.

The Supreme Court, in an opinion written by Justice Skinner, affirmed the decree. The Baileys had actual notice Stanford had conveyed the property, and notice of the occupancy of the premises by the Menards and Doolittles. After eighteen years of such notice, their acquiescence is an estoppel, both as to them and to those claiming under them. Even though the improvements were only on one of the lots, the continued possession was of two lots, since they were held as one property.

The court was also influenced by Pennsylvania laws. Skinner wrote: "Our statute is a copy of the Pennsylvania Act of 1715; and that was so construed by the courts of that State at the time of its adoption in this State. We, therefore, adopt the construction which before had been given the same words, and we are satisfied it is the only true interpretation of the words."

People ex rel. Lanphier & Walker v. Hatch
orig. ed. 19 Ill.283

(Ill. Rep.: People ex rel. Lanphier & Walker v. Hatch 19 Ill.282)
December Term 1857

The legislature passed an "Act to create senatorial and representative districts, and apportion the representation in the General Assembly of this state." It was properly signed by the leader of each house, and sent to the governor for his action. He inadvertently signed it, thinking it was another matter. He had intended to veto it. His secretary sent the signed bill back to the "House of Representatives" as was the informal custom. As soon as it was announced in the House that he had signed it, the governor sent a message of disapproval. This action is brought by the authorized printers of the approved legislative acts in the form of a writ of mandamus to require the Secretary of State to release a copy of the bill, directly to the printer. Lincoln (and Grimshaw) represented the Secretary of State.

The Supreme Court, in an opinion written by Justice Caton, said the governor may sign and erase his signature. The fact his secretary reported it was passed was not binding on the governor. It had been his practice for the secretary to report his signature, but this was merely a courtesy, and not binding on the governor. Justice Breese wrote a separate opinion, concurring with the majority. He said, "A power to rectify an error at the proper time, exists with all departments of the government, for they are all liable to err. It is an afirmity of our nature, from which a governor cannot claim exemption.

Wade et al. v. King et al.
orig. ed. 19 Ill.301

(Ill. Rep.: Wade et al. v. King et al. 19 Ill.300)
December Term 1857

Nicholas King filed his bill in equity against the personal representatives of heirs of William and Joseph King, to obtain his portion of personal and real property held by them. On the hearing, the court rendered a decree settling the rights of Nicholas as between him and the defendants to that bill, and specially reserving to the heirs and representatives of Joseph, their rights as against the heirs and representatives of William. In the hearing on this bill, the complainants (the heirs of Joseph) offered to read certain depositions taken in the former suit, and the court refused to allow them to be read. Lincoln argued against the admission of this evidence, and was successful.

The Supreme Court, however, in an opinion written by Justice Skinner, reversed the decree and remanded the cause. The rule is that depositions in a former suit in chancery between the same parties, involving the same questions, are admissible as evidence, where the questions are again presented for the judicial decision, if the parties interested had an opportunity of testing the truth of the testimony. And this, although the parties are not identical, and although there may not be complete mutuality, in respect to their relation to each other, or to the subject matter litigated, if the same matter is an issue in both cases.

Kester v. Stark et al.
orig. ed. 19 Ill.328

(Ill. Rep.: Kester v. Stark et al. 19 Ill.327)
December Term 1857

Abner Stark left equal interests in land to each of his twelve children when he died. The children had various transaction among themselves, and some moved to other states. This action was brought to apportion the rights of each, and the commissioners appointed to make the partition, made a report that was affirmed by the court. Certain parties with interests derived from some of the transactions by the heirs were not made parties and sought to interplead, even though the commissioners had made their report and the matter was about to be concluded. The court refused to allow them to participate in the case. Lincoln and Herndon represented some Starks, who were the attempted interpleaders.

The Supreme Court, in an opinion by Justice Caton, reversed the judgment and remanded the cause. The proper parties were not before the court, so the matter must be reheard. An interpleader may be filed under a statutory partition suit, or an action in chancery on the same issue, any time before the case is disposed of. Until that time, it is before the court, and entirely subject to its control and jurisdiction; and any previous orders or proceedings may be changed, altered or amended, to meet the exigencies of new facts which may be brought before the court by new parties, by their interpleaders. Here the proceeding was not yet finally determined, but was still pending; and the interpleader was filed in proper time.

The St. Louis, Alton & Chicago Railroad Company v. Dalby orig. ed. 19 Ill.353

(Ill. Rep.: The St. Louis, Alton & Chicago Railroad Company v. Dalby 19 Ill.352)

December Term 1857

This action was brought in Logan County by Joseph Dalby, represented by Lincoln, against the railroad for trespass against his person. He and his wife got on the train at Elkhart, Illinois to ride to Lincoln. He tried to buy their tickets at the Elkhart railroad station, because the fare was three cents a mile when bought there. However, the station master was out of three cent tickets, and at Dalby's request, he was given a note stating that fact. The Dalbys got on the train, and the conductor told them they would have to pay four cents a mile, which was the proper fare when tickets were bought on the train. Dalby refused, and the conductor and two coachmen injured him severely, and threatened to put him and his wife off the train at an intermediate point (Broadwell). He paid both the fares on the basis of four cents a mile. The jury awarded him $1,000.00, and the railroad appealed.

The supreme court, with the opinion written by Justice Caton, affirmed the judgment. The major arguments of the railroad are that it was not liable for the consequences of the excessive use of force of any of its employees, and in addition, a corporation could not be sued for inflicting unlawful physical harm to a person anyway. Justice Caton first pointed out that Dalby had tried to follow the rules of the railroad to justify the three cents fare. The force used by the three railroad employees was unjustified, unreasonable and actionable. Caton said the "great question" was whether a private corporation can be liable for assault and battery. Private corporations had been known for some time, but were few in number, and were "very little studied by the courts," and "it has been reserved for our own times to see them so enlarged and multiplied as to engross to themselves, almost exclusively, many of the most important branches of industry and commerce." Corporations are given powers by law, and "It follows, as necessary legal consequence, that if, by the exercise of the powers either expressed or implied, which they possess, they commit a particular wrong, they must be held responsible for such wrong, and the courts must necessarily adopt the known and appropriate remedy for the redress of such wrong." Caton continued, "This principle of applying known remedies to the exigencies of new cases as they arise is one of the great pillars of strength of the common law, without which, it would have fallen and broken to pieces, by its own rigidity, centuries ago."

The railroad argued that the corporation had no authority to order an unlawful act to be done, thus any unlawful act by an agent was his responsibility, and not the corporation's. Caton answered this: "It is not to be presumed that the legislature would ever grant or suffer such (corporate) rights to exist, if the restraining influence of a just responsibility for the abuse of those powers were not to attach to their exercise." There is some precedent in cases holding assault against a person could not lie against a corporation," a corporation cannot beat or be beaten." However, "The idea that a corporation cannot be liable for beating because it has no body to be beaten, must be founded on the assumption that no party can inflict an injury which it is not capable of receiving. We confess to a want of respect when such whimsical notions are advanced by grave and learned Judges. As well might it be said that a man cannot commit a rape because he cannot be the subject of one."

Laughlin v. Marshall
orig. ed. 19 Ill.390
(Ill. Rep.: Laughlin v. Marshall 19 Ill.390)
December Term 1857

Laughlin deposited $500 each at two different times with Manchester, a private banker in Cincinnati, Ohio, and was given certificates of deposit. These were both endorsed by Laughlin and transferred to Marshall in Danville, Illinois. Four days later one of these certificates was presented by Marshall to Manchester, and it was refused; and due notice of this was give by Marshall to Laughlin. Two days later the second certificate was presented, but Manchester had closed his business and vanished. Laughlin contends Marshall was not diligent enough because when the notes were transferred to Marshall, Laughlin had adequate money in Manchester's private bank to pay the certificates. Judgment awarded to Marshall. Lincoln and Herndon represented Marshall on the appeal at least.

The Supreme Court, in an opinion written by Justice Caton, affirmed the judgment. First he stated a certificate of deposit is in fact, and in law, a promissory note for the payment of money, as settled in the case of Bank of Peoria v. Farnsworth, 18 Ill.563. Secondly, the only remaining question is whether or not Marshall was guilty of negligence or unnecessary delay in presenting these certificates for payment. He said, "The Circuit Court found that he was not, and we do not feel authorized to disturb that finding."

People ex rel. Koerner & Yates v. State Bank by Ridgley et al.
orig. ed. 21 Ill.65
(Ill. Rep.: People ex rel. Koerner & Yates v. State Bank by Ridgley et al. 21 Ill.64)
January Term 1859

Ridgley, Manly, and Calhoun were appointed by the governor in 1847 to be trustees of the State Bank of Illinois, which "closed its affairs" in that year. They continued in that capacity, and in 1857 the governor, with the advice and consent of the Senate, duly removed Ridgley et al. and appointed Koerner, Brown and Yates. However, Ridgley et al. continued to hold the books etc. and operate as trustees. The People, on behalf of Koerner, bring an application for a **quo warranto** (a common law writ asking "by what authority etc.") to compel Ridgley et al. to turn over the books and responsibilities, in the Sangamon circuit court, and by agreement the matter was taken to the Supreme Court. The People were represented by White, State's Attorney, and Lincoln. Logan, Hay, and McClernand represented Ridgley et al.

The Supreme Court, in an opinion written by Justice Breese, denied the application. **Quo warranto** is a criminal proceeding, and was not the proper form of action here. It was contended this incumbents were "officers" rather than trustees, and the governor has the power to remove public officers. However, these appointees are truly trustees--their duty is to the creditors of the bank and its stockholders. If any proccceding is brought against them for not properly discharging their duties, it must be brought by a bill in chancery, and by a creditor or stockholder of the bank.

Tonica & Petersburg RR Co. v. McNeely, adm. of Sathoff orig. ed. 21 Ill.72

(Ill. Rep.: Tonica & Petersburg RR Co. v. McNeely, adm. of Sathoff 21 Ill.71)

An association was formed to organize a railroad, and to sell subscriptions for stock. One of the subscribers died before the incorporation of the railroad. His administrator refused to pay for the stock, and the railroad brought this action for payment. Judgment was rendered for the adminstrator.

The supreme court, in an opinion written by Justice Caton, reversed the judgment and remanded the cause. A subscription made in contemplation of a charter to construct a railroad is a valid contract between the parties. The object of the contract is lawful, and it is founded upon a good consideration, which is the mutual promise expressed in the contract. It was a legal obligation, which may be enforced according to its terms.

Tonica & Petersburg RR Co. v. Stein orig. ed. 21 Ill.96

(Ill. Rep.: The Tonica and Petersburg Railroad Company v. Stein 21 Ill.95)

December Term 1859

The railroad had an organizational meeting, which Stein attended along with other prospective members. The evidence indicated Stein agreed to take one share of stock on the condition that the depot would be located at a particular place. He did not sign the subscription book, but someone else signed for him, alleging he had Stein's authority to do so. The railroad successfully sued Stein before a justice of the peace in Menard county, which was appealed to the Menard circuit court, who reversed the lower court and gave judgment to Stein. Lincoln and Herndon represented the railroad on the appeal, and Stuart and Edwards represented Stein.

The Supreme Court, in an opinion written by Justice Breese, affirmed the circuit court. Parol evidence by Stein was admissable since it was not offered to explain a written instrument (when parol, or oral, evidence is inadmissable). The inquiry was whether he subscribed at all. The jury found he did not subscribe in such a manner as to bind him, and the Supreme Court was satisfied the jury decided correctly.

School Trustees of McLean County v. Allen & Allen orig. ed. 21 Ill.120

(Ill. Rep.: Trustee of Schools v. Allen et al. 21 Ill.120)

January Term 1859

In 1850 the school administrators of town, 23N, R1E, sold a portion of the school lands to the Allens. Eight years later the school trustees bring this action in equity to find the sale illegal and void, alleging the prerequisites of the law had not been complied with on the sale. The court ruled for the Allens. Lincoln represented the Allens on the appeal, at least, and Stuart and Edwards represented the school trustees.

The court, in an opinion written by Justice Breese, affirmed the decree. Breese presented the several alleged irregularities offered by the trustees, and said: "This case, as shown by the proofs in the cause, is wholly destitute of any indication of any fraudulent act or intent, in any quarter by any party. The most that can be said about it is, there are omissions to perform certain acts which the statute required; but which not being performed, in the absence of fraud, should not be permitted to invalidate" the sale. Then: "The testimony shows that full value was paid for the land at the time it was sold. It is only by the wonderful and magnificent improvements that have been made in that beautiful region since 1851, that has so enhanced the value of all the land in that region, that this sale is sought to be disturbed. It may be a misfortune and loss to the county that the sale was made so soon, but being made fairly and not in violation of any law, it must stand."

Crabtree v. Kile & Nichols
orig. ed. 21 Ill.180

(Ill. Rep.: Crabtree v. Kile et al. 21 Ill.180)
January Term 1859

Kile and Nichols sold Crabtree eighty-one head of fat cattle, and Crabtree gave his note for $2,550. Kile et al. warranted the cattle free from a disease, called "milk sick or trembles," and Crabtree shipped them to New York City. During the journey about forty of the cattle died, and many of the rest were sick. Kile et al. bring an action in assumpsit on the note, and the Edgar circuit court awards them a judgment for the total amount. Witnesses were allowed to impeach the credibility of one of Crabtree's witnesses at the trial. Lincoln and Herndon represented Kile and Nichols on the appeal, at least.

The Supreme Court, in an opinion written by Justice Walker, reversed the judgment and remanded the cause. Where a vendor, having title sells with warranty as to quality, when a consideration is given and possession is taken under the sale, the vendee may rely upon the contract of warranty to recover for any loss resulting from effects covered by it. He may bring an independent suit, or it may be set off, in an action on the contract for the sale of them. This is what Crabtree tried to do here; and when, and if, the cause is retried he may do it then. The damages are the difference between the contract price agreed upon for healthy animals, and their value as diseased animals at the time of delivery, together with any other immediate injury resulting from the breach of warranty. As for the court allowing witnesses to impeach the credibility of one of Crabtree's witnesses, a well established rule of law is that the credit of a witness for veracity may be impeached by general evidence. But his general reputation is the subject of inquiry, not particular facts as were stated by witnesses in this trial. The impeaching witness must be able to state what is generally said of the person to be impeached, among his associates. That was not done here, so the impeaching witnesses should not have been heard.

President & Trustees of Petersburg v. Metzker
orig. ed. 21 Ill.205

(Ill. Rep.: Town of Petersburg v. Metzker 21 Ill.204)
January Term 1859

Metzker was tried before a police justice in Petersburg for assault, and fined $10. He appealed to the Menard circuit court, which dismissed the sentence because the ordinance establishing the fine was improper. The charter of Petersburg provided the town could establish punishment for any crime, consistent with any punishment established by the state for like crimes. For this particular crime involving Metzker, the fine established by the city was from $5 to $50. The law of the state fixed the minimum for this crime at $3. Lincoln and Herndon represented the town of Petersburg on the appeal at least.

The Supreme Court, in a short opinion written by Justice Breese, affirmed the judgment. The corporation by its charter, can prescribe no greater punishment for an assault and battery committed in the town "limits than is provided by the State for the same offense." The charter controls the exercise of the power by the town corporation. The city should have set the minimum fine at $3.

Young et al. v. Ward
orig. ed. 21 Ill.223

(Ill. Rep.: Young et al. v. Ward 21 Ill.223)
January Term 1859

A note signed by Reim and Young et al. was made payable to Alfred Ward or Charity D. Ward for $250, and is in default. An action of assumpsit is brought in the name of Charity D. Ward. Young et al. plead action brought only by Charity was improper, and that Reim (not Young et al.) had defrauded them. Judgment for Charity. Lincoln and Herndon represent Charity on the appeal at least.

The Supreme Court, in an opinion written by Justice Walker, affirmed the judgment. Walker said there is no doubt the suit should have been brought in the name of the husband alone, or in their joint names. However: "The husband and wife being in law regarded as one person, the legal effect of the note was that the husband was the payee, and the note was not payable in the alternative, to one of two persons, and the objection that there was uncertainty as to who was the payee, and therefor void, does not apply."

Secondly, Young et al. claimed Reim had lied to them to induce them to join in the note. But since the Wards were innocent of any participation in any possible fraud, they were not affected by the fraud. "It is the duty of the maker to see that his negotiable paper does not improperly get into circulation, and failing to do so, he must suffer the consequences of his negligence."

Smith v. Smith et al.
orig. ed. 21 Ill.244
(Ill. Rep.: Smith v. Smith 21 Ill.244)
January Term 1859

Isaac Smith made a wager with Moffitt, two days after the presidential election. Moffitt bet his buggy against $110 put up by Isaac that Fillmore had received the most votes in New York State. The stakeholder, Alexander, determined Isaac had won, returned his $110, and awarded him the buggy. However, in the meantime, sore-loser Moffitt, had sold the buggy to John H. Smith, who brings this action in replevin to recover the buggy. The Bond circuit court awarded the buggy to John H., who was represented by Lincoln and Herndon on the appeal at least.

The Supreme Court, in an opinion written by Justice Caton, reversed the lower court and remanded the cause. Firstly, the wager is not against public policy. The event had already occurred. Caton said: "Nor did the event which was to determine the wager depend upon any chance, accident, effort or skill. It was a fact irrevocably fixed as the number of grains of wheat in a measure standing on the table, or the date of a coin held in the hand. Such a contract the parties had an undoubted right to make, by the common law, and it is not forbidden by our statute." Secondly, a stakeholder (Alexander), unless some other mode has been provided, is the proper person to decide who has won a wager.

Thus, ownership of the buggy properly transferred to Isaac Smith, and John H. Smith cannot recover it. In remanding the cause for a new trial, if John H. wanted one, Justice Caton remarked, "and the proof satisfactorily shows that John H. Smith purchased with full knowledge of the defendant's right to the property." It seems logical to assume Lincoln and Herndon did not advise him to try again.

Terre Haute and Alton RR Co. v. Earp
orig. ed. 21 Ill.291
(Ill. Rep.: The Terre Haute and Alton Railroad Company v. Earp 21 Ill.290)
January Term 1859

Earp subscribed to ten shares of railroad company's stock, which constructed a line from Terre Haute, Indiana to Alton, Illinois. Afterwards it bought controlling interest in the Belleville and Illinoistown Railroad Company and constructed a line from Alton to Illinoistown.

Earp refused to pay for his stock and this action in assumpsit is brought in the Shelby circuit court. Lincoln and Herndon represented Earp on the appeal at least.

The Supreme Court, in a short opinion written by Justice Caton, reversed the lower court, and remanded the cause. Justice Caton started the opinion as follows: "The principles by which this case must be determined, have already been settled by repeated decisions of this court, and we do not feel compelled to discuss them again at length." After a short recitation of the facts, he said: "That it was for the interest of the plaintiff to obtain control of that road, and thus secure a continuous route to Illinoistown, may be easily appreciated, etc." Then: "If what we have said in the cases of Alton and Sangamon Railroad Company v. Barrett, 13 Ill.504, (and three other cases), has not shown satisfactory reasons for the rule of law which we hold on the subject, we despair of doing so now."

Lincoln and Herndon did convince Justice Walker, however, who wrote a strong dissenting opinion. Any fundamental change in the charter of a railroad company, releases subscribers for shares from payment of the subscription. But the alteration to exonerate the subscriber must be one that removes the prevailing motive for the subscription, or else materially and fundamentally alters the responsibilities and duties of the company, in a manner not provided for or contemplated by either the charter itself or the general laws of the sate. Walker concluded: "This change is not a mere change of location, still maintaining its points of terminus according to the original design, but is superadding other roads leading to other points of termination, and I think the alteration of the charter removes the prevailing motive that induced the subscription, and changes essentially and materially the terminus of the road."

Brundage v. Camp
orig. ed. 21 Ill.330

(Ill. Rep.: Brundage v. Camp 21 Ill.239)
January Term 1859

Brundage agreed to sell two mules to Crouch for $300. Crouch wanted to take the mules with him, and offered Brundage a note to be delivered a few days later. Crouch took the mules, sold them to Camp, and never delivered a note or any money to Brundage. Brundage brings this action in the Sangamon circuit court of replevin to recover possession of the mules. Judgment for Camp, who is represented by Logan and Hay on the appeal at least, and Lincoln and Herndon represented Brundage.

The Supreme Court, in an opinion written by Justice Breese, affirmed the judgment. Breese reviewed many pertinent cases submitted by counsel for each side, and concluded the most recent cases supported the rights of a good faith purchaser (as was Camp) in the most recent decisions. The sale was conditional upon Crouch paying for the mules, but the delivery of the mules was not. The good faith purchaser should be protected. Breese summed it up as follows: "It seems to us that any other rule would be attended with great inconvenience an embarrassment, in such a community as ours, where it is impossible to inquire into the various neighborhood transactions of our people, of which the sale of personal property forms so important a part. Information cannot be had of the private arrangements between parties, not placed on record, and only to be established through imperfect memories. A sale and delivery of a chattel, so far as a bona fide purchaser from the first vendor is concerned, without any notice of any reserved claims or rights on the property, ought to be sufficient for his protection."

Constant v. Matteson et al.
orig. ed. 22 Ill.546

(Ill. Rep.: Constant v. Matteson et al. 22 Ill.546)
April Term 1859

Miller and Scott sold to Wichersham certain goods, wares and merchandise for the purpose of furnishing and fitting up the St. Nicholas Hotel in Springfield. Miller and Scott wanted security, and Matteson endorsed a note for half the balance, and Constant endorsed as surety for the other half. Wichersham gave Matteson and Constant separate mortgages for the property required. Wichersham then bought additional goods from Miller and Scott, and told them he could have Matteson and Constant as sureties; Miller and Scott gave up the original notes, in anticipation of subsequent guaranteed notes from the three parties. Matteson and Constant didn't endorse the new notes, and contend they are released from the original notes. Wichersham borrows money from several others, and gives them various mortgages on the same property. Constant also advanced additional money, and took additional mortgages as security. Constant, Matteson and Dodge (another secured creditor) took possession of the property, and sold it, holding the money for the benefit of the three. Miller and Scott aren't paid, and they file two bills in the Sangamon circuit court, one against Wichersham and Matteson, and one against Wichersham and Constant for payment. The court sorted out who was owed what, and Constant, believing he received less than he was due, brings this appeal against all the others. Logan and Hay represented Constant on the appeal at least, and Stuart and Edwards and Lincoln and Herndon represented Matteson et al.

The court in an opinion written by Justice Walker, reversed the decree, ascertaining for itself who really should get what, and entered a "proper decree to which the parties are entitled under this record." Constant received more than he had in the first decree. There were many interests owed money by Wichersham, and one of the things that gave Constant, Matterson and Dodge priority was the taking of possession of the property. If there are several mortgages, all over due, and the mortgagor holds the property contrary to the conditions of them, any mortgagee who first takes possession of the property, acquires a preference over the others, without regard to the date of the mortgage. Miller and Scott released their claims against Matteson and Constant, albeit involuntarily.

Walters v. Smith
orig. ed. 23 Ill.342

(Ill. Rep.: Walters v. Smith 23 Ill.283)
December Term 1860

Walters executed a promissory note to Fullenwider for $1,300 payable on a day certain. Fullenwider assigned the note to Smith, who brings this action of assumpsit as the note is past due and unpaid. Walters claims there was an agreement with Fullenwider, that Smith knew about, that Walters would not be liable on the note unless Fullenwider gave him certain notes due Fullenwider which Walters was to collect. Judgment was rendered for Smith, since Walters evidence was rejected because it was only about oral agreements, and Fullenwider was a principal witness. Herndon represented Walters on the appeal at least.

The supreme court, in an opinion written by Justice Caton, affirmed the judgment. The pertinent Illinois statute allowing the failure or want of consideration of a note to be proved by parol (oral) evidence, does not authorize proof to change the terms of the note or contract so as to show the maker was not to pay the note absolutely, but only on certain conditions. Also the endorser (Fullenwider) is not a competent witness to impeach the note, or to show failure of consideration.

Leonard v. Villars
orig. ed. 23 Ill.377

(Ill. Rep.: Leonard v. Villars 23 Ill.322)
January Term 1860

Villars brought an action in equity to foreclose a mortgage against Leonard. Leonard's wife was not included as a necessary party. The decree of foreclosure was granted, with interest also granted, which included $16.80 of interest computed on interest. Lincoln represented Villars on the appeal at least.

The supreme court, in an opinion written by Justice Walker, reversed the decree and remanded the cause. Mrs. Leonard should have been included as a party. She had a right of dower along with her husband's right of redemption. A decree which would attempt to deprive her of these rights, unless she was a party to the record, and properly before the court, could not bind her any more than would a decree against any other person over whom the court had no jurisdiciton. Also to compute interest on interest has been found by all counts to be compounded interest, and in violation of law.

Cass v. Perkins
orig. ed. 23 Ill.382

(Ill. Rep.: Cass v. Perkins 23 Ill.326)
January Term 1860

Ford borrowed $600 from Rodham and gave him a mortgage on some houses and other personal property. Rodham assigned his interest in both to Cass. The mortgage debt became due on July 1, 1859, and Cass took possession of the property on July 4, 1859. However, on June 25, 1959 an execution against Ford was placed in the hands of Perkins, the Sheriff of Sangamon county. On July 6, 1859, Perkins seized the subject property under the execution, and Cass brings an action of replevin to recover the property. Judgment for sheriff Perkins. Lincoln & Herndon represented Cass on the appeal at least.

The Supreme Court, in an opinion written by Justice Walker, affirmed the judgment. Cass waited too long to recover the property from Ford. Perkins was entitled to believe Ford owned the property because it remained in his possession as long as it did after the note was in default; thus constituted an unreasonable delay. The court said there was no general rule as to what constitutes reasonable or unreasonable time in matters like this. Walker said: "No general rule can be established, but the mortgagee must act with promptness, and must use every reasonable effort to reduce the property into his immediate possession after a default of payment, or other condition broken, by which he becomes entitled to possession. Upon a default in payment, the title vests absolutely in the mortgagee, and to permit it afterwards to remain in the custody of the mortgagor is equally a fraud upon creditors and purchasers . . . It would thereby enable the mortgagor, as the apparent owner of the property, to acquire credit by means of its possession, sell it to innocent purchasers, and perpetrate the very frauds which the law designed to prevent."

Ritchey v. West
orig. ed. 23 Ill.385

(Ill. Rep: Ritchey v. West 23 Ill.329)

January Term 1860

West sued Dr. Ritchey for injuries resulting from alleged malpractice of Ritchey as a physician. The facts are not presented in great detail, but West ended up with a deformity and inability to use one of his hands, after Ritchey treated him. Testimony was given that the splints were not adequate, and Ritchey never saw his patient after the initial treatment. Judgment in the Adams circuit court was entered for West. Lincoln and Herndon represented Dr. Ritchey on the appeal at least.

The judgment was affirmed in an opinion written for the Supreme Court by Justice Walker. The opinion stated several errors apparently committed in the trial court by Dr. Ritchey's attorneys. Firstly, the evidence could not be reviewed since, "No question can arise on the correctness of the decisions of the court below in admitting or reflecting evidence, in this case, as no exceptions were preserved in the record: We shall therefore decline their examination." Secondly, the application for a new trial because of newly discovered evidence was faulty, because in such an application, "it is not sufficient for the party to state that he has been informed and believed that the witness will testify to the facts, but the truth of such facts must be verified by affidavit."

The principle of law in this case is that when a person assumes the profession of physician and surgeon, he must, in its exercise, be held to employ a reasonable amount of care and skill. And whether the injury results from a want of skill, or the want of its application, he will, in either case, be equally liable. Ritchey failed one or both of these tests here; failing either one was sufficient to support the judgment against him.

Kelleher & Kelleher v. Tisdale
orig. ed. 23 Ill.405
(Ill. Rep.: Kelleher v. Tisdale 23 Ill.354)
January Term 1860

Tisdale brought an action of assumpsit against Daniel and Dennis Kelleher, as partners, for goods sold and delivered. Dennis alone was served, and he filed a plea denying the partnership. Judgment for Tisdale for $1,306.58. Herndon represented Tisdale on the appeal at least.

The supreme court, in an opinion written by Justice Breese, reversed the judgment. Tisdale had an obligation to prove the partnership existed, and the supreme court opined there was not sufficient proof of a partnership between the Kellehers. Tisdale must have had a weak case, because the record prepared by the attorneys was inadequate, and could have lost the appeal. However, the court overlooked the inadequacy, and still reversed the Piatt circuit court; "The abstract in this case, which is quite voluminous, does not give the instructions of the court, which are the only matters assigned for error, but refers us to the pages of a more voluminous record for them. We will not, hereafter, consider a case in which the abstract is so defective as this is. It is unpardonable, under such a rule of court as exists here, that counsel should impose on the court a labor which they are required to perform themselves, and which they must perform, or suffer the consequences."

Tomlin v. Tonica & Petersburg RR Co.
orig. ed. 23 Ill.429
(Ill. Rep.: Tomlin v. The Tonica and Petersburg Railroad Company 23 Ill.374)
January Term 1860

The railroad brought this action in assumpsit against Tomlin for failing to complete his subscription to buy 10 shares of stock at $100 per share. The pleadings recited the various formalities of the procedure, several of which being held inadequate on the appeal. Tomlin thought the railroad was going to be built on property adjoining his, but it was built a mile and a half further away, which explains his reluctance to pay for his subscription. The court held for the railroad. Herndon and Cowan represented the railroad on the appeal at least.

The supreme court, in an opinion written by Justice Caton, reversed the judgment and remanded the cause. As the case was presented, the railroad did not adequately prove the procedure in seeking the subscription as proper. Perhaps it was, or perhaps it wasn't. In either event when, and if, the case were retried, the attorneys for the railroad had to do a better job of presentation to prevail.

Miller v. Whittaker; Young v. Miller
orig. ed. 23 Ill.453

(Ill. Rep.: Miller v. Whittaker; Young v. Miller 23 Ill.400)
January Term 1860

These are two cases in Chancery in Logan county which involved the same basic facts, and which were combined on appeal. Lincoln and Herndon, and Logan & Hay represented Miller on the appeal at least, and Stuart & Edwards and Young represented Whittaker & Young.

The first case was brought by Whittaker against Miller to rescind a contract. Miller, as agent for Flinchbaugh, sold the exclusive patent rights to a cast iron cemetery monument for most of the counties in Illinois. Whittaker transferred title in certain land and gave notes to Miller. Whitttaker contends fraud was present, and in addition that "at the time of the purchase, (he) was so intoxicated and stupefied by the use of liquor as to not know what he was doing; that Miller not only knew this, but in a great measure caused and prolonged it to enable him to get an advantage." A decree was entered rescinding the contract, and causing Miller to surrender the notes and reconvey the land.

The second case was also a motion in chancery, by Young against Miller, to set aside the exclusive rights to the same patent for the state of Michigan; again alleging fraud. Young transferred title to 160 acres of land as consideration. Miller admitted the sale and the representations, but claimed they were but the expression of opinions, and denied the charge. The court here held for Miller, and dismissed the bill. There is no evidence of intoxication in this case, which is possibly the reason the outcome was different than in the Whittaker case.

The supreme court, in an opinion written by Justice Caton, wrote a short opinion, reversing both decrees. Flinchbaugh was a necessary party. The consideration received in the Whittaker case was received in trust for Flinchbaugh, and his rights could not be protected without his presence. Also Whittaker did not offer to reconvey the title to the patents back to Miller in the pleading, which was necessary. The Young case was also reversed, because Flinchbaugh was not a party. Both cases were reversed, and the suits remanded with leave to the complainants (Whittaker and Young) to amend their bills and make Flinchbaugh a party.

The next record of the cases resurfacing in the supreme court was at the January term, 1864, when each case was retried in accordance with the orders from the Supreme Court, decrees were rendered at those trials, and each appealed separately.

Miller v. Young, 33 Ill.355 was the first reported. The opinion recites the earlier case, and that then Young's bill was amended to include Flinchbaugh, and to offer to reconvey the patent rights. The court entered a decree against Flinchbaugh (who didn't enter an answer) and Miller for a recision and reconveyance of the land and notes. Miller makes this appeal on the ground the decree is not supported by the evidence. Herndon represented Miller on this appeal at least, and Morrison represented Young. The supreme court, in an opinion written by Justice Beckwith, reversed the decree. There was no fraud. The patent was proper. Then: "It is essential to the validity of a patent for a design, that it should be a new and an original one, but the law does not require that it should be useful." The record was not complete enough to judge whether the patent was novel. Any statements made by Miller about the durability and probable sales of the patented articles were mere matters of opinion.

In Miller v. Whittaker, 33 Ill.386, the decree was amended in the circuit court to add Flinchbaugh and to offer to reconvey the patent, as ordered by the supreme court. Herndon represented Miller on this appeal, and Conkling represented Whittaker. In this case the decree against Miller (and Flinchbaugh) was affirmed, in contradiction of Miller v. Young appealed in the same term. In this appeal the record was inadequate, and the court held since there was no error shown by the record, the decree of the court below is affirmed. When the cause below was amended in accordance with the orders of the supreme court in the previous case, by the consent of the defendant (Miller), he did not file an answer. He was not required to, but he was at liberty to do so if he chose. The record in the present case "contain a transcript of the bill, certain depositions, and the decree, but none of Miller's answer. We do not know what allegations of the bill were admitted, or what were denied, and with no knowledge of the contents of the answer, we are unable to say that the allegations of the bill were not admitted. The pleading in every case must be brought before us." This case seems to have been lost by inadequate pleading, when it should have been won. The same court had held Miller's acts were not fraudulent. Herndon represented Miller in each, but the attorneys for the appellees were different. Perhaps one knew more law than the other, and recognized a fatal error in Herndon's presentation of the appeal in the Whittaker case, which could have also been present in the Young case.

The supreme court obviously knew of the prior Young case, but was not allowed to consider anything other than what was presented in the record.

Ferraria et al. v. Vasconcelles et al.
orig. ed. 23 Ill.456

(Ill. Rep.: Ferraria et al. v. Vasconcelles et al. 23 Ill.403)
January Term 1860

In 1851 a religious body, named the Free Portuguese Church, was organized in Jacksonville. The group was "under the care of the Free Church Presbytery of Glasgow, Scotland." In 1852 they bought land, and built a church building, financed by the members, with a large portion of the cost donated by "the old Presbyterian Churches in the Eastern States." In 1856 the church was dismissed by the presbytery of Glasgow, and, on application, was taken and received under the care of the Old School Presbytery of Sangamon. In 1858 Vasconcelles and others decided to withdraw from the church. They elected trustees and took possession of the church, excluding all who didn't secede. Ferraria et al. say they were the properly constituted trustees, and bring this action in equity to recover peaceable possession of the church. Vasconcelles et al. stated the church had held a meeting, and 89 voted to remain in the presbytery, and 106 voted against; thus the majority ruled to leave. The petition of Ferraria et al. was dismissed.

The Supreme Court, in an opinion written by Justice Walker, reversed the decree and remanded the case for further proceedings. The group who left the church attempted to form a religious society, but did not comply with the Illinois statutes specifying how this had to be done. Thus they had no official standing. Secondly, the group who left didn't agree with all the Presbyterian principles which had been followed by the Free Portuguese Church since it had been organized. In this case involving a division of the religious society, or secession, the title to the church property remains with that portion which adheres to the tenets and discipline of the organization to whose use the property was originally dedicated, although it may be minority.

Radcliff et al. v. Pierce; Radcliff et al. v. Reese et al.; Radcliff et al. v. Crosby et al.; Radcliff et al. v. Watson et al.; Radcliff et al. v. Usher et al.; Radcliff et al. v. Johns

orig. ed. 23 Ill.473

(Not in Illinois Reports)
January Term 1860

In each of these cases petitions were granted by six different parties for decrees giving them mechanic's liens against Radcliff et al. for work they performed on Radcliff et al's property, but not paid for. The decrees were granted.

The supreme court, with an opinion written by Justice Caton combined all six, and reversed all six decrees. The facts indicated that the petitions failed to show that the work was to be completed within two years from the time when the contracts were made. Caton said "It has been repeatedly decided by this court, that this objection is fatal, for which the decrees must be reversed and the suits remanded."

Gill et al. v. Hoblit

orig. ed. 23 Ill.473

(Ill. Rep.: Gill v. Hoblit 23 Ill.420)
January Term 1860

Hoblit brought an action in assumpsit against Gill and two others in Logan county. Two summonses were issued, one in Logan county against the two others, and another directed to the sheriff of Cook county for all three. This second summons commanded the sheriff of Cook county to "summons George Michael and Elijah Wicklin and Richard T. Gill, if they should be found in your county, personally to be and appear before the circuit court of said county, on the first day of the next term thereof, to be holden at the Court House in Lincoln, on the third Monday in the month of September next, etc." The Cook county sheriff found Gill, and served him. Gill did not appear in Logan court on the appointed day, and a default judgment was rendered against him. Gill appeals, and Lincoln & Herndon represent Hoblit on the appeal at least.

The supreme court, in an opinion written by Justice Caton, reversed the judgment and remanded the cause. The summons was faulty. It commanded Gill to appear before the Cook circuit court, to be "holden" in Lincoln, which was impossible. Caton said: "He was bound to obey the summons, or if that was impossible, he was bound to do nothing."

Caton said this issue had been decided in Orendorff v. Sanberry, 30 Ill.91, and that the court had been asked to reconsider that opinion. Caton said that opinion was still the law, concluding his opinion thereby: "We adhere to our former decision, and reverse the judgment and remand the cause."

Langworthy, heirs of v. Baker, adm. of Langworthy orig. ed. 23 Ill.484

(Ill. Rep.: Unknown Heirs of Asabel Langworthy v. Baker 23 Ill.430)
January Term 1860

This was an application, by Baker, administrator of Asabel Langworthy, deceased, against the unknown heirs of the deceased, for an order to sell six quarters of land to pay debts. Langworthy died in 1834, and in 1855. David P. Wells requested letters of administration be issued by the county circuit to Baker, the public administrator of McDonough county, which were issued. Wells presented a promissory note executed by Asabel Langworthy to N.B. and H. Wells for $618.28 in 1828 and assigned by N.B. Wells to Truman Roberts of New York. The amount of this debt was increased by $989.24 of accumulated interest. The court ordered the six quarters of land to be sold for $270 to David P. Wells. Herndon represented Baker on the appeal at least.

The supreme court, in an opinion written by Justice Breese set the decree aside. Breese said: "We think, before this court (the county court of McDonough county) could get jurisdiction of this case to act, it should have affirmatively appeared to the court, that there was no relative in the State or creditor, to whom administration might be committed. (There was a statement later in the opinion that there was a female heir who had resided in the State for at least ten years.) It should further have affirmatively appeared, that the application for the appointment of an administrator on the estate, was made by a party interested in the estate. Neither of these facts, and they are fundamental facts, are shown, . . .: We think, on the facts presented by the record, the county court had no jurisdiction of the subject matter, and the proceedings are consequently void. In addition any claim for a debt so long after the debtor has died, is much too late." It is not necessary to decide what shall be a reasonable time for that purpose [presenting a claim against an estate], for here the delay is twenty seven years, leaving no room either from adjudged cases, or the analogies of our law, for question. Then Breese said: "The order to sell the land to pay this debt should not have been allowed, and the heirs at law can contest it here. We might well advert in general terms to prominent facts in this case, which leave the strongest possible impression that the whole proceeding was void as having been contrived of fraud to swallow up a large estate on a debt which the law presumes was paid. In the first place, the old note is assigned by the surviving payee, N.R. Wells, without recourse, to one Roberts, one D.P. Wells filed the claim in court, and N.B. Wells made the affidavit of the death of Langworthy, and D.P. Wells enters himself as security on the bond of the administrator. The administrator interposes no defense to a claim he knew he could successfully defend, obtains the order to sell the land, and six quarter sections, in all nine hundred and sixty acres are sold to D.P. Wells for the trifling sum of two hundred and seventy dollars. There is no proof of the actual value of the lands before us, but from our general knowledge of the counties in which they are located, we feel well satisfied that they would average at least ten dollars per acre. Thus by the contrivance of these parties, a valuable inheritance, in justice and right belonging to the plaintiff in error below, the only child and heir at law of the deceased Langworthy, for the merest trifle, is wrested from her if the proceedings be valid." Then in conclusion: "We can consider this case in no other light than as a concocted fraud - fraudulent in its inception, and in its consummation, and we would be remiss in our duty did we not declare all the proceedings void. The decree ordering the sale is set aside." Justice Walker apparently thought so much of this case, he adds: "I concur in the conclusion arrived at in this case."

Kinsey v. Nisley et al.
orig. ed. 23 Ill.505

(Ill. Rep.: Kinsey v. Nisley et al. 23 Ill.452)

January Term 1860

Kinsey brought an action in assumpsit against Nisley and others, upon a promissory note for $200. Defendants pleaded usury, and the court ruled the note was usurious, declared the contract forfeited, and assessed the statutory penalty against Kinsey: "The plaintiff shall forfeit three-fold the amount of the whole interest reserved, discounted or taken, and shall have judgment and execution for the balance only after deducting three-fold the amount of said interest, one-third part of which shall be paid to the defendant, and the remaining two-thirds shall be paid into the county treasury of the count in which such suit shall have been instituted." This was the penalty provided in the act of 1845, and when the interest laws of the state were revised in 1849, the legal interest note was raised from 6% to 10%, with no mention made of what the penalty should be. Kinsey, represented by Lincoln & Herndon on the appeal at least, contended since the 1849 act did not include any specific penalty, the provision for such in the 1845 act was repealed.

The supreme court, in an opinion written by Justice Breese, didn't agree with Lincoln & Herndon, and affirmed the judgment. Justice Breese, after stating the 1849 act raised the legal limit form 6% to 10% said. "This, and this only, was the intention of the legislature, as we gather it from the particular provisions of the act, and the general context. The acts of 1845 and 1849 are in pari materia [on the same subject], and must be construed so that both may stand, if that be possible. This is a familiar principle in construing statutes."

People ex rel. Ballou v. Dubois
orig. ed. 23 Ill.547
(Ill. Rep.: People ex rel. Ballou v. Dubois 23 Ill.498)

Ballou was duly elected as circuit court judge for the county of Bureau in the twenty-third judicial district in 1857, for a constitutional term of six years. In 1859 the legislature passed an act moving the county of Bureau out of the twenty-third judicial district, and Bangs was elected circuit court judge. Ballou reported for duty, but Bangs had taken over the court, leaving Ballou no place to work. Ballou brought an action of quo warranto in the circuit court to recover his office, but lost. While that appeal was pending. Ballou demanded his salary from Dubois, the State Auditor, who refused to pay him. This action was brought directly to the supreme court for a writ of mandamus directing Dubois to pay Ballou's salary.

The supreme court in an opinion written by Justice Caton, granted the mandamus. It was the intention of the legislature to place the judges above and beyond the legislative control or interference, except by impeachment. It is the constitution which creates the office of circuit judges, and not the legislature.

Bissell v. Ryan
orig. ed. 23 Ill.566

(Ill. Rep.: Bissell v. Ryan 23 Ill.517)
January Term 1860

This action was brought by Ryan against Bissell for medical services. Bissell had children of his brother in law living with him, and one became sick. Dr. Ryan was called to render medical services, and Bissell refused to pay, contending his brother in law should pay. The court held for Ryan. Two of the questions involved on the appeal were: first, one of the jurors had served on another jury within the past year, and under a statute of 1859 this was improper. Although requested to dismiss the juror, the judge allowed him to serve. Second, Ryan contended it was the custom and usage for the head of the family to pay medical expenses for those who lived with him, and offered proof of this by the testimony of one Dr. Helm. Herndon and Hay represented Bissell on the appeal at least.

The supreme court, in an opinion written by Justice Breese, reversed the judgment and remanded the cause. Justice Breese, in commentary on the mistake in allowing the juror to serve, in explaining the need for the regulatory statute, said: "There had grown up in our State, a formidable corps of professional jurors; persons who having no honest means of livelihood, or resorting to them, if they had, were found, at every term, hanging around the court-houses, importuning the sheriffs and their deputies, and seizing every occasion to be put upon juries - making their living, in fact, by jury service." He felt strongly this was wrong and was properly stopped - and should not have happened here. Secondly, to establish a usage, it ought to be so general, uniform and frequent, as to warrant an inference that the party against whom the right is claimed, had knowledge of it, and contracted with reference to it. It will rarely happen that one witness will sufficiently establish a usage, and Dr. Helm did not do so here.

Gregg et al. v. Sanford
orig. ed. 24 Ill.17

(Ill. Rep.: Gregg et al. v. Sanford 24 Ill.17)
January Term 1860

Sanford made a contract with Edmistons for them to acquire hogs to sell in Madison, Indiana, with Sanford advancing $5,000 for that purpose. The hogs were acquired and in the possession of the Edmistons, who had also given Sanford a chattel mortgage on the hogs to be acquired. The mortgage was not recorded. Gregg et al. obtained a judgment against the Edmistons, and the sheriff levied on the hogs as the property of the Edmistons. This action is brought by Sanford for an injunction to restrain the levy on this judgment. The court ordered the injunction be perpetual, and the hogs not sold under the levy. Sanford was represented by Lincoln and Herndon on the appeal at least.

The Supreme Court, in an opinion written by Justice Breese, reversed the lower court, and dismissed the bill. Breese agreed with Lincoln and Herndon that property acquired after the execution of a mortgage can be subject to the mortgage (as was the case here), but the mortgage had not been recorded; and third parties, with no actual or constructive notice of the mortgage, could enforce rights against the mortgaged property, if in the possession of the mortgagee (the Edmistons). Sanford would have prevailed, if the mortgage had been recorded, as the chattel mortgage act requires.

Fridley et al. v. Murphy
orig. ed. 25 Ill.146

(Ill. Rep.: Fridley et al. v. Murphy 25 Ill.131)
January Term 1861

This was an application by Murphy, administrator of the estate of John Findley, deceased, to sell real estate to pay debts of the estate. Murphy proved the death, who were the heirs, that there was insufficient personal property to pay the debts, and the appointment of a guardian ad litem, (a special guardian appointed by the court to protect the rights of minor children). The sale was made, and the guardian ad litem approved it. The application was granted. Herndon represented Murphy on the appeal at least.

The supreme court, in an opinion written by Justice Caton, reversed the judgment and remanded the cause. He said: "The order for the sale of these lands shows affirmatively that no proof was heard by the court in support of the allegations of the petition, but the court acted alone upon the answer of the guardian ad litem, which admitted the truth of the allegations of the petition. This was not sufficient to justify the action of the court. Independent of the answer, the court should have been satisfied by proof that the facts actually existed which would require a sale of the land."

Columbus Machine Manufacturing Co. et al. v. Dorwin
Columbus Machine Manufacturing Co. et al. v. Ulrich
orig. ed. 25 Ill.169

(Ill. Rep.: Columbus Machine Manufacturing Co. et al. v. Dorwin 25 Ill.153)

(Ill. Rep.: Columbus Machine Manufacturing Co. et al. v. Dorwin 25 Ill.153)

January Term 1861

Two petitions were filed for mechanics liens against the Columbus Machine Manufacturing Co. et al. who were represented by Lincoln and Herndon on the appeal at least. The Sangamon circuit court awarded decrees to each complainant against the company. The petitions were both objected to for the same defect in the filings since they stated no time within which the contracts were to be performed; so the appeals were combined.

The Supreme Court, in an opinion written by Justice Caton, reversed the decrees, and remanded the suits. The entire opinion is: "The petitions in both these cases present the same defect which we have so often decided to be fatal. They state no time within which the contracts were to be performed, as is required by statute. This may be remedied by amendments, after the cases are remanded."

Lockridge v. Nuckolls
orig. ed. 25 Ill.178

(Ill. Rep.: Lockridge v. Nuckolls 25 Ill.159)

January Term 1861

Lockridge was the administrator of the estate of James Nuckolls. John Nuckolls brings an action of assumpsit against Lockridge, upon a promissory note, endorsed to him by Charles Nuckolls, apparently signed by James Nuckolls during his last illness. Lockridge alleges fraud, and judgment was rendered for John for $183.43. The court refused to hear evidence of the fraud. Stuart and Edwards, and Herndon, represented Lockridge on the appeal at least.

The supreme court, in an opinion written by Justice Walker, reversed the judgment and remanded the cause. Under the practice act of the state, the evidence offered by Lockridge of the possible fraud should have been admitted.

People ex rel. City of Springfield v. Power
orig. ed. 25 Ill.187

(Ill. Rep.: The People ex rel. The City of Springfield v. Power 25 Ill.169)

January Term 1861

The legislature passed an act that declared that after certain expenditures are allowed the County of Sangamon and the city of Springfield, the surplus of county taxes shall be divided between the city and the remainder of the county in proportion to the amount collected from each, with the city's portion to be applied to repair streets, and building and repairing bridges, in the city. The county judge, Power, refused to make these allocations, and Springfield brings this application directly to the supreme court for a mandamus to compel Judge Power to act. The county believes the legislature cannot control the revenue of a county, such revenue being the property of the counties, and not to be taken away from them without their consent, and to be used an appropriated in such manner only as the county courts of the respective counties may direct.

The supreme court, in an opinion written by Justice Breese, granted mandamus. Justice Breese said: "While private corporations are regarded as contracts which the legislature cannot constitutionally impair, as the trustee of the public interest, it has the exclusive and unrestrained control over public corporations: and as it may create, so it may modify or destroy, as public exigency requires, or the public interests demand. The whole capacities, powers and duties, are denoted from the legislature, and subordinate to that power."

Osborn v. McCowen
orig. ed. 25 Ill.218

(Ill. Rep.: Osborn v. McCowen 25 Ill.201)

January Term 1861

Osborn made a promissory note payable to McCowen for $530.10 payable one day after it was made. The note provided that if Osborn did not pay the note when due, he owed penalty interest of 20% until it was paid. McCowen brought an action in assumpsit, and was awarded a judgment for the amount of the note plus twenty percent interest.

The supreme court, in an opinion written by Justice Caton, reversed the judgment and remanded the cause. The form of the note was not usurious, but when the note was given it was not the intention of either party the note would be paid at maturity, but to provide for 20% interest to be paid - which is usurious. Caton said: "It presents so palpable a case of an attempt to evade the statute (against usury), that it will not even bear discussion."

Campbell et al. v. Brunk et al.
orig. ed. 25 Ill.225
(Ill. Rep.: Campbell et al. Brunk et al. 25 Ill.210)
January Term 1861

One school district corporation brought an action against another school district corporation. Judgment was rendered against the trustees of one corporation in favor of the trustees of the other. Stuart and Edwards and Herndon represented the corporation who won the case, on the appeal at least.

The supreme court, in a short opinion written by Justice Breese, reversed the judgment and remanded the cause. When a suit is brought by one corporation against another, it is erroneous to render judgment against the individuals composing the one corporation in favor of the individual members of the other.

Rusk v. Newell
orig. ed. 25 Ill.226
(Ill. Rep.: Rusk v. Newell 25 Ill.211)
January Term 1861

Newell's agent, Pruitt, collected $1,000 from Rusk for some hogs Newell sold him. Pruitt was indebted to Rusk for $1,000, so he gave Newell's money to Rusk to discharge that debt. Newell brings an action of assumpsit against Rusk to recover the $1,000. Judgment for Newell.

The Supreme Court, in an opinion written by Justice Breese, affirmed the judgment. Rusk knew Pruitt was Newell's agent.

Justice Breese said "We make no comment on the morality of the transaction," which was very generous.

Scott et al. v. Keeling
orig. ed. 25 Ill.358
(Ill. Rep.: Scott et al. v. Keeling 25 Ill.316)
January Term 1861

Keeling brought an action to enforce a mechanic's lien against Scott et al., and was awarded a judgment. Herndon represented Keeling on the appeal at least.

The supreme court in a per curiam report, reversed the judgment and remanded the cause. The entire opinion is: "The petition in the case is insufficient. Both the petition and proof show that no time was specified by the contract within which it should be performed."

State v. Illinois Central RR Company
orig. ed. 27 Ill.64
(Ill. Rep.: The State of Illinois v. The Illinois Central Railroad Company 27 Ill.64)
November Term 1861

The State brought this action against the railroad for taxes alleged to be due the State for the year 1857 and unpaid. The railroad charter provided it would pay 5% of is gross proceeds to the State; and after the expiration of six years from the grant of its charter, it was required to furnish a list of its stock, property and assets. It provided such a list for 1857, and the State assessed taxes of $108,000 (5% of its gross revenues), and $132,000, based on its list of property. The major question in the case is as to the evaluation of its property. The railroad paid $37,600 (in addition to the $108,000) based upon its valuation of its property. This is an original suit in the supreme court, with agreed facts, to determine the proper evaluation of the property. White, States Attorney, Logan, and Hay represented the State, and J.M. Douglas and Lincoln represented the railroad.

The supreme court in an opinion written by Justice Breese, held for the railroad. The basic difference was the State assessed the land at prospective value, and the railroad at its present value. Breese said. "The most experienced and intelligent railroad men in the West, were fully examined on all the elements of value, as subsisting in a railroad concern, and in this road particularly." Present value should be used; as the railroad property increases in amount and in profitable use, it will be evaluated each year on the same basis. Justice Breese then observed: "In this country at least, hope is so seductive, and the future so bright, and so full of promise, there is the greatest danger that the most prudent man may be mistaken, and the most considerate be misled, and it is much safer to rely upon practical demonstration, to determine the present value of such property, rather than speculatively, enter into the unknown future, whose dark veil is not given to us to lift, and look beyond. It is safer surely, to say, that, when the future shall be revealed, and practically exhibit an increased value of the property, then would be the proper time to assess it at such increased value." Then: "The road is doing its best, and it is proved, it has no net income - no profit on its cost, and is not a good investment at a value greater than that fixed by its owners, and proved on the trial."

Gibson v. Roll (1st appeal)
orig. ed. 27 Ill.88

(Ill. Rep.: Gibson v. Roll 27 Ill.87)

January Term 1862

Gibson brought an action of ejectment against Roll. Roll traced his title to the heirs of Jewett, deceased. Gibson traced his title to the sale of the same property by the administrator of Jewett. Roll argued the interests of the heirs, who were minors at the time were not foreclosed by the sale, because they were not properly notified of the sale: thus the heirs could convey the land. The administrator had published one notice of the sale, but did not specify the names, or existence of, any minor heirs. Judgment for Roll, who is represented by W. B. Herndon and Gross on the appeal at least. E. B. Herndon represented Gibson on the appeal.

The supreme court, in an opinion written by Justice Caton, reversed the judgment and remanded the cause. The statute says one of the ways an administrator may bring into court all adverse parties is to publish a notice to all parties interested, to come in and show cause why the land should not be sold, according to the prayer of the petition. This was done in this case by the administrator, and the sale is binding on the heirs, even though minors at the time.

See subsequent activity on this case Gibson v. Roll 30 Ill.172.

Trumbull v. Nicholson
orig. ed. 27 Ill.149

(Ill. Rep.: Trumbull v. Nicholson 27 Ill.148)
January Term 1862

Benjamin Trumbull obtained a judgment against Taylor, and execution was issued. Zane was Benjamin's attorney. Benjamin assigned the judgment to his brother, Lyman, and so informed Zane. Nicholson, the sheriff of Logan county, received $125 in bank notes and two checks for current bank notes on the Springfield Marine and Fire Insurance Bank amounting to $231, which aggregated the $356 total judgment, which were accepted by Zane. Since the notes on the Springfield bank were depreciated in value, Lyman preferred not to accept them, and brought this action to order the sheriff to deliver the execution in full value. A decree was entered allowing the sheriff (Nicholson) to pay the $125 in bank notes, and the checks amounting to $231, which he had delivered to Zane, to Lyman in satisfaction of the execution. Herndon represented Lyman Trumbull, on the appeal at least.

The supreme court, in an opinion written by Justice Caton, reversed the decree, and remanded the cause. If an attorney should accept from the sheriff depreciated money, in satisfaction of an execution, the owner of the judgment is not bound by such acceptance: and may compel the sheriff to return the amount in legal currency. If the sheriff has been injured by the conduct of the attorney, he must look to him for redress. Also an assignment of a judgment, is a revocation of the authority of the plaintiff's attorney to received the money on execution, or to control the judgment.

McHenry v. Yokum & Yokum
orig. ed. 27 Ill.160

(Ill. Rep.: McHenry v. Yokum & Yokum, adm. of Yokum 27 Ill.160)
January Term 1862

Yoakum bought certain land from McHenry, and gave him a note for $1,485.40 in exchange for a warranty deed. $900 was paid on the note before Yoakum died. McHenry is awarded the balance by a probate court. The administrator of Yokum's estate appeals to the Menard circuit court claiming an additional offset of $350 because of a dower right of a Mrs. Penny in the land. The circuit court allows this offset, and McHenry, represented by Herndon & Cowan, appeal questioning the method of computing the value of the dower right.

The supreme court, in an opinion written by Justice Caton, affirms the judgment. The consideration for the note had failed by the amount of the value of the dower right. Caton said: "But the plaintiff (McHenry) thinks it is impossible to compute the exact value of this dower interest, so as to determine the extent to which the consideration has failed. The proof clearly shows what was the annual value of the dower and the age of the doweress. From this it is as easy to compute the cash value of the dower, as it is the interest on a note of hand, from tables which have been formed with great care, from well established facts, and these tables are recognized and acted upon by all courts, at least in this country and in England, whenever occasion requires."

Coon et al. v. Nock
orig. ed. 27 Ill.235

(Ill. Rep.: Coon et al. v. Nock 27 Ill.234)
January Term 1862

Coon et al. made three promissory notes to Lockland, who assigned them to Nock before maturity. The notes are past due and Nock brings an action of assumpsit to collect. Coon et al. deny the liability, and serve notice they intend to prove usury. Coon calls Lockland to testify, and asks him to testify there was no consideration for the notes, and that they had not been delivered to Nock. Nock objects to the admission of this testimony, and the judge excludes it. Judgment for Nock for $1,381.68, and Coon appeals on the issue the judge ruled incorrectly in refusing this testimony.

The Supreme Court, with Justice Walker writing the opinion, affirms the judgment. There was no attempt to prove usury. Instead Coon tried to prove no consideration for the assignment, and that they had not been delivered to Nock. The is an entirely different defense. A case in the first Illinois report held that the assignor of a note was not competent to prove the fact of the assignment, or any other fact, in a suit on the note against the maker. That case is decisive on the question. Lockland, the assigner, was not competent to prove those facts, even if they constituted a defense.

Rankin v. Simonds
orig. ed. 27 Ill.352

(Ill. Rep.: Rankin v. Simonds 27 Ill.352)
January Term 1862

Simonds sued out an attachment against Elliott, and took a process of garnishment against Rankin and Green. Rankin answered that he had funds of Elliott's, but that he had delivered to Elliott a note against the Hannibal and St. Josephs Railroad Company for collection, and that Elliott owed the railroad company an amount greater than the amount of the note, and had not collected the note. Rankin wanted to set off the amount of the note against the claim against him as garnishee. Judgment was rendered against Elliott, and the court ordered the sum to be collected from Rankin as garnishee. Herndon represented Simonds on the appeal at least.

The supreme court, in an opinion written by Justice Caton, reversed the judgment and remanded the cause. The garnishee has a right to set up as an offset any claim he could set off in an action brought by the defendant against him. However, the note against the railroad which had not been paid could have been withdrawn by Rankin at any time, and thus would no be allowed as an offset. Caton also observed the judgment had not been entered in proper form as specified in McLagan v. Brown 11 Ill.519, where it held the judgment against a garnishee should be entered in favor of the defendant in the attachment, for the benefit of such attaching creditors as are entitled to share in the proceeds. Here the judgment was entered against Rankin, not in favor of Elliott, but in favor of Simonds. Since the funds in Rankin's hands were greater than the judgment against Elliott, Simonds could have recovered more than the amount of the judgment in the form in which the judgment against Rankin was entered.

Lilly v. Wagoner, cons. of Wagoner
orig. ed. 27 Ill.395

(Ill. Rep.: Lilly v. Waggoner cons. of Waggoner 27 Ill.395)
January Term 1862

This was a bill in chancery brought in 1858 by George Wagoner, conservator of the estate of Elisha Wagoner, to set aside a conveyance of land from Elisha to Lilly in 1851, upon the ground Elisha was insane at the time. Elisha was declared insane in 1858, after evidence on both sides was presented, the judge entered a decree declaring the deed void, ordering a reconveyance of the land to Wagoner, and that the purchase price be returned to Lilly with interest. Herndon and Bromwell represented Wagoner, and Thornton and Stuart, Edwards and Brown represented Lilly on the appeal.

The supreme court, in an opinion written by Justice Walker, reversed the decree, and dismissed the bill. All persons of legal age are presumed to be sane, and a deed executed several years before the maker was found to be insane, has the legal presumption of validity in its favor. Walker said, "The law has never required the high order of reasoning powers that mark the gifted, or a large portion of the human family would be thus deprived of the legal capacity to transact their own business." The evidence showing the insanity of a party at the time of execution of a deed, must preponderate, or the legal presumption in favor of sanity, will sustain the act. One of the witnesses testified that Elisha, in 1851, was "about like the other Wagoners," and there wasn't enough evidence of Elisha's disability in 1851 to support George's contention. Certainly George had difficulty proving Elisha was insane in 1851, when none of the other Wagoners, especially George, were.

Titus et al. v. Ginheimer et al.
orig. ed. 27 Ill.462

(Ill. Rep.: Titus et al. v. Ginheimer et al. 27 Ill.462)
January Term 1861

The trustees representing the bond and mortgage holders of the Chicago, Alton and St. Louis Railroad, bring an action for an injunction against the enforcement of a judgment recovered by Ginheimer against the railroad. The sheriff sought to execute the judgment against the personal property, including the cars, locomotives, and a tank-house. The trustees contend these items are part of the reality, and thus not subject to seizure on an execution. The bill was dismissed.

The Supreme Court, in an opinion written by Judge Walker, reversed the decree, and issued a temporary injunction against the execution until a new hearing could be held. The precedent in Illinois, in a case decided at the then present term of the court, held that railroad cars and locomotives, when on the road, are part of realty, and cannot be executed upon. The tank-house is a structure to hold water for the locomotives, and also is realty.

Gibson v. Roll
orig. ed. 30 Ill.172 (rehearing)

(Ill. Rep.: Gibson v. Roll 30 Ill.172)

January Term 1863

This was an appeal brought from a rehearing of the case remanded in Gibson v. Roll (27 Ill.88). In that case, Gibson brought an action of ejectment against Roll, who was in possession of the land under authority title traced to the heirs of Jewett, deceased. Gibson traced his title to the sale of the same property by the administrator of Jewett. Roll argued the interests of the heirs had not been foreclosed by the sale since they had not been properly notified the property was to be sold. They were minors, and had not been listed in the notice of the sale. The court held for Roll. The supreme court in the first appeal, in an opinion written by Justice Caton, reversed that judgment and remanded the cause for rehearing, stating it was not necessary to name the minor heirs in the notice, and if the administrator had followed the statute, the sale was good, and Gibson had proper title and would be entitled to eject Roll.

In the second hearing an additional question was raised bearing on whether or not the administrator had properly followed the statute. The statute required notice to be published for three successive weeks, the first publication to be at least six weeks before the presentation of the petition. Here the notice was first published on July 24th, stating the sale would be made on September 3rd, which was less than six weeks from July 24. However, apparently in an attempt to correct the time period problem, the petition to sell the property wasn't made until September 9th. Judgment was rendered for Roll again, on the grounds the sale was void because of faulty procedure.

The Supreme court, in an opinion written by Justice Caton, affirmed this judgment. The notice was insufficient to give the court jurisdiction, and the sale was void. The notice was void on its face, and the delay in presenting the petition to September 9 did not correct it. Caton said "When the notice is published as required by statute, those interested are bound to appear and attend upon the court during the whole of that day, either to resist the application then, or to hear the order of the court fixing another time for hearing the proof; but if during that day no petition is presented, they may well presume that the purpose of presenting it is abandoned, and go about their business. It would be a great hardship to require them to attend during a whole term, lasting perhaps for several weeks, to see if some move would not be made in the matter. We think the court decided properly in rejecting the deed, and its judgment is affirmed."

W.H. Herndon represented Roll on this appeal, as well as in the appeal of the original case. E.B. Herndon, W.H. Herndon's brother, represented Gibson in both cases. Gibson's delight in having the first case against him reversed and remanded for another trial was short-lived, because on the rehearing and appeal it was established the proper procedures had not been followed in the actions supporting his claim.

Miller v. Young
orig. ed. 33 Ill.355

(Ill. Rep.: Miller v. Young 33 Ill.355)
January Term 1864

Flinchbaugh had a patent or a design for the form and ornamental part of a cast iron cemetery tomb, and Miller, as his representative, sold exclusive rights to this patent in the state of Michigan, to Young, who agreed to convey 160 acres of land in Logan county to Miller. Young brought an action to rescind the deal, which was dismissed. Upon appeal (Young v. Miller, 23 Ill.453) the dismissal was reversed and the cause remanded with leave for Young to amend the bill, adding Flinchbaugh as a party, and to offer to reconvey the patent. This was done, and the court issued a decree in favor of Young requiring recision of the contract and for Miller to reconvey the land. Miller is represented by W.H. Herndon.

The supreme court, in an opinion written by Justice Beckwith, reversed that decree and dismissed the entire matter. It is essential to the validity for a patent for a design that it should be new and original, but the law does not require that it must be useful. The evidence was not adequate to prove the design was neither new nor useful, and statements made by Miller as to the durability and probable sale of the tombs were mere matters of opinion.

Miller v. Whittaker
33 Ill.386

(Ill. Rep.: Miller v. Whittaker 33 Ill.386)
January Term 1864

Whittaker was awarded a decree requiring Miller to rescind a contract wherein he transferred to Whittaker rights in a certain patent to a cast iron cemetery monument, with Whittaker claiming he was intoxicated when the contract was made, and that fraud had been committed. The case was originally appealed as Miller v. Whittaker (23 Ill.453), reversed and remanded with leave for Whittaker to bring another action to rescind. Again he was successful and Miller again appealed. Miller was represented by W.H. Herndon.

The supreme court, in an opinion written by Justice Beckwith, affirmed the decree. In this appeal the record was inadequate, and since no errors were shown in the record, the decree of the circuit court was affirmed.

In Miller v. Whittaker, and Young v. Miller (23 Ill.453) both decrees were appealed and decided at the same time. This case is reported in more detail as part of the summary of the prior case, and we refer the reader to that case for a complete history of this matter, as well as that involving Young with Miller.

White v. Primm
orig. ed. 36 Ill.416

(Ill. Rep.: White v. Primm 36 Ill.416)

January Term 1864

Primm, a long term resident of Menard County, Illinois was served by a Missouri constable in an action brought before a justice of the peace court in St. Louis, Missouri. Judgment was rendered against him and White brings this action in Sangamon County Illinois, to enforce the judgment. Primm represented by W.H. Herndon on this appeal, contended the service was improper, as he had been only temporarily in St. Louis when the personal service was made. A Missouri statute specified personal service could be effected "by leaving a copy of the summons at the usual place of abode of the defendant, with a white member of the family above the age of fourteen years." This would not have been a proper personal service under common law. Judgment in the Sangamon circuit court was rendered for Primm because the personal service was not proper.

The supreme court, in an opinion written by Justice Lawrence, affirmed the judgment. The hotel where Primm was staying could not be considered as his "usual place of abode." The statute was in derogation of the common law, and must be strictly construed.

Illinois Central RR Co. v. Allen
orig. ed. 39 Ill.205

(Ill. Rep.: The Illinois Central Railroad Company v. Allen 39 Ill.205)
January Term 1866

Allen brought an action in 1859 against the railroad for damages caused by a pond forming on one section of his land due to a ditch being clogged by the railroad, and to another section of land due to washing of mud and to improper construction of the railroad. The railroad defended itself by proving Allen had brought an action of trespass against it in 1854 for mud washing down onto the section of land for which he makes this new claim, and was awarded $762.50. Judgment was awarded him of $25.

The supreme court, in an opinion rendered by Justice Lawrence, reversed the judgment. The recovery of the prior damages precluded any further action against the railroad for injury to the same tract of land covered by the prior suit as for the damage to the other tract of land; the change in the ditch was at the request of Allen, and thus he is precluded from bringing a suit for damages caused by such change.

Lincoln had left Springfield in 1861, never to return. His involvement here undoubtedly occurred in the prior case, since he represented the Illinois Central Railroad at that time. The railroad's counsel in this case, as stated in the report, were Moore & Greene.

LINCOLN and the COMMON LAW
Alphabetic Index

LINCOLN and the COMMON LAW
Topic Index

Procedure (cont.)

Railroads

12 95